The Television Horrors
of Dan Curtis

The Television Horrors of Dan Curtis

Dark Shadows, The Night Stalker
and Other Productions,
1966–2006

JEFF THOMPSON

Foreword by Jim Pierson

McFarland & Company, Inc., Publishers
Jefferson, North Carolina, and London

Unless otherwise noted, each photograph is courtesy
Jim Pierson and Dan Curtis Productions.

LIBRARY OF CONGRESS CATALOGUING-IN-PUBLICATION DATA

Thompson, Jeff, 1958–
The television horrors of Dan Curtis : Dark shadows,
The night stalker and other productions, 1966–2006 /
Jeff Thompson ; foreword by Jim Pierson.
p.   cm.
Includes bibliographical references and index.

ISBN 978-0-7864-3693-4
illustrated case binding: 50# alkaline paper

1. Curtis, Dan, 1927-2006 — Criticism and interpretation.
2. Horror television programs — United States — History
and criticism.   I. Title.
PN1992.4.C87T46   2009
791.4502'33092 — dc22 [B]   2009000143

British Library cataloguing data are available

On the cover: A rare alternate take from a 1968 photo session
for *Dark Shadows* with Jonathan Frid as Barnabas Collins and
Grayson Hall as Dr. Julia Hoffman

Manufactured in the United States of America

McFarland & Company, Inc., Publishers
Box 611, Jefferson, North Carolina 28640
www.mcfarlandpub.com

To my parents,
Sonia and E.D. Thompson;
to my sister and brother-in-law,
Lee Anne and Jeff Parsley;
to my nieces and nephews,
Katy, Kevin, Kameron, Kelly, and Kimberly;
and

to Dan Curtis

Table of Contents

Foreword: The Fearless Master

by Jim Pierson

I first met Dan Curtis in the late 1980s, not long after I graduated from college. He was just finishing directing and producing the biggest dramatic program in television history, an adaptation of Herman Wouk's massive World War II novel *War and Remembrance*. To say that I was in awe of the man would be an understatement. I had never met such an intimidating figure.

His passion was enormous, his energy was staggering, and I think that his sheer willpower was nothing short of supernatural. Of course, those are qualities that everyone admired in Dan. In addition to his legendary lack of patience, he could also scare the hell out of you. But that didn't last. Once you knew what Dan expected of you and how to make it happen, you came to realize that he was really a world-class motivator, mentor, and creative genius. Dan could be tough, as many friends and colleagues know, but once he responded

Dark Shadows Festival chairman Jim Pierson and director Dan Curtis attend the Museum of Television and Radio tribute to Curtis's 40th anniversary (Beverly Hills, California, 2004). Curtis holds the book that Pierson wrote about him.

1

with that nod of approval, or his million-dollar smile, or the words, "Good job, son," I can't imagine a more rewarding validation.

Starting in 1990, I had the extreme pleasure and challenge of working in production and marketing for Dan Curtis Productions, beginning with the prime-time revival of Dan's legendary *Dark Shadows* series. I'm so grateful for all of the incredible opportunities and adventures that Dan brought to my life during those years — and beyond. (Even now, as this scholarly analysis of Dan's career goes to press, a major motion picture adaptation of *Dark Shadows* starring Johnny Depp is being developed.) Dan's legacy in film and television is vast, varied, and far from dull. From war epics to Westerns to human dramas to horror tales, Dan knew how to tell great stories, and he could do it all. He was the ultimate fearless leader.

Preface

"I ran home from school to watch *Dark Shadows*." Throughout the 1980s and 1990s, the bumper of each of my automobiles bore a sticker making that proud claim. Finally I ran out of replacement stickers, but my enthusiasm for *Dark Shadows* and the entire, diverse body of work of the *auteur* Dan Curtis will never expire. My love for Curtis's horror films, *Movies of the Week,* and miniseries has carried me across four and a half decades and to the creation of this book.

I first ran across ABC-TV's *Dark Shadows* on WSIX-TV 8 in Nashville on Monday, September 25, 1967, when I was in the third grade and at home sick. Amazingly, the very first scene that I watched—David Collins, a boy my age, dreaming that he and his young friend Sarah see the vampire Barnabas Collins emerge from his coffin—became the very first clip on MPI Home Video's VHS release, *The Best of Dark Shadows,* 22 years later. From that moment in 1967, I was hooked on *Dark Shadows*—even more fervently than I was enthralled by *The Edge of Night* and *The Secret Storm*—and I followed *Dark Shadows* until its 1971 cancellation, often by running home from school so as not to miss a moment.

Just watching Dan Curtis's Gothic soap opera was not enough. In the late 1960s and early 1970s, I collected *Dark Shadows* games, puzzles, bubble-gum cards, View-Master reels, 45 RPM and LP records, model kits, and the unusually-named 1974 *Dan Curtis Giveaway* mini-comic books featuring not only Gold Key's *Dark Shadows* but also Gold Key's *Dagar the Invincible, Grimm's Ghost Stories, Occult Files of Doctor Spektor, Ripley's Believe It or Not, Star Trek, Turok Son of Stone,* and *Twilight Zone* titles. One of my prized possessions—along with my Buck Rogers Atomic Pistol—was a Barnabas Collins Halloween mask that few if any other *Dark Shadows* fans seemed to have (at least in those pre–Internet days). My *Dark Shadows* memorabilia collection grew and grew until in 1998 it took over the entire guest bedroom of my then-new home. Today, the *Dark Shadows*-related portraits and memorabilia—especially a Joan Bennett wall with eight pictures—spill out of the so-called *Dark Shadows* room and have traveled all the way to the upstairs playroom (named for a room inside the Collinwood of 1840) and its adjoining *Psycho* bathroom (the subject of quite a few Nashville newspaper and television news features).

In the late 1960s and early 1970s, if I was not reading my school books — or comic books such as *Justice League of America, Superman's Girlfriend Lois Lane, Amazing Spider-Man,* and *Fantastic Four*— I was reading Dan "Marilyn" Ross's 32 Paperback Library novels based on *Dark Shadows,* as well as Ross's novelization of Dan Curtis's 1970 film *House of Dark Shadows.* My love for Dan Ross's writing and storytelling techniques then caused me to begin reading dozens of Ross's non–*Dark Shadows* Gothic novels, historical romances, mystery novels, and nurse romances. Ultimately I read 120 of Ross's 358 published novels and began using a few of Ross's 600 published short stories in my developmental-English classes at Tennessee State University, where I have taught since 1985. In 1989–1990, I wrote my TSU master's thesis about four of Dan Ross's greatest historical novels, including *China Shadow* and *Moscow Mists,* and I received my M.A. degree in May 1991. Of course *Dark Shadows* and Dan Curtis were mentioned in the thesis, but they were not the focal points. My extensive writing about *Dark Shadows,* Curtis's other works, and the *Dark Shadows* comic books and memorabilia had been published in more than one dozen different *Dark Shadows* fanzines — including *The World of Dark Shadows, The Collinsport Call, Dark Shadows Announcement,* and *Shadows of the Night*— beginning in 1975 and continuing for more than two decades.

In 1983, I began attending the annual Dark Shadows Festival fan conventions in New Jersey, New York, California, and elsewhere, and although I never had the pleasure of meeting Dan Curtis himself, I started meeting many of the actresses, actors, writers, and producers who had brought *Dark Shadows* to life every afternoon on ABC-TV between 1966 and 1971. I also met and befriended Marilyn and Dan Ross and my fellow *Dark Shadows* fans — women and men of all ages and from across the United States and Canada. Many of them became my pen pals and lifelong friends, and some of them joined me in acting out humorous skits based on *Dark Shadows* at subsequent Dark Shadows Festivals. After Dr. Laura Brodian Freas and I co-founded the Collinsport Players acting troupe and wrote the first scripts, many other fans became writers and directors of the troupe's satirical, costumed plays. All the while, I was building on my knowledge of Dan Curtis's television horror through my interaction with the fans, the Rosses, and the TV stars themselves.

In the 2000s, I was enrolled in the doctoral program of the English department of Middle Tennessee State University, and it was time to write my doctoral dissertation. I considered writing about *film noir* in general and *Chinatown* in particular, for that *film-noir* classic — as well as *Somewhere in Time, The Piano Lesson,* and several of Dan Curtis's short films (segments from *Trilogy of Terror, Dead of Night,* and *Trilogy of Terror II*)— is a movie that I show to my Tennessee State University students every semester. However, before I wrote the actual dissertation in 2006–2007 and received my Ph.D. in May 2007, two events occurred that changed the topic of my dissertation from *film noir* to Dan Curtis.

First, in May 2005, I wrote seven entries for Midnight Marquee Press's 2008 multi-author book about loss of identity in science-fiction, fantasy, and horror movies. I chose to focus on loss of identity in five of Dan Curtis's films —*House of Dark Shadows, Night of Dark Shadows, Burnt Offerings, Trilogy of Terror,* and *Trilogy of Terror II*— as well as in E.W. Swackhamer's *Death at Love House* (very similar to *Night of Dark*

Shadows) and Gordon Hessler's *The Strange Possession of Mrs. Oliver* (another *Trilogy of Terror*-style vehicle for Karen Black). I found that I really enjoyed serving as, in the words of editor Anthony Ambrogio, "the Dan Curtis man" for the loss-of-identity book.

Second, in March 2006, Dan Curtis died. I first learned the sad news from an e-mail edition of Marcy Robin's *Shadowgram* newszine. Then my friend Bob Tinnell, the noted filmmaker (*Frankenstein and Me*) and comic-book creator (*The Black Forest*), suggested to his friend Jeff Vaughn that I write Dan Curtis's obituary for *Scoop*, Diamond Galleries' weekly e-newsletter that Vaughn published. I wrote the death notice for the March 31, 2006, edition of *Scoop*; then, my two-part article about the *Dark Shadows* comic books and newspaper comic strip appeared in the April 7 and 14 editions of *Scoop*; and I was interviewed in the May 5 *Scoop*, about my lifelong interest in *Dark Shadows*, soap operas, *Planet of the Apes*, comic books, *Somewhere in Time*, film music, *Highlander*, memorabilia, and more.

Suddenly I realized that I should write my MTSU doctoral dissertation about the horror films and television of Dan Curtis! Many dissertations and books had covered *film noir*, but just as I had broken new ground with my M.A. thesis by expanding the scholarship concerning Dan Ross, I now had the chance to bestow some much-deserved recognition on one of the most remarkable writer-producer-directors of the 1970s and beyond. Before my dissertation there had been only a few works spotlighting Dan Curtis, most notably *Produced and Directed by Dan Curtis* by Jim Pierson, *The Night Stalker Companion* by Mark Dawidziak, and Darren Gross's articles about the two *Dark Shadows* movies for various magazines, websites, and books.

In 2006–2007, I accomplished the daunting yet thrilling and enjoyable task of writing at least a few sentences about every single Dan Curtis production and at least a few pages or more about

Dead of Night (1977): Elisha Cook, Jr. (left; as Karel) and Patrick Macnee (as Dr. Gheria) pose for this rare publicity photo in 1973. Their television film *No Such Thing as a Vampire* did not air until March 1977.

Curtis's 16 major horror productions. Much of my information came from my own knowledge, writings, and life experiences pertaining to *Dark Shadows, The Night Stalker,* and their fandoms. I also found a great deal of material in my several decades' worth of back issues of Marcy Robin's *Shadowgram* newszine and Kathy Resch's *World of Dark Shadows* fanzine. Still more information came from the aforementioned writings of Dawidziak, Gross, and Pierson, as well as from our fellow *Dark Shadows* experts Jeffrey Arsenault, Mark Booher, and Charles Ellis. I could always rely on them to remind me of such arcane facts as how, in the early 1970s, *House of Dark Shadows* was released or re-released on double bills with such unusual films as *The Brotherhood of Satan, Dusty and Sweets McGee, Every Little Crook and Nanny, The Traveling Executioner,* and (in 1976) Dan Curtis's own *Burnt Offerings.* For their added insights into television, horror movies, and comic books, I could count on Scott Gibson, Dr. Jonathan Lampley, and Patrick Murphy. At the same time that I was writing my Dan Curtis dissertation, Dr. Lampley was writing his dissertation — soon to be a McFarland book — about the horror films of Vincent Price.

I cannot overemphasize the invaluable assistance of Jim Pierson in the preparation of my doctoral dissertation, which now has become this McFarland book. While Dan Curtis *was* all things *Dark Shadows* and 1970s TV horror, Jim Pierson, in Curtis's absence, *is Dark Shadows.* Through his leadership of the Dark Shadows Festival and his vital involvement with Dan Curtis Productions, MPI Home Video, and film preservation, Jim Pierson has been a major force in perpetuating *Dark Shadows* and the entire body of work of his mentor Curtis, whom Pierson has called "the ultimate fearless leader." As I was writing my dissertation, I often wrote letters or e-mails to Jim and asked him questions about Dan Curtis minutiae. In his replies, Jim revealed little-known facts; for instance, according to Jim, in 1973, Curtis shot "No Such Thing as a Vampire" for Metromedia and ABC as part of a weekly mystery anthology series. "Originally titled *Inner Sanctum,* it never aired," Jim Pierson explained, "and Dan bought back the half-hour and folded it into his 1977 NBC 90-minute *Dead of Night* TV-movie pilot." An even more obscure fact which only Jim Pierson could tell me is that in 1972, Dan Curtis had signed Jack Palance to host a syndicated Viacom TV series tentatively titled *Classic Mystery Ghost Stories with Jack Palance.* According to Pierson, "Unfortunately, no tape seems to exist, but wraparound intros were taped with Jack for a pilot presentation." Jim also provided background information about *The CBS Golf Classic, Frankenstein, The Great Ice Rip-Off, Supertrain, Me and the Kid,* the Dark Shadows Festival, and much more. I extend a very special thank you to Jim Pierson not only for helping me and encouraging me along the way but also for writing the foreword to this book and for supplying me with almost every single photograph found herein. Unless otherwise noted, each photograph is courtesy of Jim Pierson and Dan Curtis Productions.

One of the hallmarks of my writing style is lists, and here is by far the longest list in this book. For their expertise, assistance, encouragement, love, and/or friendship, I wish to thank Forrest J Ackerman, Jo Addie, Anthony Ambrogio, Jeffrey Arsenault, Dr. Jane Asamani, Dr. Linda Badley, Dennis Baker, John Barcus, Joyce and Bill Barry, Karen Black, Robert Bloch, Mark Booher, Sharon Bradley, Ken Bramming, Dr. Will

Brantley, Stephon Brisco, Dave Brown, Bill Byrge, Robert Cobert, Joe Collins, Richard Cowl, Dan Curtis Productions, Jenny and Mike Darrell, Mark Dawidziak, Alison and Andy Egan, Charles Ellis, Eileen Farrar, Robert Finocchio, Dr. Laura Brodian Freas, Jonathan Frid, Scott Gibson, Elva and John Griffin, Dr. Johanna Grimes, Darren Gross, Dr. Karen Gupton, Guy Haines, Richard Halpern, Craig Hamrick, Jonathan Harrison, Arlena Hayden, Joan Higgins, Penny Holdren, Dr. Marian Hollings, Dr. Bob Holtzclaw, Joe Integlia, Jack Jackson, Laurel Jenkins-Crowe, Sherri Justice, Barbara Kannard, David Lackey, Dr. Jonathan Lampley, the Lipper family, Peter Macchia, Stuart Manning, Richard Matheson, Dan McEachern, Rev. Martin McGeachy, MPI Home Video, Patrick Murphy, Lois Nixon, Michelle and John Noel, William F. Nolan, the Parsley family, Jim Pierson, Cheryl and Jeff Podolsky, Dr. Jo Helen Railsback, Dr. Monetha Reaves, Kathy Resch, Marcy Robin, Marilyn and Dan Ross, Helen Samaras, Chris Schlueter, Kathryn Leigh Scott, Bill Shepard, Dan Silvio, Brenda Smith, Cindy and Brian Smith, Barbara Steele, Brinke Stevens, Harriet Stich, Dr. Tom Strawman, Susan and Gary Svehla, Donna Thomas, the Thompson family, Bob Tinnell, Mike Turner, Larry Underwood, Joshua Vance, Jeff Vaughn, Muninn and Thor Venetis, Steve Vertlieb, Shirley and David Wadell, Dr. Warren Westcott, Tim Wiley, Ann Wilson, Emma Wisdom, Kenneth Wright, Reed Young, the stars of *Dark Shadows,* my colleagues and students at Tennessee State University (where I often show Dan Curtis's "Graveyard Rats"), my co-workers and listeners at WAMB-AM 1200 (where I often play Robert Cobert's "Quentin's Theme"), and *you.* Finally, I thank the people to whom this book is dedicated: my parents, my sister, my brother-in-law, my three nieces, my two nephews, and, of course, Dan Curtis. To paraphrase what Forrest J Ackerman always said about Lon Chaney, Sr., "Dan Curtis Shall Never Die!"

Jeff Thompson
Spring 2009

Introduction: Dan Curtis and Television Horror

While the decade of the 1970s is often considered the final golden age of American cinema — offering landmark films such as *Chinatown* (1974) and *Nashville* (1975) — remarkable films were also being made for American television. These include *The Autobiography of Miss Jane Pittman* (1974), *The Execution of Private Slovik* (1974), and *The Legend of Lizzie Borden* (1975), as well as made-for-TV horror movies such as *The Screaming Woman* (1972), *Gargoyles* (1972), *Satan's School for Girls* (1973), and *The Dark Secret of Harvest Home* (1978). One of the era's most significant television directors, in terms of impact, ratings, innovation, quality, and influence, was the Emmy and Directors Guild of America award-winning *auteur* Dan Curtis.

From his beginnings as one of the chief architects of ABC-TV's *Dark Shadows* (1966–1971), Dan Curtis could be considered an *auteur* (i.e., the predominant author of his productions and the one most responsible for their tone and vision) because of his intense involvement in numerous aspects of his works, from producing, directing, and editing to writing, script-doctoring, and set-decorating. Furthermore, Curtis was able to tap into the mood of a particular cultural movement, whether it was the seventies-era fascination with demonology (as evidenced in his *Norliss Tapes* and *Dead of Night* in 1973 and 1977, respectively) or the late-eighties/early-nineties interest in New Age mysticism (as manifested in his drastic updating of the Maggie Evans character for the 1991 *Dark Shadows*). Curtis had the ability both to follow and to shape trends — this is seen when his made-for-TV movies in the 1970s perpetuated the subgenre of the occult/suspense movie of the week, when he emphasized the feminist aspects of his 1977 telefilm *Curse of the Black Widow,* and when he assembled a multicultural cast for his 2004 *Dark Shadows* remake.

Curtis further distinguished himself by his attraction to multifaceted projects. *The Night Stalker* (1972) was equal parts newspaper procedural, *film noir,* and horror. *Supertrain* (1979) was a blend of comedy, drama, and mystery, and *Me and the Kid* (1993) brought together elements of slapstick comedy, crime drama, and kids' adventure. Curtis demonstrated great confidence in choosing the stories that he felt personally suited to tell, e.g. *When Every Day Was the Fourth of July* (1978), *The Long Days of Summer*

(1980), *Me and the Kid* (1993), and *The Love Letter* (1998). He engaged in self-reflection before and after making a film, as his forthcoming quoted comments and letters demonstrate, and he was always ready to defend his material if he felt it was being overlooked or dismissed, as his emphatic editorials about *Frankenstein* (1973) and *War and Remembrance* (1988, 1989) proved to 1990s readers of the *Los Angeles Times*.

Dan Curtis became an *auteur* when, during his 1966–1991 heyday, every film project that he wanted to make received a green light from networks or studios. All he had to do was talk to ABC executive Brandon Stoddard about making *Dark Shadows,* and Curtis received a 26-week commitment. He pitched something as offbeat as *The Norliss Tapes* (1973) or *The Great Ice Rip-Off* (1974) to a TV executive like Michael Eisner or Barry Diller, and it became a movie of the week. Years later, Brandon Stoddard implored Curtis to direct the mammoth *War and Remembrance.* Not only did studio executives such as Stoddard want to work with Curtis time and again, but actors clamored to make a second, third, or even fourth film with the director, thereby establishing Curtis alongside Woody Allen or Robert Altman as an *auteur* with a recognizable stock company of regular performers.

Finally, Curtis mastered the ability to manipulate the restrictions of the television and film industries and to mitigate their various pressures. For example, Curtis successfully negotiated with Polish authorities to film part of his *War* epic at Auschwitz, and then he successfully negotiated with ABC executives and censors to allow him to show the horrors of the Holocaust, unsanitized and unedited, on national television. The unflinching Auschwitz death-camp scenes are the somber hallmark of *War and Remembrance.*

By the close of the 1980s, Curtis had been duly recognized as a prodigious director because of his decade-long work in bringing to television Herman Wouk's epic World War II novels *The Winds of War* (in 1983) and *War and Remembrance* (in 1988 and 1989). However, well before those Herculean accomplishments, Curtis had made an indelible mark on television horror. Themselves influenced by classic Gothic-horror literature, Universal monster movies, or Hammer vampire movies, the many horror productions of Dan Curtis went on to influence books such as *The Vampire Contessa* (1974) and *Interview with the Vampire* (1976); films such as *Dark Mansions* (TV-1986), *Bram Stoker's Dracula* (1992), and *Men in Black* (1997); and television series such as *Strange Paradise* (1969–1970), *The X-Files* (1993–2002), *Passions* (1999–2007), and *Dante's Cove* (debuted 2005).

The impact of Dan Curtis's work cannot be denied. His daytime Gothic serial *Dark Shadows* mesmerized an entire generation of baby boomers and made a teen idol of Barnabas Collins, the reluctant vampire. J. Gordon Melton, author of *The Vampire Book: The Encyclopedia of the Undead* (1994), notes that the three most significant vampires in all of popular culture are Bram Stoker's Dracula, Dan Curtis's Barnabas, and Anne Rice's Lestat.[1] The Barnabas character has starred in two television series, one TV pilot (never aired), one theatrical film (*House of Dark Shadows* [1970]), more than two dozen paperback novels, more than three dozen comic books, and even a modern ballet — and on July 27, 2007, *Variety* announced Johnny Depp's intention to portray Barnabas Collins in a motion picture for Warner Brothers. Subscribers to Marcy Robin's *Shadowgram* had heard the news the day before.

Curtis's made-for-TV movies, including *The Night Strangler* (1973), *Dracula* (1974), and *Trilogy of Terror* (1975), often scored blockbuster ratings—none more so than Curtis's production of *The Night Stalker*, the telefilm which introduced Carl Kolchak, another TV character as culturally significant as Barnabas Collins. On Tuesday, January 11, 1972, an amazing one-third of all TV households in the United States watched *The Night Stalker*.[2]

The films of Dan Curtis brought great innovation to the horror landscape of the 1970s and beyond. First, TV-movies such as *The Night Stalker* (1972), *The Night Strangler* (1973), *The Norliss Tapes* (1973), *Curse of the Black Widow* (1977), and *Trilogy of Terror II* (1996) unleashed age-old horrors onto the modern world. A vampire stalked showgirls in modern-day Las Vegas. An immortal killer struck Seattle every twenty-one years. A legendary spider-woman claimed her male victims under the full moon. Second, all five of the aforementioned movies added *film-noir* sensibilities to the mayhem, and *The Night Stalker* and its sequel mixed humor with horror. Finally, in those two films and *The Norliss Tapes,* as well as on *Dark Shadows,* Curtis reinvented for modern audiences the Van Helsing/vampire-hunter character in the forms of Carl Kolchak, David Norliss, and Professor Stokes.

The on-screen credit, A DAN CURTIS PRODUCTION, almost always meant very high quality. *The Winds of War* (1983), *The Last Ride of the Dalton Gang* (1979), and *Melvin Purvis, G-Man* (1974) are television classics in the war, Western, and gangster genres, but Curtis invested just as much quality in his horror output—perhaps never more so than in his acclaimed adaptations of *The Strange Case of Dr. Jekyll and Mr. Hyde* (1968), *Frankenstein* (1973), *The Picture of Dorian Gray* (1973), *Dracula* (1974), and *The Turn of the Screw* (1974). *Dr. Jekyll and Mr. Hyde* was nominated for six Emmy Awards, and all five productions received glowing reviews from such publications as the *Boston Globe, Los Angeles Times, Hollywood Reporter, Variety,* and others. Critics and scholars alike praised these adaptations for their overall fidelity to the classic texts. Radu Florescu, author of *In Search of Frankenstein* (1975), called Curtis's production of Mary Shelley's novel "the most faithful rendering the screen has yet seen."[3] Numerous Dracula scholars, from Florescu and Raymond McNally to Donald F. Glut and Lyndon W. Joslin, have commended Curtis's *Dracula* for its faithful interpretation of Bram Stoker's novel. At the same time, director Curtis, writer Richard Matheson, and actor Jack Palance brought to *Dracula* a human quality especially appealing to 1970s audiences. Curtis and his frequent co-writers, including Matheson, William F. Nolan, and Earl Wallace, almost always struck a balance between timeliness and timelessness.

Curtis's horror productions were highly influential on works which followed them. In February 2006, the *Los Angeles Times* credited *The Night Stalker* and *The Night Strangler* "with inspiring contemporary entertainment, including *Buffy the Vampire Slayer* and *Men in Black. X-Files* creator-producer Chris Carter has often cited Carl Kolchak as the primary inspiration for *The X-Files*."[4] NBC-TV's *Passions* (1999–2007) and BBC America's *Hex* (2004–2007) are supernatural serials which echo the themes of witchcraft and the occult portrayed on *Dark Shadows.* From time to time, *Passions* even played some of Robert Cobert's music from *Dark Shadows,* and in one February 2006 episode, the witch Tabitha Lenox (played by Juliet Mills) declared that Barnabas Collins was one of her old boyfriends. *Hex* imitated *Night of Dark Shadows* (1971) by hanging a witch from a tree on the grounds of a haunted manor house.

Another important accomplishment of the horror television of Dan Curtis is that it served as a bridge from classic horror to modern horror. Curtis's productions utilized elements from both styles: "classic," as exemplified by Gothic novels, Universal monster movies of the 1930s and 1940s, and Hammer horror films of the 1950s and 1960s; and "modern," as embodied in groundbreaking films such as *Psycho* (1960), *Peeping Tom* (1960), *Homicidal* (1961), *Repulsion* (1965), *Rosemary's Baby* (1968), and *Night of the Living Dead* (1968), as well as the mid–1970s emergence of Stephen King and Anne Rice in the burgeoning field of horror literature. According to Mark Twain scholar and *Cleveland Plain Dealer* film and television critic Mark Dawidziak,

> Keep in mind that *Dark Shadows* hit the air long before horror regularly claimed the number-one spot at the movie box office or on the *New York Times* best-seller list. There just wasn't much horror around in those days, and fright fans jumped on anything that came into view. They relied on old Universal shockers from the 1930s and the occasional Hammer horror film from England, as well as Forrest J Ackerman's *Famous Monsters of Filmland* magazine. Along with *Dark Shadows,* they all kept the flame alive, bridging the gap between the horror boom of the 1950s (the golden age of Ray Bradbury, Richard Matheson, Robert Bloch, and Charles Beaumont) and the horror explosion of the 1970s and 1980s in print (Stephen King, Anne Rice, Dean Koontz, Clive Barker) and on screen (filmmakers George Romero, Wes Craven, Tobe Hooper, John Carpenter). The influence and impact were immense.[5]

Meanwhile, at about the same time (1966–1977) that Curtis was producing *Dark Shadows* and then filming his horror classics, Koontz and Barker were writing books such as *Demon Seed* (1973) and *The Books of Blood* (1981), and Romero, Craven, Hooper, and Carpenter were making revolutionary modern-horror films such as *Night of the Living Dead* (1968), *Last House on the Left* (1972), *The Texas Chainsaw Massacre* (1974), and *Halloween* (1978). Ackerman's *Famous Monsters* magazine chronicled these works, as well as the output of Dan Curtis. Pictures from the *Dark Shadows* TV series or movies appeared on the cover of *Famous Monsters* four times (issues #52, 59, 82, and 88).

The change from classic horror (often based in myths or legends and combined with atmosphere) to modern horror (often based in reality or verisimilitude and coupled with shock value) began in 1960 with Alfred Hitchcock's *Psycho* in America, Michael Powell's *Peeping Tom* in England, and Mario Bava's *Black Sunday* in Italy. The first two films depict murder in shockingly realistic terms, and all three blend horror and lust. Horror-film critic Bruce Kawin maintains that *Peeping Tom* and *Psycho,* as well as Hitchcock's earlier *Vertigo* (1958) and *Rear Window* (1954), exemplify "the core of the shift into the sixties themselves."[6] Kawin adds that Hitchcock's films, "along with Powell's *Peeping Tom,* most prefigure [...] such sixties horror films as *Targets* (Peter Bogdanovich, 1968) and *Kwaidan* (Masaki Kobayashi, 1965)."[7]

Another important year was 1963, when Hitchcock's *The Birds* heralded the many apocalyptic-horror films to come and Roger Corman's *X—The Man with the X-Ray Eyes* combined science fiction, horror, and paranoia years before *Alien* (1979) or *The X-Files* (1993–2002). Of course, classic-horror films were still being made in 1963. Two examples are Robert Wise's *The Haunting* in America and Anton Leader's *Children of the*

Damned in England. They are the more traditional stories of ghosts in a haunted house or evil children in the *Turn of the Screw* mode.

Horror-film critic Isabel Pinedo identifies four characteristics of modern horror as a disruption of normalcy, a violation of boundaries, a disruption of the social order, and an open-ended final outcome.[8] *The Birds* (1963) fits this description in that the birds' deviant, hostile behavior disrupts normal human life in Bodega Bay when the birds cross their natural boundaries by attacking people and reducing the community to chaos. The film ends with *no* real ending as the birds seem to be on their way to conquering humanity. On an even more realistic note, Norman Bates of *Psycho* (1960) is the very epitome of normalcy gone awry. His serial murders violate the boundaries of law and decency, and they threaten civility and society. Although Norman himself is apprehended and put away, he is seen as merely one representative of a much greater, more widespread psychosis threatening civilization.

In the year 1968, modern horror (and modern science fiction) took hold with a vengeance and proved that a new kind of film was here to stay. It was the year of Richard Fleischer's *The Boston Strangler,* George Romero's *Night of the Living Dead,* Franklin Schaffner's *Planet of the Apes,* Roman Polanski's *Rosemary's Baby,* and Stanley Kubrick's *2001: A Space Odyssey.* Horror-film critic Gregory Waller observes that *Rosemary's Baby* and *Night of the Living Dead* are "the two films that could be said to have ushered in the modern era of horror."[9] Waller contends that these landmark movies "challenged the moral-social-political assumptions, production values, and narrative strategies of Hammer and AIP films" because they "situated horror in the everyday world of contemporary America."[10] Dr. Frankenstein in his laboratory is not as relevant or horrific to modern America, Waller contends, as the Satanist cabal next door or the zombies on the porch. With these films, horror had come home to roost and fester.

While Polanski's and Romero's films indeed are the touchstones of modern horror, neither they nor *The Exorcist* (1973), *The Texas Chainsaw Massacre* (1974), and *Jaws* (1975) could be possible without Robert Bloch's 1959 novel and Alfred Hitchcock's 1960 film *Psycho*— for better and for worse the grandfather of modern horror and its powerful sub-genre, the slasher film. Countless horror movies that have come after *Psycho* owe a conscious or subconscious debt to Hitchcock's film, which upended the classical idea of clear-cut good and evil found in many Universal, Hammer, and American International pictures. *Psycho* also countered Hammer's Technicolor costume melodramas with stark, black-and-white minimalism and realism, and it turned narrative structure inward by, in the words of horror-film critic Paul Wells, "directly implicating the viewer in an amoral universe grounded in the psychic imperatives of its protagonists."[11] Marion Crane steals $40,000, but does that make her all bad? Norman Bates kills people, but does even *that* make *him* all bad? According to Wells, *Psycho* "is the moment when the monster [...] is conflated with the reality of a modern world in which humankind is increasingly self-conscious and alienated from its pre-determined social structures."[12]

In a CBS-TV special on June 12, 2001, the American Film Institute acknowledged the supreme importance of *Psycho* by placing it at number one on the AFI's list of "America's Most Heart-Pounding Movies," i.e. thrillers in the horror, science-fiction, fantasy, *film-noir,* Western, and suspense genres. Without *Psycho* (#1) and its innovations, there might never have been *Jaws* (#2), *The Exorcist* (#3), *The Silence of the Lambs* (#5), *The Birds* (#7), *Rosemary's Baby* (#9), *Fatal Attraction* (#28), *Carrie* (#46), *The Sixth Sense* (#60), *Halloween* (#68), *The Omen* (#81), *Poltergeist* (#84), or *Night of the Living Dead* (#93)—or, at least, not in exactly the same way that each of those movies came to be. Bloch, Hitchcock, and *Psycho* ushered in a new way of looking at, talking about, and rebelling against the seeming complacency and conformity of the Eisenhower era. How safe, sweet, and idyllic is one's home and community if, at any moment, the boy next door can start killing people, birds can make war on humans, a woman can bear Satan's son, or zombies can march on the town?

Burnt Offerings (1976): Dan Curtis, to the right of a cameraman, directs Oliver Reed and Lee Harcourt Montgomery in the swimming pool at Dunsmuir House in Oakland, California. This "rough-house" scene is one that audiences remember well.

Dan Curtis was making his horror classics at a time when cinematic horror and science fiction were becoming more quasi-realistic and brutally terrifying. Although *House of Dark Shadows* (1970) was much bloodier than any of his other films, its horrors still were not equivalent to the barbarity depicted in *Last House on the Left* (1972) or *The Texas Chainsaw Massacre* (1974). In 1997, Curtis said, "Anybody can make a gory, slasher type of horror movie. That's easy, and it's not really horror. Those things are abominations as far as I'm concerned."[13]

Curtis's idea of horror was much more classical—suspense, mystery, dread, shadows, and fear of the unknown. With the possible exceptions of the bloodletting of *House of Dark Shadows* (1970) and the violent climax of *Burnt Offerings* (1976), Curtis always endorsed the less-is-more *suggestion* of horror. He took his cues from Mary Shelley, Bram Stoker, and Richard Matheson's literate descriptions of terror; from the atmospheric Gothicism of the Universal movies; from other classic-horror films such as *The*

Uninvited (1944) and *The Innocents* (1961); and perhaps from the admittedly more daring but usually tasteful Hammer horrors, such as *The Curse of Frankenstein* (1957) and *Horror of Dracula* (1958). Curtis's films also presented a traditional Judeo-Christian ethos of good and evil, right and wrong.

Curtis and Matheson worked so well together because their vision of terror was similar. Matheson preferred to be called a terror writer rather than a horror writer because he considered horror to be merely blood-and-guts gore. To Matheson, terror was the creeping dread and fear exemplified in Jacques Tourneur's *Night of the Demon*, a.k.a. *Curse of the Demon* (1957), from a story by M.R. James. "You can get many points made through terror," Matheson insisted in a 2006 DVD interview. "You can get away with a lot more — and it's a lot more frightening — when you don't have it right in front of you."[14]

Dan Curtis became a master at blending modern horror and classic horror in his works. In *The Night Stalker* (1972), a vampire drives a rented car through Las Vegas, but he goes home to his coffin in the typical old, dark house. In *The Night Strangler* (1973), a serial killer terrorizes Seattle, but he retreats to a conventional mad-scientist laboratory. In *The Norliss Tapes* (1973), fascination with demonology (in vogue, in both theory and practice, in the early 1970s) causes a man to take on the characteristics of a vampire. In *Scream of the Wolf* (1974), the possibility of a werewolf in present-day California sets the stage for a re-enactment of the classic 1924 short story "The Most Dangerous Game." In *Burnt Offerings* (1976), a modern family becomes engulfed in the classic terrors of a haunted house. In *Curse of the Black Widow* (1977), everything old is new again as 1970s Southern California is attacked by something out of a 1950s monster movie. Even *War and Remembrance* (1988, 1989) blends the abominations of Auschwitz with the nostalgia of World War II.

This book will analyze and make connections among the major horror movies of producer-director Curtis's body of work. It will provide insight into the making of the films — often in the form of an oral history as Dan Curtis, Richard Matheson, William F. Nolan, Robert Cobert, Darren McGavin, Jack Palance, Karen Black, Barbara Steele, and the stars of *Dark Shadows* tell the story in their own words. It will place Curtis's films in the broader context of twentieth-century popular culture, underscoring the ways in which culture influenced — and was influenced by — these movies and television programs. Reviews of the productions (from the *New York Times, Hollywood Reporter, Films in Review, Chicago Sun–Times, Variety,* and many other publications) will be presented, as will the life, the works, and personality of this Connecticut-born director who in the 1960s produced *The CBS Golf Classic* and *Dark Shadows,* in the 1970s helmed more than one dozen TV horror classics, in the 1980s directed two of the finest miniseries in television history, in the 1990s returned to his horror roots with remakes of *Dark Shadows* and *Trilogy of Terror,* and in the 2000s concluded his career with the topical, emotional docudramas *Saving Milly* and *Our Fathers.*

Chapter I, "The Career of Dan Curtis: An Overview," offers information about every Dan Curtis production, from golf shows to *Our Fathers* (2005). The 16 horror films are mentioned only in passing because they are the subjects of their own in-depth chapters. All of Curtis's non-horror films and miniseries are showcased more fully, as are the media's reports of his death.

Chapter II, "Curtis's Dream: *Dark Shadows*," examines the 1966–1971, 1991, and 2004 television projects. The chapter explores the 21 *Dark Shadows* episodes Curtis directed in 1968 and 1969, and it demonstrates how the original *Dark Shadows* (into which Curtis had considerable writing input) served as his creative springboard to adapt the literary horror classics *Frankenstein, The Picture of Dorian Gray, Dracula,* and *The Turn of the Screw* in 1973–1974. For example, *Dark Shadows* featured a synthetic man not unlike Frankenstein's creation, a werewolf whose curse was negated by a *Dorian Gray*-like portrait, Barnabas Collins and other vampires in the tradition of *Dracula,* and possessed children such as those in Henry James's novel. Conversely, Curtis's 1968 production of *The Strange Case of Dr. Jekyll and Mr. Hyde* inspired him to feature a Jekyll-and-Hyde character in the *Dark Shadows* TV show's 1970 Parallel Time story-line (the plotline which also was an inspiration for *Night of Dark Shadows*). Also examined will be Curtis's career-long trait of doubling (begun by shooting the same *Dark Shadows* scenes twice and making two *Dark Shadows* movies) and the literary antecedents to the many complicated *Dark Shadows* storylines themselves, including *Jane Eyre, The Crucible,* "The Cask of Amontillado," "The Tell-Tale Heart," "The Pit and the Pendulum," "The Premature Burial," *Rebecca, Wuthering Heights, The Lottery,* and the Cthulhu mythos of H.P. Lovecraft.

Chapter III, "Big-Screen Shadows: *House of Dark Shadows* and *Night of Dark Shadows*," reveals the genesis of Dan Curtis's movie career. The chapter details the making of the movies, the possible influence of Hammer films on *House of Dark Shadows* (1970), and the cultural significance of the downbeat ending of *Night of Dark Shadows* (1971), a film which barely survived the drastic cuts imposed on it by MGM and the MPAA.

Chapter IV, "Curtis and the Classics: *The Strange Case of Dr. Jekyll and Mr. Hyde, Frankenstein, The Picture of Dorian Gray, Dracula,* and *The Turn of the Screw,*" takes a detailed look at each adaptation in relation to the classic text. The chapter points out each production's overall fidelity to the novel and explains and contextualizes the changes which Curtis and his writers (including Matheson and Nolan) made and why such changes were necessary and/or desirable.

Chapter V, "The Kolchak Papers: *The Night Stalker* and *The Night Strangler*," chronicles the evolution of Carl Kolchak's adventures from an unpublished novel to the highest-rated made-for-TV movie in history up to that time. The chapter illuminates both films' unique blends of classic horror and modern horror, and it spotlights the highly successful Dan Curtis/Richard Matheson collaboration which spanned six projects.

Chapter VI, "In the *Night Stalker* Vein: *The Norliss Tapes* and *Scream of the Wolf*," adds writer William F. Nolan to the Curtis/Matheson mix and reveals why these two telefilms are much more than mere imitations of the Kolchak-versus-monster formula. One film benefits from its strong sense of place (a characteristic of many of Curtis's films), and the other reveals an unexpected sexual undercurrent of a type still considered shocking in 1974. Both films are additional examples of Curtis's ability to mix traditional and modern elements of horror: they are in tune with their times, and they are aware of their literary underpinnings. Because one movie was never released on video and the other has been relegated to public-domain DVDs, both are ready for reappraisal.

Chapter VII, "A Trilogy of Trilogies of Terror: *Trilogy of Terror, Dead of Night,* and *Trilogy of Terror II,*" compares and contrasts Matheson and Nolan's TV adaptations and the actual short stories by Matheson, Henry Kuttner, and Jack Finney. The chapter discusses Sigmund Freud's idea of scopophilia and Laura Mulvey's idea of the male gaze, and it measures the three films' relevance to audiences of 1975, 1977, and 1996.

Chapter VIII, "Curtis's Pre–*War* Farewell to Horror: *Burnt Offerings* and *Curse of the Black Widow,*" examines what is perhaps Curtis's greatest horror film and perhaps his most underrated horror movie. The chapter points out that while these films are definitely horror movies, they also are remarkable family dramas, and one of them is decidedly feminist. Of these final horror films that Curtis made before he turned his attention to *The Winds of War* and *War and Remembrance,* one exemplifies Curtis's ideas of what a horror movie should be and should do, and the other was co-written by someone who would win the Academy Award for Best Screenplay less than a decade later.

Finally, "Conclusion: Dan Curtis and the Emergence of Participatory Fan Culture," summarizes the legacy of Dan Curtis, including *Dark Shadows* fandom, and the lasting importance of this major but often unsung figure in American television horror and popular culture. This book's goal is to assert, assure, and ensure the esteemed place of Dan Curtis and his movies on the canvas of popular culture.

CHAPTER I

The Career of Dan Curtis:
An Overview

Three of Dan Curtis's greatest loves defined the producer-director's career. Curtis loved golf, Gothic horror, and World War II. In his television career, he created golf series, *Dark Shadows* and memorable made-for-TV horror films, and the epic miniseries *The Winds of War* (1983) and *War and Remembrance* (1988, 1989). Curtis's associates remember the fearless director practicing his golf swing in his office, constantly searching for great horror properties to film, and executing the mammoth shooting schedules of the two *War* miniseries with the zeal of an army general. "Even when he directed *Dark Shadows*," actor Jonathan Frid recalled in his talk at the 1993 Dark Shadows Festival, "he approached it as if we were doing *The Winds of War!*"

Curtis was born Daniel Mayer Cherkoss, the only child of Mildred and Edward Cherkoss, on August 12, 1927, in Bridgeport, Connecticut. He gained a half-brother from his dentist-father's second marriage after his mother's death. When Curtis dramatized his childhood in 1930s Bridgeport in two award-winning made-for-TV movies, *When Every Day Was the Fourth of July* (1978) and *The Long Days of Summer* (1980), he added a fictitious younger sister Sarah to his TV family — just as he had given Barnabas Collins of *Dark Shadows* a little sister Sarah.

After serving in the Naval Reserve in 1945, he

A young Daniel Mayer Cherkoss (Dan Curtis) smiles broadly.

attended Syracuse University and graduated with a bachelor's degree in sociology in 1950. Two years later, he married Norma Mae Klein, his wife until her death in March 2006 (just 20 days before Curtis's own). Cathy and Tracy, two of the Curtises' three daughters, survived their parents; Linda Curtis died tragically in 1975.

Beginning a career in television in the 1950s, Curtis worked in film sales (TV syndication) for NBC for eight years. "I sold *Douglas Fairbanks Presents* and *Hopalong Cassidy* reruns," as well as *Victory at Sea* and *Dragnet* reruns, Curtis explained.[1] Between 1952 and 1960, Curtis advanced from the position of Eastern field salesman to central sales manager to Eastern sales manager to regional/national sales manager and finally to director of sales. Then he spent two years in the show-packaging department at MCA, where he sold *Union Pacific* episodes and the Grace Kelly TV special *A Look at Monaco* to local television stations. When he sold the cartoon series *Linus! The Lion-Hearted* to CBS, Curtis made a cameo voice appearance in one episode as Big-Time Talent Agent, who kidnaps a singing group led by Billie Bird (voiced by Carl Reiner). His experience in selling syndicated reruns prompted him to save all 1225 episodes of *Dark Shadows* for future sales. All but one of the episodes still exist and are available on VHS and DVD.

In 1962, the 35-year-old Curtis formed his own company, Dan Curtis Associates (soon renamed Dan Curtis Productions), and created *Golf Challenge* for ABC-TV. The show featured Arnold Palmer and Gary Player in a best-ball competition. In 1963, CBS, wanting to cultivate its own golf audience, asked Curtis to create and executive-produce *The CBS Match-Play Golf Classic* (later called *The CBS Golf Classic*). "CBS and I owned the show 50–50," Curtis revealed.[2] It was he who devised the practice of wiring golfers with throat microphones so that the TV audience could hear the players' immediate reactions to their shots (including occasional obscenities when they missed).

The CBS Golf Classic aired for a decade, from December 28, 1963, to April 21, 1973, and brought Curtis his first Emmy Award (for Achievement in Sports) in the 1965–1966 season. Curtis executive-produced the show until 1967; Frank Chirkinian was his producer-director. The series eventually went from one hour to 90 minutes (and from black-and-white to color), and the prize money rose from $166,000 to $225,000. Most of the tournaments took place on golf courses in California, New Jersey, or Ohio. The Emmy Award-winning Curtis, now earning $100,000 per year, was well on his way to becoming a noted television producer.

Known for getting bored easily, Curtis soon yearned to try his hand at dramatic television. One night in the summer of 1965, he went to sleep and had a dream which changed the course of television popular culture and the fortunes of third-place ABC. In his dream, Curtis saw a dark-haired young woman riding a train toward a house of dark shadows by the sea and her destiny. She was a present-day Jane Eyre, soon to be caught up in the intrigues and deceptions of a wealthy, eccentric family and its secrets.

Curtis pitched his Gothic idea to ABC executives Brandon Stoddard and Leonard Goldberg. He was supposed to meet with them to discuss a different idea for a series, but his dream of the girl on the train would not leave his mind. Curtis gave ABC that idea instead, to which Goldberg replied, "Dan, haven't you just rewritten *Jane Eyre?*" Curtis's comeback was, "Is anybody doing it on TV right now?"[3]

After briefly considering *Dark Shadows* as a nighttime program, Curtis and ABC decided to present it instead as a daytime soap opera. Its stars would be Hollywood film actress Joan Bennett, New York stage actor Louis Edmonds, and (as the girl on the train) newcomer Alexandra Moltke. In the wake of the November 1965 premiere of NBC-TV's *Days of Our Lives,* with classic Hollywood star Mac-Donald Carey heading the cast, Curtis decided to seek Bennett, an even more celebrated movie star, for the anchor role of Elizabeth Collins Stoddard. *Dark Shadows* debuted on June 27, 1966.

However, after ten months of low-rated episodes which ABC publicity had unsuccessfully promoted as "a modern tale told in the classic tradition of the Gothic novel," *Dark Shadows* was in danger of cancellation. After Curtis's young daughters urged their father to make it scarier, Curtis resolved to introduce the kind of creature that scared *him* the most: an evil vampire named Barnabas

Dark Shadows (1966–1971): Joan Bennett (seated; as Elizabeth Collins Stoddard), Louis Edmonds (as Roger Collins), and Alexandra Moltke (as Victoria Winters) pose for a picture on Monday, June 13, 1966, as they tape the first episode of *Dark Shadows* (which aired two weeks later).

Collins (played by Jonathan Frid). The ratings skyrocketed for the next three years (until 1970) and saved the show from a premature cancellation as it told arcane tales of vampires, witches, werewolves, and time travel.

One of the many elements that made *Dark Shadows* so memorable was its distinctive music, composed by the Emmy Award-nominated composer Robert Cobert. "I met Dan Curtis in 1966," Cobert recalled, "and there was an immediate rapport, so I was hired and wrote all of the music for *Dark Shadows*"— 20 hours of music cues in all.[4] As for the unforgettable theme song, Cobert said, "I whistled the whole theme to Dan as he was putting golf balls on his office floor. His face lit up, and he said, 'I love it!' We then recorded it with a five-piece orchestra"— alto flute, double bass, vibes, harp, and Yamaha synthesizer.[5]

Julliard-educated Cobert had broken into television in the early 1960s by writing music for dramatic specials (*The Scarlet Pimpernel, The Heiress*), game shows (*To Tell the Truth, The Price Is Right*), and soap operas (*The Young Marrieds, The Doctors*). After *Dark Shadows,* Cobert went on to compose the music for almost every Dan Curtis production. Only *When Every Day Was the Fourth of July, The Long Days of Summer, Saving Milly,* and three unsold pilots feature music by composers other than Cobert. In terms of

Tuxedo-clad composer/conductor Robert Cobert laughs with Dan Curtis during the filming of Cobert's cameo appearance in *War and Remembrance* (1988, 1989).

their long creative partnership, Curtis and Cobert were the Alfred Hitchcock and Bernard Herrmann or the Steven Spielberg and John Williams of television.

"As the rapport not only held, but grew," Cobert recalled, "I did for Dan, due to his incredible versatility, an unbelievable variety of projects. The best thing about working with 'Big D' is that he'll let me try anything I want to do musically — even when he is violently opposed to my idea — and then make a truly open-minded decision."[6] Dan Curtis called Robert Cobert "the most brilliant composer around, and he's never let me down. The guy just writes dead-perfect scores."[7] A best-selling soundtrack LP of Cobert's *Dark Shadows* music was released in July 1969 and stayed on the *Billboard* music chart for 19 weeks.

"I have absolutely fond memories of *Dark Shadows,*" Curtis declared. "We had a great time, and I loved all of those people; we were like a big family. We were trailblazers in those days. We gave ABC a daytime schedule. It was great fun."[8]

Seeing others direct his spooky brainchild inspired Dan Curtis the producer to become Dan Curtis the director. After spending some time in England and Canada in 1967 to produce the Emmy Award-nominated *The Strange Case of Dr. Jekyll and Mr. Hyde* (starring Jack Palance and seen on ABC on January 7, 1968), Curtis returned to the New York studios of *Dark Shadows* and directed a total of 21 daily episodes in 1968 and 1969. "The first time I ever directed was the greatest nightmare that ever happened," Curtis insisted.[9] "I took about two weeks on *Dark Shadows* where I taught myself how to direct — I almost sank ABC while I was doing that — but I've produced *and* directed almost everything I've done since."[10]

His first experience as a director was on episodes #457–461 in March 1968. These episodes delivered the climax of the popular storyline set in 1795–1796, revealing how and why Barnabas Collins became a vampire. Later, Curtis occupied the director's chair for another 1796 interlude, then for three 1969 episodes of a *Turn of the Screw*-like storyline introducing Quentin Collins as a ghost, and finally for six episodes in the 1897 storyline. That saga revealed how and why Quentin became a werewolf. It also changed history by preventing both Quentin's death in 1897 and his existence as a ghost in 1969. Quentin had overcome the werewolf curse and become immortal through a *Dorian Gray*-like portrait, and Dan Curtis had added *director* to his producing and writing credits. His accomplishments throughout the 1970s built on his *Dark Shadows* success and caused the *Los Angeles Times,* in 1978, to crown him "the master of the macabre."[11]

The 1970s began with Curtis's direction of the 1970 MGM theatrical feature *House of Dark Shadows* at the Lyndhurst estate in Tarrytown, New York, while the *Dark Shadows* TV series continued. The film was a more horrific retelling of the TV storyline of Barnabas Collins's release from his chained coffin. Half of the TV cast (including Jonathan Frid and Grayson Hall) filmed the movie while the other half (including David Selby and Lara Parker) carried the TV show.

Just as *Dark Shadows* had gone up like a rocket after the introduction of Barnabas, it eventually came down just as abruptly. Later in 1970, some of the audience — as well as Curtis — "became disenchanted" with the TV show, in Curtis's words.[12] Indeed, the viewership had fallen from 18 million to 12 million.[13] Curtis admitted that he lost interest in *Dark Shadows* during the last six months of the show.[14] The final episode, set in the alternate universe of 1841 Parallel Time, aired on April 2, 1971. Five days after the TV series wrapped, Curtis began directing *Night of Dark Shadows* (MGM, 1971) on the Lyndhurst estate. This film was a Gothic story in the tradition of *Rebecca* (1940) and *The Haunted Palace* (1963).

Later in 1971, Norma and Dan Curtis and their three daughters spent time on the West Coast before they permanently relocated from New York to California in 1972. For the next eight years, Curtis produced and/or directed a string of highly successful made-for-TV movies which captivated an entire generation of baby boomers and their parents.

First came *The Night Stalker* (ABC, January 11, 1972), the telefilm which introduced the character of Carl Kolchak (Darren McGavin), a rumpled, seedy reporter on the trail of a vampire in modern-day Las Vegas. Based on a novel by Jeff Rice, scripted by the great fantasy author Richard Matheson (*I Am Legend, The Shrinking Man, Somewhere in Time*), produced by Curtis, and directed by John Llewellyn Moxey (*The House That Would Not Die, The Last Child, Genesis II*), *The Night Stalker* scored an enormous viewership (a 33.2 rating and a 54 share) and (as of late 2008) is the fifteenth-highest-rated made-for-TV movie.[15]

Curtis himself directed *The Night Strangler* (ABC, January 16, 1973), his and Matheson's follow-up to *The Night Stalker,* again starring McGavin as Kolchak. It premiered on the same night as *Frankenstein* (on ABC's *Wide World Mystery,* January 16–17, 1973), a faithful adaptation produced and co-written by Curtis (with Sam Hall) and directed by Glenn Jordan (*Les Miserables, Dress Gray, Barbarians at the Gate*). A possible third Kolchak telefilm, *The Night Killers,* never materialized, and Curtis was not involved in ABC-TV's short-lived series *Kolchak: The Night Stalker* (1974–1975).

Attempting to recreate the reporter-versus-the-supernatural magic of the Kolchak films, Curtis directed *The Norliss Tapes* (NBC, February 21, 1973) from a script by the noted science-fiction author William F. Nolan (*Logan's Run* and its sequels). Next came Curtis's late-night production of *The Picture of Dorian Gray* (ABC, April 23–24, 1973), written by John Tomerlin (*The Twilight Zone*) and again directed by Glenn Jordan. *Scream of the Wolf* (ABC, January 16, 1974), directed by Curtis, was yet another Curtis/Matheson effort in Curtis's own TV subgenre of writer-investigates-murders.

Making another ratings and critical splash was *Dracula* (CBS, February 8, 1974), directed by Curtis, written by Matheson, and starring Jack Palance as the vampire count. This adaptation was the first American film to link Count Dracula with the real-life Vlad Tepes as theorized in the then-current book *In Search of Dracula*, by Raymond McNally and Radu Florescu (1972). It also echoes Karl Freund's *The Mummy* (1932) and Curtis's own *Dark Shadows* (1966–1971)—and presages Francis Ford Coppola's *Bram Stoker's Dracula* (1992) and the animated adventure *The Batman Versus Dracula* (2005)—with its subplot of Count Dracula's attraction to a present-day woman who may be the reincarnation of his long-lost love. A bloodier cut of Curtis's *Dracula* was released theatrically in Europe.

Curtis's two-picture foray into gangster movies began with *Melvin Purvis, G-Man* (ABC, April 9, 1974), co-starring Dale Robertson as the FBI agent and Harris Yulin as Purvis's adversary Machine Gun Kelly. Released theatrically overseas as *The Legend of Machine Gun Kelly,* this Dan Curtis/American International co-production was an outgrowth of AIP's 1973 theatrical film *Dillinger,* co-starring Warren Oates as John Dillinger and Ben Johnson as Melvin Purvis. John Milius, one of Roger Corman's many protégés, had written and directed *Dillinger,* a film publicly protested by J. Edgar Hoover, while Milius and novelist William F. Nolan co-wrote but Curtis directed *Melvin Purvis, G-Man.* The *Los Angeles Times* proclaimed *Purvis* to be "spunky, provocative, and far superior to *Dillinger,* the theatrical feature that preceded it."[16] The *Times* continued, "Here, motivation and character are made to count for much more than mere violence. Its development creates confrontations both revealing and ambiguous, which have been directed by Dan Curtis with a sense of edginess and insight."[17]

Dan Curtis (right) converses with a cameraman during the filming of *Melvin Purvis, G-Man* (1974).

Critic Leonard Maltin characterized *Melvin Purvis, G-Man* as "a wonderful send-up of the type of gangster movie they don't make any more."[18] A sequel followed on ABC one and a half years later, and *The Fugitive* creator Roy Huggins followed Curtis's lead by executive-producing the 1974 TV-movie *The Story of Pretty Boy Floyd*. Later in 1974, Quinn Martin, another famous executive producer, joined the trend with *The FBI*

The Great Ice Rip-Off (1974): (from left to right) Lee J. Cobb (as Willy Calso), Grayson Hall (as Helen Calso), and Gig Young (as Harkey Rollins) take a rest stop during their characters' bus trip down the California coast. *The Great Ice Rip-Off* was released briefly, and only in Canada, in the early days of home video.

Versus Alvin Karpis, Public Enemy Number One.

In 1973 and 1974, Dan Curtis productions became a fixture on ABC-TV's late-night *Wide World Mystery* schedule. In addition to *Frankenstein* and *The Picture of Dorian Gray,* Curtis produced the 1974 thrillers *Shadow of Fear* (directed by Herb Kenwith), *The Invasion of Carol Enders* (directed by Burt Brinkerhoff), *Come Die with Me* (also directed by Brinkerhoff), and *Nightmare at 43 Hillcrest* (directed by Lela Swift). The most notable *Wide World Mystery* production of 1974 was *The Turn of the Screw* (April 15–16), directed on location in England by Curtis from a script by William F. Nolan. For this adaptation, Nolan gave Henry James's governess a name—Jane Cubberly—and Curtis recruited actress Megs Jenkins, who had played Mrs. Grose in Jack Clayton's *The Innocents* (1961), to play Mrs. Grose once again in Curtis's version.

Curtis's final telefilm of 1974 was *The Great Ice Rip-Off* (ABC, November 6), a clever heist comedy written by Andrew Peter Marin (*Bad Ronald*). Lee J. Cobb, Gig Young, and Grayson Hall co-starred in the story of four diamond thieves who use a Seattle-to-San Diego bus as their getaway vehicle. Unbeknownst to the thieves, one of the other passengers is a retired police officer. *Variety* applauded director Dan Curtis's "light touch" and asserted that *The Great Ice Rip-Off* "has enough sharp corners to keep viewers alert, and Curtis's eye for human foibles manages to get laughs. Curtis picks up credit for being able to derive amusement from a caper film after the onslaught of the genre in recent years."[19] In the months before the TV-movie's premiere, audiences had seen such theatrical capers as *The Hot Rock* (1972), *The Getaway* (1972), *The Sting* (1973), *Charley Varrick* (1973), *The Taking of Pelham One Two Three* (1974), and *Bank Shot* (1974).

When scholars and viewers alike think of the works of Dan Curtis, the programs that immediately come to mind are *Dark Shadows* (1966–1971), *The Night Stalker* (1972),

The Winds of War (1983), and *Trilogy of Terror* (ABC, March 4, 1975), another ratings smash which made a huge impression on the popular-culture consciousness. Curtis, Matheson, and Nolan collaborated on this anthology of three Matheson short stories, all starring Karen Black. The third segment of *Trilogy of Terror* is the one that viewers remember most strongly. "Amelia," based on Matheson's 1969 short story "Prey," is the story of the tiny, ferocious-looking Zuni fetish doll that comes to life and stalks Black through her apartment. Black has called *Trilogy of Terror* "a little legend all to itself."[20] That legend has lived on through reruns and home video in the 1980s, Curtis's *Trilogy of Terror II* in the 1990s, and a collectible Zuni fetish doll action figure in the 2000s.

Curtis's other TV-movie of 1975 was another adventure of Melvin Purvis, G-man, as co-written by Bronson Howitzer (*Alias Smith and Jones*) and William F. Nolan. ABC-TV launched its 1975–1976 season with *The Kansas City Massacre* (September 19), pitting Purvis (Dale Robertson again) against Pretty Boy Floyd (Bo Hopkins), Baby Face Nelson (Elliott Street), and John Dillinger (William Jordan). *Variety* praised the film's "splendid cast" (also including John Karlen, Scott Brady, Harris Yulin, Sally Kirkland, Robert Walden, and James Storm) and "Dan Curtis's inventive direction [which] reconstructs the era [1933] with relentless authenticity."[21] *The Kansas City Massacre* surpassed *Melvin Purvis, G-Man* in plot, characterization, action, music, and period detail. Curtis considered a third Purvis project, *The Legend of Johnny Dillinger,* and/or a Melvin Purvis TV series, neither of which ever materialized. It was not until 2009 that Purvis (Christian Bale), Floyd (Channing Tatum), Nelson (Stephen Graham), and Dillinger (Johnny Depp) lived again, this time in Michael Mann's *Public Enemies.*

Instead of a third Purvis project, Curtis returned to his horror roots — and the big screen — with the 1976 United Artists feature *Burnt Offerings,* an extremely faithful filming of Robert Marasco's 1973 Gothic-horror novel of the same name. The impressive cast included Karen Black, Oliver Reed, Bette Davis, Burgess Meredith, and Eileen Heckart. In addition to directing *Burnt Offerings,* Curtis co-wrote the script with William F. Nolan. Both the film and Curtis won Saturn Awards from the Academy of Science-Fiction, Fantasy, and Horror Films. Thirty years later, in a DVD interview, Karen Black insisted, "There's no one better at this genre than Dan Curtis."[22]

However, after mastering horror for more than a decade, Curtis left the genre for more than a

Dan Curtis directs a shoot-out in *The Kansas City Massacre* (1975).

dozen years after his two 1977 telefilms. *Dead of Night* (NBC, March 29) was another trilogy of terror and the final full-fledged Dan Curtis/Richard Matheson collaboration. Two of the stories (about vampirism and black magic) were by Matheson, while Matheson adapted the third from a 1956 short story by Jack Finney, a respected fantasy author who since the 1950s had specialized in stories of time travel (*Time and Again, From Time to Time, The Woodrow Wilson Dime,* "Second Chance," "The Third Level"). In 1969 Curtis had used the title *Dead of Night* for an unsold pilot about psychic investigators (ABC, August 26). This first *Dead of Night*, also known as *A Darkness at Blaisedon* (directed by Lela Swift), essentially had been an attempt to duplicate *Dark Shadows* in prime time. In the 1990s, Curtis filmed another Jack Finney story, "The Love Letter," and remade, shot for

When Every Day Was the Fourth of July (1978): The characters played by Katy Kurtzman (Sarah Cooper) and Geoffrey Lewis (Albert "Snowman" Cavanaugh) share a special but misunderstood friendship.

shot, "Bobby," one of the 1977 *Dead of Night* segments.

Six months after *Dead of Night*, ABC launched its 1977–1978 season with *Curse of the Black Widow* (September 16), Curtis's homage to 1950s-era monster movies. Anthony Franciosa headed a veteran cast (June Allyson, Sid Caesar, Jeff Corey, June Lockhart, Vic Morrow) in a tale of a private investigator, a femme fatale, and a giant spider. Dan Curtis's own personal golden age of horror (1966–1977), beginning with *Dark Shadows* and *The Strange Case of Dr. Jekyll and Mr. Hyde,* now concluded with *Dead of Night* and *Curse of the Black Widow.* Curtis felt that he had reached the point where he "didn't want to try to squeak another door."[23]

Curtis next turned his directorial attention to the aforementioned *When Every Day Was the Fourth of July* (NBC, March 12, 1978), a nostalgic, semi-autobiographical film about the Cooper family of Bridgeport, Connecticut, in the summer of 1937. In a story reminiscent of *To Kill a Mockingbird,* attorney Ed Cooper (Dean Jones) defends his young daughter's friend, Albert "Snowman" Cavanaugh (Geoffrey Lewis), a brain-damaged World War I veteran, when "Snowman" is accused of murder. The character of young Daniel Cooper (Chris Petersen) is based on Daniel Cherkoss — Dan Curtis himself. Writer Lee Hutson (*The Children Nobody Wanted*) scripted the film, from a story by Hutson and Curtis.

In its glowing review of the telefilm, the *Los Angeles Herald-Examiner* declared, "It's an absolute gem. It will touch all of your emotions. It will grip you with suspense. It will amuse you. It will warm your heart."[24] The *Los Angeles Times* concurred that *When Every Day Was the Fourth of July* was "pretty wonderful."[25] Curtis told the *Times* that this was the movie that he

Supertrain (1979): Dan Curtis steered the multimillion-dollar vehicle through only the two-hour pilot and four subsequent hour-long episodes. Curtis—and many of the viewers—left *Supertrain* before episodes 5 through 9 were made.

had wanted to make for the last 20 years.[26] The film won the 1978 Golden Halo Award for Family Film Entertainment from the Southern California Motion-Picture Council, as well as a Certificate of Commendation from the Horizon House Institute in Philadelphia "for exemplary work in bringing mental-health issues to the American public."[27] An award-winning sequel appeared, this time on ABC, two years later.

Curtis ended his extremely successful decade of the 1970s with two acclaimed TV-movies — and his only real flop. NBC-TV's *Supertrain* (February 7–July 28, 1979) was one of the most expensive and high-profile failures in the history of television — "the biggest money-loser in TV history at the time," according to Jim Pierson. Designed as an answer to ABC-TV's *The Love Boat* (1977–1986), *Supertrain* was an anthology series of comedy, drama, and mystery about the passengers and crew of a futuristic, atomic-powered locomotive that crossed the country in 36 hours at a speed of 200 miles per hour. Some of the show's elaborate sets were of the train's 14' × 22' swimming pool, the gymnasium and steam room, and the seventies-style discotheque. The sets, along with detailed miniatures of the train, inflated the show's budget to ten million dollars.[28]

"Frankly, I thought *Supertrain* was the worst idea I'd ever heard," Curtis remembered. "I thought they were out of their minds. But a good friend at NBC said, 'Everybody wants you to do this thing called *Supertrain*.' And they convinced me to do it — against my better judgment."[29]

Curtis executive-produced the first five of the show's ten episodes, but he directed only the pilot episode (later released on VHS as *Express to Terror*). After that highly-rated debut episode (starring Steve Lawrence and Don Meredith), *Supertrain* plummeted in the ratings, and NBC pulled the show after only four more Wednesday-night episodes. At this point Curtis left the show, and NBC brought back a slightly revamped *Supertrain* for five additional episodes and several reruns (April-July 1979) on Saturday nights (opposite ABC's popular *Love Boat* companion, *Fantasy Island*). Jim Pierson remembered, "NBC wanted *Supertrain* to be more escapism like *Love Boat,* but Dan wanted more mystery and intrigue with a touch of violence." In later years, whenever anyone asked Dan Curtis about *Supertrain,* his reply was, "Super *what?*" [30]

Curtis quickly got back on track by directing two notable made-for-TV movies. *Mrs. R's Daughter* (NBC, September 19, 1979) showcased a tour-de-force performance by Cloris Leachman as a mother determined to bring her daughter's rapist to justice.

Mrs. R's Daughter (1979): Season Hubley of *Family* (left) and Cloris Leachman of *Phyllis* play daughter and mother in Dan Curtis's bleak drama.

When the judicial process breaks down, Mrs. Randell wages a year-long battle against legal conundrums and continuances. Emmy Award-winning writer George Rubino (*The Last Tenant*) based his teleplay on an actual incident. Two months later, during the crucial November-sweeps period, NBC aired the three-hour event, *The Last Ride of the Dalton Gang* (November 20, 1979), Curtis's only Western and one of his personal favorites of his films. The producer-director originally planned the film as a two-part, four-hour miniseries called *Raid on Coffeyville,* but he decided to reshape it as a tighter, one-night feature.

The Last Ride of the Dalton Gang, written by future Oscar winner Earl Wallace (who had written *Curse of the Black Widow* and *Supertrain*), tells the light-hearted story of the Dalton brothers' experiences as deputies-turned-horse thieves, train bandits, and bank robbers. Curtis mixed the rollicking tone of *Bonnie and Clyde* (1967) with the fatalism of *The Wild Bunch* (1969) and the nostalgia of classic Hollywood Westerns. Playing the Dalton brothers were Cliff Potts, Randy Quaid, Larry Wilcox, Mills Watson, and Don Collier. Royal Dano portrayed their father Lewis Dalton, and Jack Palance played their nemesis Will Smith. The cast also included Sharon Farrell, Bo Hopkins, Dale Robertson, John Karlen, and Harris Yulin. The film won the Western Heritage Award for Outstanding Fictional Television Program from the National Cowboy Hall of Fame. "This picture really got me ready for *The Winds of War*," Curtis observed, because of its large cast, complex action sequences, and

The Last Ride of the Dalton Gang (1979): The group of outlaws includes Matt Clark (standing, left, as Bitter Creek), Cliff Potts (seated, center, as Bob Dalton), Bo Hopkins (seated, right, as Billy Doolin), and Randy Quaid (standing, right, as Grat Dalton).

period detail.[31] The National Cowboy Hall of Fame gave the Wrangler Award to composer Robert Cobert for his free-wheeling, panoramic music score.[32]

Dean Jones and the Cooper family of Bridgeport, Connecticut, returned in *The Long Days of Summer* (ABC, May 23, 1980), another semi-autobiographical work, directed by Curtis and co-written by Lee Hutson and Hindi Brooks (*Family*). During the summer of 1938, the Coopers, who are Jewish (like Curtis's own Cherkoss family of Bridgeport), confront anti–Semitism from the local German-American Club. The family is distressed further when a German Jew (Donald Moffat) escapes to America and reveals Nazi Germany's growing atrocities against the Jews. This film's historic subject matter — the Holocaust, a whistle-stop appearance by President Franklin Roosevelt (Stephen Roberts), the Joe Louis-Max Schmeling fight, and a Golden Gloves boxing match between young Daniel Cooper (Ronnie Scribner) and an older boy — begins to evoke an era which Curtis, some years later, brought fully to life in his two epic war miniseries.

Like its predecessor (*When Every Day Was the Fourth of July*), *The Long Days of Summer* received the Golden Halo Award for Family Film Entertainment from the Southern California Motion-Picture Council. The *Los Angeles Herald-Examiner* ranked the "extraordinarily good" film number three in the top ten television programs of 1980.[33] *The Los Angeles Times* declared that the film "has the sort of honesty and reality that is lacking in most TV series."[34] Both *The Long Days of Summer* and *When Every Day Was the Fourth of July* were unsold pilots for a *Waltons*-style family TV series to be called *The Coopers*. Two years later, writer Hutson and executive-producer Curtis re-teamed for another unsold pilot, *The Big Easy* (ABC, August 15, 1982), directed by Jud

Taylor (*The Last Tenant*), and starring William Devane as New Orleans private investigator Jake Rubidoux.

The 1970s saw Dan Curtis dominate television horror; the 1980s propelled him even higher in the TV firmament as he became king of the miniseries. He spent almost the entire decade on the two greatest achievements of his career and two of the most impressive filmmaking feats in history: the ABC miniseries *The Winds of War* (1983) and

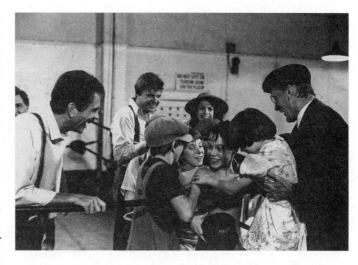

The Long Days of Summer (1980): Dean Jones (as Ed Cooper), John Karlen (as Duane Haley), extras, Ronnie Scribner (as Daniel Cooper), Louanne (as Sarah Cooper), and Donald Moffat (as Josef Kaplan) share a pivotal scene.

War and Remembrance (1988, 1989), based on the best-selling novels by Herman Wouk.

In 1980, ABC executive Barry Diller asked Curtis to take on the Herculean task of bringing to television *The Winds of War,* Wouk's sprawling novel of an American Naval family in the years 1939–1941. Wouk himself was against the idea after being greatly displeased by Hollywood's filmings of his novels *The Caine Mutiny* in 1954 and especially *Marjorie Morningstar* in 1958 and *Youngblood Hawke* in 1964. Wouk felt that Hollywood had trivialized the latter two works, and he did not want to see a watered-down screen version of his 1971 masterpiece *The Winds of War,* an 888-page opus which he had begun researching in 1960.[35]

Nevertheless Curtis, once a Naval Reserve officer, and Wouk, a four-year naval officer on minesweepers, met and convinced each other to film *The Winds of War* from a screenplay by Wouk. Unaccustomed to writing for the screen, Wouk gladly accepted pointers from Curtis, by now a master at doctoring the scripts of his projects. Earl Wallace served as story editor. "We all worked closely on the screenplay," Curtis recalled, "with Herman having the final word on everything. He even told ABC how many commercials and *what kind of* commercials they could run during the thing!"[36]

The miniseries's running time of nearly 15 hours (scheduled in an 18-hour block on ABC) was the equivalent of seven motion pictures. Curtis originally planned to direct only parts of the epic and use other directors to fill in the rest, but ABC wanted a single director — Curtis — and his singular *auteur's* vision. Curtis remembered,

> I kept thinking, "What am I going to do?" I talked to my wife about it, and then I said, "I'll just start directing this thing, and then when I start to wear myself out, I'll bring in other directors and fight about it then." Norma said, "As long as you promise me you won't direct the whole thing!" I said, "Promise you? There's no way I could direct the whole thing." Well, I directed the whole thing.[37]

Curtis filmed the $40 million production for more than one year at 267 locations in six countries: the United States, England, West Germany, Austria, Italy, and Yugoslavia. "We shot as much as we could in Yugoslavia," Curtis explained in a DVD interview. He remembered,

> The people were wonderful in Yugoslavia. It was still a communist country, and the people were very impoverished. But it had this tremendous innocence. Wherever you went, people were happy to see you. We found quaint villages like where we shot the Jewish wedding, and we actually used the real rabbi and the real cantor. Ali [McGraw] loved the flower markets and the food markets. The food was great.[38]

At that time the most enormous project in television or film history, *The Winds of War* consisted of 4000 camera set-ups, more than one million feet of film, and 1785 scenes in Wouk and Curtis's 962-page script. There were 285 speaking roles and thousands of extras spread across Europe.[39] Curtis had actualized the Old Hollywood expression, "a cast of thousands." Heading the cast along with Ali McGraw were Robert Mitchum, Polly Bergen, Jan-Michael Vincent, Victoria Tennant, David Dukes, Peter Graves, Chaim Topol, Jeremy Kemp, and John Houseman. Character actors from Anton Diffring, Andrew Duggan, Jerry Fujikawa, and John Karlen to Charles Lane, Ferdy Mayne, Barry Morse, and Richard X. Slattery made appearances, and Ralph Bellamy reprised his 1960 *Sunrise at Campobello* role of President Franklin Delano Roosevelt.

Playing Morse's on-screen wife was Barbara Steele, a then-fortyish icon of 1960s-era European cinema (*8½, The Hours of Love, Young Torless*) and Italian horror (*Black Sunday, The Horrible Dr. Hichcock, An Angel for Satan*). Steele was living in Los Angeles and at loose ends after the 1980 death of her husband, Oscar-winning screenwriter James Poe (*Around the World in 80 Days*). She met Curtis through a mutual friend, British ICM agent Maggie Abbott, and he hired her to peruse stock footage of World War II for possible use in *The Winds of War*. Curtis and Steele began a successful professional relationship which lasted until his death. Steele became associate producer of *The Winds of War*, full producer of *War and Remembrance* and *Saving Milly*, co-producer of *Our Fathers*, and co-star of the 1991 *Dark Shadows* revival.

"*The Winds of War* and *War and Remembrance* were such vast projects of staggering complexity, covering all of World War II and the events leading up to it," Steele observed. She explained,

> This involved years of shooting, pre-production, and post-production. It was the equivalent of making 18 motion pictures back to back, involving so many people, countries, currencies, and shifting world events that it seemed unimaginable and even mad to me that one man could have the desire and the passion — let alone the energy — to be able to translate these two epic books to the screen with a commitment involving years and years of work. But Dan never faltered in his vision. He was like a rabid wolf in his intensity and determination. Of course, the whole operatic landscape suited his personality so perfectly; it's as if he were born for these projects. They were both beautiful and terrible.[40]

Steele commended the solid cast of *The Winds of War*, headed by Robert Mitchum as Captain Victor "Pug" Henry. "Mitchum had a stubborn independence," she declared, and he effectively evoked the war era.[41] Similarly, Polly Bergen was well suited for the role of Rhoda Henry, Pug's restless wife. Bergen, a voracious reader, had read both *The*

Winds of War and its 1042-page sequel, *War and Remembrance* (1978), and strongly desired to play Rhoda. She received Emmy nominations for her work in both miniseries. "I loved working with Dan," Bergen recalled. "He was enormously supportive, a terrific and very loud director, and I had complete trust in him. He could be very difficult, but he never was with me. I would work with him any day of the week."[42]

Once fearful that he would tire of shooting *The Winds of War,* Curtis later

Polly Bergen (as Rhoda Henry), Peter Graves (as Palmer Kirby), and Dan Curtis converse on the set of *The Winds of War* (1983).

declared, "It was the toughest thing I ever did, but I *never* got tired. I could have kept shooting forever. Making *The Winds of War* was one of the greatest experiences of my life. Recreating history where it actually happened was the most exciting experience."[43] Curtis remembered with special fondness shooting the meeting between Roosevelt (Bellamy) and Churchill (Howard Lang) aboard the *Prince of Wales* (actually the U.S.S. *Missouri*) and recreating the attack on Pearl Harbor (actually the Oxnard, California, naval base)—*on December 7,* 1981—two decades before Michael Bay's *Pearl Harbor* (2001) and well before the conveniences of CGI special effects.

Curtis's efforts paid off remarkably when *The Winds of War,* broadcast on ABC-TV, February 6–13, 1983, commanded more than 140 million viewers. It delivered a 38.6 rating and a 53 share, and it remains the third most-watched miniseries of all time, after *Roots* in 1977 and *The Thorn Birds* later in 1983.[44] *The Winds of War* appeared on 17 different magazine covers and made headlines around the world. "The reviews were phenomenal," Curtis beamed. "I'd never even *seen* reviews like the ones we got."[45] *Variety* called *The Winds of War* "striking television" and "an impressive look at history in the making" and praised its "enormous sweep" and "unerring ring of truth."[46] *Newsday* called it "really something extraordinary and special,"[47] and the *Philadelphia Enquirer* proclaimed it to be "television in its finest hour."[48] The *Detroit News* added,

> Producer-director Dan Curtis treads knowingly between the television form known as docudrama and the old movie romances. He tastefully employs 1940s movie conventions (the recurring, heavy love-theme music; the camera turning around the kissing couple), but he knows he's directing for the little screen, not the big one. His emphasis is on the telling close-up, the intimate set piece. His action sequences are just enough to convey cold or

smoke or carnage. Some of the outdoor shots are beautiful — a delicately lighted Geneva, the Kremlin as seen from a frozen hill, the leafy richness of Sienna. The total effect is remarkably evocative of the period.[49]

Robert Cobert's music score, with its love theme, marches, waltzes, and ethnic music, ran longer than 2000 manuscript pages. The love theme has joined Cobert's equally haunting "Quentin's Theme" from *Dark Shadows* as a staple on what the broadcasting industry calls beautiful-music radio stations.

The Winds of War was nominated for the Emmy Award for Outstanding Limited Series, and Dan Curtis was nominated for Outstanding Directing in a Limited Series or Special for his direction of "Into the Maelstrom," the seventh and final episode of the blockbuster miniseries. *The Winds of War* received 11 other Emmy nominations in various Limited-Series categories: cinematography, art direction, special visual effects, costumes, film editing, film sound editing, film sound mixing (three separate nominations), supporting actress (Polly Bergen), and supporting actor (Ralph Bellamy). Bergen and Bellamy lost to Jean Simmons and Richard Kiley, both of *The Thorn Birds,* and Curtis lost to director John Erman for *Who Will Love My Children?* (ABC, 14 February 1983).

In one of the most startling upsets in Emmy history, *both* the high-profile *Winds of War* and *Thorn Birds* lost the Outstanding Limited Series award to the Royal Shakespeare Company's syndicated TV adaptation of Charles Dickens's *Nicholas Nickleby,* a production which ABC, CBS, and NBC had turned down. However, *The Winds of War* did win Emmy Awards for cinematography (Charles Correll), costumes (Tommy Welsh et al.), and special visual effects (Roy Downey et al.). Although it did not win any of its four Golden Globe nominations, the miniseries won Spain's TP de Oro award for best foreign series, and Dan Curtis himself received the Torch of Liberty award from the Anti-Defamation League.[50]

By the time that ABC-TV reran *The Winds of War* on September 7–14, 1986 as a kick-off to its 1986–1987 season, Curtis was already two-and-one-half years into his work on the miniseries's even more staggering sequel, *War and Remembrance,* again based on a Herman Wouk novel. This time Curtis and Earl Wallace wrote the dramatic, personal scenes involving the novel's characters, and Herman Wouk wrote the historical scenes. Returning as sole director was, of course, Dan Curtis, who remembered,

> When I finished *The Winds of War,* which turned out to be 18 hours, I swore I would never, ever do *War and Remembrance.* But *Winds* was such a huge hit that I knew *War and Remembrance* was going to be made. I wasn't going back into television. I figured I had done all the television I was ever going to do. I could never be able to top myself. I might as well get into the feature business, which is where I wanted to be. [ABC executive] Brandon Stoddard kept after me [to direct *War and Remembrance*], and I kept saying, no, no, no, no, no. One day, my wife and I were driving to Palm Springs. I was an unhappy guy, and she said to me, "You want to do *War and Remembrance,* don't you? I know you really want to do it." I said, "Yeah, maybe I do; I miss all the action and the excitement." Norma said, "Well, then, why don't you do it?"[51]

Curtis went to *War* again in early 1984 and began pre-production on the continuing story of the Victor Henry family in the years 1941–1945. This miniseries would recreate the most crucial events of World War II with stunning accuracy and power. History-making moments at Midway, Guadalcanal, Stalingrad, Yalta, El Alamein, the Battle of the Bulge, Babi Yar, Leyte Gulf, Iwo Jima, and Hiroshima would live again under Curtis's meticulous direction. The 21-month-long shooting schedule would consume almost all of 1986 and 1987, with a cast/crew wrap-party/dinner aboard the *Queen Mary* in Long Beach, California, on January 8, 1988.[52]

While viewers found the naval battle sequences thrilling, the submarine sequences technically impressive, and the characters' romantic entanglements satisfying, the defining segments of *War and Remembrance* were the devastating recreations of the Holocaust — filmed at one of the actual places where the genocide occurred. After two years of delicate negotiations with the Polish government, Curtis and his cast and crew were allowed to film harrowing Holocaust scenes at the Auschwitz concentration camp in January and May of 1986.[53]

"Auschwitz was the worst," Curtis admitted. "There's no way to describe the feeling" of recreating the unspeakable horrors of the Nazis' "final solution" on the very ground where it happened — and with some of the actual survivors.[54] As a boy, Curtis's associate producer Branko Lustig had been imprisoned in Auschwitz. Many of the extras who played the doomed Jews herded naked into gas chambers were also survivors of the camps. In January 1986, Herman Wouk himself visited Curtis in Poland and observed one night of the grueling filming at Auschwitz. The writer came away deeply moved and convinced that he and Curtis had captured the atrocity exactly as it must have happened.[55]

"When we do the extermination of 30,000 Jews at Babi Yar, you'll never see anything like it in your life," Curtis told the *Los Angeles Times* in September 1986. "As tough as it was for us, it was even tougher for the German crew because they couldn't come to terms with the fact that their forebears really did this."[56]

The Holocaust scenes were unflinching in their brutality, nudity, and horror. "One of the conditions that I had before I agreed to do *War and Remembrance*," Curtis stipulated, "was that ABC had to give me carte blanche." He insisted,

> I would not be edited in terms of pulling punches because I felt that to show the Holocaust in anything but its most brutal form would be a crime — and I didn't want to be part of that — so what I needed to know was there wasn't going to be anybody who was going to be censoring me or anybody who was going to stop me from doing what I had to do. ABC agreed to that. I met with the Standards and Practices people, and we had an understanding.[57]

While *The Winds of War* was the equivalent of seven motion pictures, *War and Remembrance*— more than 23 hours of footage spread across 29 hours of television — approximated 11 movies in one. The final cost of the gigantic miniseries was $140 million, at that time the most expensive motion picture ever made and exceeded only in more recent years by *Titanic* (1997) and various fantasy films which have cost more than $200 million. Wouk, Curtis, and Wallace's 1492-page script contained 2070 scenes which took 1,852,739 feet of film to shoot.[58]

ABC touted the miniseries as having been filmed in more than ten countries, i.e. England, France, West Germany, Switzerland, Austria, Poland, Yugoslavia, Italy,

Canada, the United States (including Hawaii), and the Bahamas. Although 757 sets were built and used, many scenes were filmed at the actual locations, such as The Eagle's Nest (Adolf Hitler's headquarters), the Paris Opera House, and the Auschwitz death camp. Rummaging through some filing cabinets at Auschwitz, Curtis found the actual blueprints and specifications for the death camp's crematoria, whose interiors were then rebuilt almost perfectly to scale on a soundstage.[59] Curtis and Wouk's goal was to tell the story of the Holocaust more vividly and accurately than ever before. "It's a way to make sure it never happens again," Curtis insisted.[60]

Most of the principal actors of *The Winds of War* reprised their roles in *War and Remembrance,* and the few recastings were changes for the better, making a good cast great. Heading the cast were Robert Mitchum, Polly Bergen, Hart Bochner (replacing Jan-Michael Vincent), Jane Seymour (replacing Ali McGraw), Victoria Tennant, David Dukes, Peter Graves, Chaim Topol, Jeremy Kemp, John Gielgud (replacing John Houseman), and Ralph Bellamy. Once again, the supporting cast was a movie and TV who's who: Eddie Albert, Brian Blessed, Mike Connors, John Dehner, Howard Duff, Nina Foch, Pat Hingle, E.G. Marshall, Ian McShane, Robert Morley, Dennis Patrick, Addison Powell, William Prince, John Rhys-Davies, William Schallert, and others. In all, there were 358 speaking roles, 2257 bit players, and 41,720 extras. Counting the almost 1700 crew members, Dan Curtis commanded an army of 46,000 people marching across Europe and North America.[61] Curtis worked indefatigably with decommissioned or still-active ships, aircraft carriers, submarines, and planes; with 35-foot-long miniature ships on a wet set at Pinewood Studios in England; and with the thousands and thousands of extras playing the difficult roles of refugees, soldiers, prisoners, and corpses.

Producer Barbara Steele (who also played the small role of Elsa) had nothing but praise for the director. She remarked,

Dan Curtis directs Robert Mitchum (right, at podium) and others in a naval scene from *War and Remembrance* (1988, 1989).

There were moments when I thought the demands would kill all of us, but never Dan, because he was working from the center of his very big heart. It's as if we were living in Beethoven's Ninth Symphony. I don't believe there is another filmmaker on the planet who could have done [the two miniseries]. It was a moment of brilliant synchronicity, and it was wonderful to witness someone work at the height of his powers in a state of sustained enthrallment. Dan knew this was his "moment," and he could put his signature so beautifully and powerfully on a devastating period of history.[62]

Polly Bergen added, "I don't think there is any other television show, movie, or miniseries that has captured the incredible scope and majesty of *The Winds of War* and *War and Remembrance*. Dan never received the kind of recognition that he deserved."[63] Auschwitz survivor and associate producer Branko Lustig declared, "Dan Curtis can be put in the category with Steven Spielberg and Ridley Scott. Nobody recreated the Holocaust better than Dan Curtis. He did it with his heart."[64]

Also adding heart to *War and Remembrance* was the 11 hours of music — 3500 manuscript pages — composed and conducted by Curtis's musical mainstay Robert Cobert. At ABC's request, Cobert repeated his *Winds of War* theme as the main-title theme of *War and Remembrance*; additionally, he composed what he called "everything from pure, romantic music to all kinds of military music to jazz."[65]

Despite Cobert's success with *The Winds of War* and essentially all of Dan Curtis's productions, Cobert initially was not guaranteed the job of scoring the sequel. In a DVD interview, the composer recalled,

> When they started *War and Remembrance*, they said, "Let's get Leonard Bernstein," or "Let's get John Williams." But Dan wanted me and *only* me. He called me up and said, "You're doing it!" Curtis asked me if I could write five minutes of music a day, and I thought about it and said, "Yeah, but I won't do it for free." When Dan told me that money was no object, I called my agent and said, "Go get 'em!"[66]

While many composers manage to perfect only one to three minutes of programmatic music per day, Cobert wrote five minutes of music each day. He dutifully worked 12 to 14 hours a day, seven days a week, from August through October 1988 in order to meet the deadline for the November 1988 episodes of *War and Remembrance*. With Curtis present in the recording studio and deliberating over every note, Cobert conducted a 50-piece orchestra in the recording of his background music. Except for a few quibbles, Curtis enthusiastically approved of every theme.

"I think Cobert's a genius, no question about it," Curtis declared. "He has an incredible knack for writing clever background music that enhances my movies all the time. He stands up there with the greatest, and somebody should start to recognize him."[67]

Finally, after almost five years in the making, *War and Remembrance* aired on ABC-TV, November 13–23, 1988 (parts 1–7), and May 7–14, 1989 (parts 8–12, called *War and Remembrance: The Final Chapter*). Because of the overwhelming length of the miniseries, its unwise division into two segments six months apart, and the ever-increasing alternative programming available on cable television, *War and Remembrance* attracted only about one-half of the 140 million viewers of *The Winds of War*. Nevertheless, commanding 55 to 75 million TV viewers is still impressive and admirable whether in 1988–1989, the 1990s, or the 2000s.

Once again the reviews were spectacularly positive. The *Washington Post* called *War and Remembrance* "monumental," "mammoth," and "tremendous."[68] *Newsday* called it "super TV,"[69] and the *Newark Star Ledger* proclaimed the "masterwork" miniseries "very simply television's finest hours."[70] Newspapers from Los Angeles to Kansas City praised Dan Curtis's brilliant directing, and *TV Guide* singled out Curtis's "unparalleled combat footage."[71] Curtis especially enjoyed the Associated Press's assessment: "Curtis has himself a masterpiece of a war movie [...] the battle scenes are stunning [...] some of the best submarine scenes since *Das Boot*. The Battle of Midway [is] worthy of a theatrical film. The concentration-camp scenes are the most powerful such depictions television has ever seen."[72]

Curtis's personal goal with the submarine scenes was to top *Das Boot* (1981), and he also strove to surpass *Midway* (1976), all World War II movies, and NBC-TV's Emmy Award-winning *Holocaust* (April 16–19, 1978). According to the *Kansas City Star*, "Curtis did not fail."[73]

Howard Rosenberg of the *Los Angeles Times* concurred, "*War and Remembrance* takes its place at the top of all TV drama." Rosenberg added, "Volume one of ABC's *War and Remembrance* is more than just a dazzling achievement in historical storytelling. It is the best serialized drama in the history of American television. This is important, landmark TV — hard to take, but even harder to ignore. ABC should be proud."[74]

Indeed, in a rich British and American television landscape which had already produced *The Forsyte Saga* (1967); *Elizabeth R* (1971); *Upstairs, Downstairs* (1971–1975); *QB VII* (1974); *Rich Man, Poor Man* (1976); *Captains and the Kings* (1976); *Roots* (1977); *Shogun* (1980); *The Winds of War* (1983); and *The Thorn Birds* (1983), being canonized by the *Los Angeles Times* as the greatest serialized drama in the history of American television was perhaps the ultimate accolade.

In January 1989, the first half of *War and Remembrance* won three Golden Globe Awards. John Gielgud and Barry Bostwick, both of whose roles had been played by other actors in *The Winds of War*, tied for Best Supporting Actor in a TV Miniseries. In his acceptance speech, Bostwick, who had portrayed Lt. Carter "Lady" Aster, said,

> I accept this award not only for myself but also for the 357 other supporting players on *War and Remembrance*. We were supporting a dream — Dan Curtis's dream — of bringing to television 29 of its finest hours, a depiction of World War II so accurate and so moving that many of its images would be forever burned into our collective consciousness. I think he's done that. I thank Dan Curtis for allowing me to color in just a very small corner of his masterpiece.[75]

Although Curtis himself did not win a Golden Globe for his direction, his masterpiece won the award for Best TV Miniseries. In his acceptance speech, Curtis said, "A whole lot of people went to war about five years ago, and we're lucky to be standing up here right now. It's just a great joy to have it all appreciated and to mean something. Thank you from the bottom of my heart."[76] Two months later, *War and Remembrance* won the People's Choice Award for best miniseries.

In September 1989, *War and Remembrance* won another victory — on Emmy night. The miniseries was nominated for 15 Emmy Awards in various Outstanding-Miniseries categories: best miniseries, direction (Dan Curtis), lead actor (John Gielgud), lead actress (Jane Seymour), supporting actress (Polly Bergen), cinematography, special visual effects, film editing, sound editing, film-sound mixing, art direction, music composition (Robert Cobert), costumes, makeup, and hairstyling. Gielgud lost to James Woods for *My Name is Bill W.,* Seymour lost to Holly Hunter for *Roe Versus Wade,* and Bergen lost to Colleen Dewhurst for *Those She Left Behind.*[77]

The miniseries's most formidable competition was *Lonesome Dove* (CBS, February 5–8, 1989), the highest-rated TV miniseries since 1985's *North and South* and, like *War and Remembrance,* itself one of the finest programs in the history of American television. *Lonesome Dove* won seven Emmys, including awards for its director Simon Wincer and its composer Basil Poledouris, at that time both big names from the world of theatrical films. Wincer had directed *The Man from Snowy River* in 1982 and *Phar Lap* in 1983; Poledouris had scored *The Blue Lagoon* in 1980 and *Conan the Barbarian* in 1982. *Lonesome Dove* was considered to be the front-runner for Outstanding Miniseries, but in an upset equaling *Nicholas Nickleby's* victory over *The Winds of War,* it was *War and Remembrance,* not *Lonesome Dove,* which was named the best miniseries of 1988–1989. In his acceptance speech, Dan Curtis admitted that the victory was "a major shock," and he thanked ABC "for having the guts to pony up the dough" to make *War and Remembrance.*[78] Ultimately, *War and Remembrance* won only three Emmys, for editing (Peter Zinner, John Burnett), special visual effects (William Schirmer et al.), and Outstanding Miniseries.[79]

Zinner and Burnett won the Eddie Award from the American Cinema Editors, and cinematographer Dietrich Lohmann won the A.S.C. Award. The U.S. TV Fan Association gave *War and Remembrance* awards for best miniseries, best director (Curtis), and best music score (Cobert). BMI (Broadcast Music, Incorporated) awarded Robert Cobert a certificate for writing the longest film score in history. (Two months earlier, BMI had given Cobert a certificate marking the one-millionth radio performance of "Quentin's Theme" from *Dark Shadows.*) Curtis won the Distinguished Service Award from the Simon Wiesenthal Center, and he was nominated for the Directors Guild Award in both 1989 and 1990. Curtis won the prestigious DGA Award in 1990, and eight years later he won the Golden Laurel Award from the Producers Guild of America.[80] Curtis had gone from filming PGA golfers at the beginning of his career to being honored by a very different PGA near the end of his career.

In May 1989, Curtis told the Associated Press, "I'm vastly relieved that I'm done with *War and Remembrance,* yet my heart is breaking. I'm so ambivalent I want to cry. I feel my mission is accomplished. I pray that the memory and impact of it will be there with us for a long time. I pray that it will make a difference."[81] He told the *Los Angeles Times,* "I feel so good about this show because I know we've accomplished something that won't be accomplished again."[82] Of course, films such as *Schindler's List* (1993), *Saving Private Ryan* (1998), and *Flags of Our Fathers* (2006) and TV miniseries such as *When Lions Roared* (1994), *Band of Brothers* (2001) and *Hitler: The Rise of Evil* (2003) have come along in the wake of *War and Remembrance,* but nothing has matched the epic, global scope of Curtis's work. As Robert Cobert bluntly put it, "We make *Schindler's List* look sick! Of course, they had only three hours, and we had 30 hours."[83]

Curtis himself stated the case more diplomatically, but just as firmly, in the March 15, 1997, edition of the *Los Angeles Times.* The director responded to a February 26 article about the NBC telecast of *Schindler's List.* Curtis's letter to the editor stated,

As the executive producer/director of the 30-hour ABC-TV miniseries *War and Remembrance,* I think it important to demur to some points made by Howard Rosenberg in his February 26 column "NBC Can't Just Rest on Laurels." When he writes that NBC's airing of *Schindler's List* intact "marks a maturation high for network television" and "never within memory has one of the major networks shown such nudity or depicted so much violence so graphically," I feel compelled to comment.

The dehumanizing of victims, on arrival at their destination of doom, by forcing them to disrobe, was central to scenes in the miniseries. We received widespread commendation for those scenes, and ABC deserves much credit for taking a pioneering risk in first allowing me to film them and then broadcasting them without cutting a single frame.

Rosenberg himself wrote on November 23, 1988, "Never before in an American TV drama has the Holocaust been so graphically, uncompromisingly, and profoundly depicted. Tonight's scenes of rotting corpses at Auschwitz and the Nazi massacre of Jews at Babi Yar in the Soviet Union are excruciatingly and revoltingly real. This is important, landmark TV — hard to take, but even harder to ignore." The Babi Yar sequence involving the slaughter of hordes of naked Jews, which was a terrible task to film, did however evoke a protest from Nobel Laureate Elie Wiesel, who thought it unendurably graphic — an opinion I respect, but to my best ability I depicted the historic truth, nothing more.

War and Remembrance, which won the Emmy as best mini-series of 1988–1989, represents several years of my hardest work as a filmmaker. If I am proud of it, perhaps it is a pardonable pride. Certainly, no one is looking for bragging rights to graphic violence and nudity, but with regard to the memory of the horrors of the Holocaust, where we pioneered, I want the record to show it.

Signed, DAN CURTIS[84]

The 1990s began for Curtis with NBC-TV's July 29, 1990, airing of *Johnny Ryan,* an unsold pilot executive-produced by Curtis but directed by Robert Collins (*Gideon's Trumpet*). Written by Mark Rodgers (*Police Story*), *Johnny Ryan,* a.k.a. *Against the Mob,* was the story of a police detective (Clancy Brown) battling organized crime in 1949 New York City. As the pilot came and went, Curtis was hard at work on the next milestone in his career: a nighttime revival of *Dark Shadows.*

In both 1988 and 1989, before and after the broadcasts of *War and Remembrance,* NBC entertainment president Brandon Tartikoff had approached Dan Curtis about resurrecting *Dark Shadows* as a lavish nighttime dramatic serial — a kind of *Dynasty* with fangs. At first skeptical about revisiting *Dark Shadows* after two decades, Curtis ultimately decided to remake the show, this time with the luxuries of time, money, and film (instead of videotape). He resolved to produce *Dark Shadows* in the much grander, more opulent way that he "and the fans had always wanted to see the series," in his words.[85]

The new *Dark Shadows,* which was a remake of both the ABC-TV daytime series and Curtis's 1970 motion picture *House of Dark Shadows,* was filmed in and around Los Angeles from March to December 1990. Curtis directed the first five of the show's 13 hours, as well as some reshoots for the twelfth and thirteenth. Armand Mastroianni (*Tales from the Darkside*), Paul Lynch (the 1980s *Twilight Zone*), Rob Bowman (*Star Trek: The Next Generation*), and Mark Sobel (*Quantum Leap*) directed hours six through 13. Curtis co-wrote the series along with original *Dark Shadows* writer Sam Hall, Hall's novelist son Matthew Hall (*Nightmare Logic*), *Beauty and the Beast* writers M.M. Shelley Moore and Linda Campanelli, *When a Stranger Calls* co-writer Steve Feke, and four others.

This time, the Hollywood star playing Elizabeth Collins Stoddard was Jean Simmons, with Roy Thinnes as her brother Roger Collins and Joanna Going as Victoria Winters. Once again Curtis's 1965 dream was put on film as the pilot episode began with Victoria's train journey to Collinsport, Maine. Barnabas Collins's release from the chained coffin occurred in that same episode. The new Barnabas was the distinguished British film actor Ben Cross, who played the vampire with more menace and danger than had Jonathan Frid. However, Cross's Barnabas also had his tortured, vulnerable side. Curtis's *War* producer Barbara Steele revisited her horror-movie roots by portraying Dr. Julia Hoffman, a key role which Sam Hall's wife Grayson Hall had played on *Dark Shadows* and in *House of Dark Shadows*. Robert Cobert, of course, returned to furnish the show with his 1960s *Dark Shadows* music cues as well as many new, eerie compositions performed by a 25-piece orchestra under his direction.

Dark Shadows (1991): Roy Thinnes (as Roger Collins) consoles Jean Simmons (as Roger's sister Elizabeth Collins Stoddard).

The first four hours of NBC-TV's *Dark Shadows* aired as a miniseries on January 13–14, 1991. The show garnered respectable ratings, especially from the coveted 18–34 and 25–54 demographics, and favorable reviews. *Variety* called it "bloody good."[86] The new *Dark Shadows* seemed destined for success—but then fate intervened and dealt the show a mortal wound.

Before the fifth hour could air in its regular Friday-night timeslot on January 18, the Persian Gulf War broke out. News coverage blanketed the TV networks for much of the week, and *Dark Shadows* was lost in the shuffle. Although the January 18 episode aired on the East Coast, it was pre-empted by war coverage on the West Coast and did not air until January 25, one hour before that night's regularly scheduled episode.[87] A nationwide February pre-emption in favor of a showing of *The Empire Strikes Back* (1980) did not help, and neither did Brandon Tartikoff's departure from NBC for Paramount Pictures. The new NBC entertainment president, Warren Littlefield, did not seem interested in *Dark Shadows,* and despite fans' "Save *Dark Shadows* Day" demonstrations across the country on May 8, 1991, *Dark Shadows* did not appear on NBC's fall schedule. The final episode had aired on March 22, 1991, and had ended with a cliffhanger: Victoria Winters had returned from her travel through time with the knowledge that the Barnabas Collins of 1790 and the Barnabas of 1991 were one and the same — and a vampire.

Dan Curtis and the fans were crestfallen that a promising new beginning for *Dark Shadows* had ended so abruptly. Curtis, who had fought NBC for the go-ahead to film 13 hours instead of a mere six, considered keeping the new show alive through a made-for-TV movie or a theatrical feature, but no such sequel materialized. (The mythos of the new series did live on for another two years in the form of a comic-book series from Innovation Comics.) The TV show received the Saturn Award for Best Genre Television Presentation from the Academy of Science-Fiction, Fantasy, and Horror Films, and it won Dee-Dee Petty and four other stylists an Emmy Award for hairstyling.[88]

The year 1992 saw one minor and one major Dan Curtis production on network television. On February 1, 1992, ABC-TV aired *Angie the Lieutenant,* a half-hour pilot starring Angie Dickinson as a police officer not unlike her signature role on NBC-TV's *Police Woman* (1974–1978). Curtis executive-produced *Angie the Lieutenant,* and *Johnny Ryan* director Robert Collins returned to write and direct this unsold pilot. At this time Curtis also made plans with Richard Matheson and Darren McGavin to revive Carl Kolchak in a *Night Stalker* reunion movie for ABC. That network, as well as two others, passed on the idea.

Next, Curtis combined his horror and miniseries expertise in the two-part CBS event *Intruders* (May 17 and 19, 1992), which he directed and co-executive-produced.

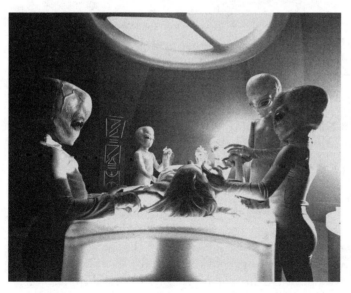

Based on the book of the same name by Budd Hopkins, *Intruders* was a horror/sci-fi docudrama based on 600 actual case studies of alien abduction. Curtis's scriptwriters came with suitable credentials for this alien fare: Tracy Torme had written for *Star Trek: The Next Generation* (1987–1994), and Barry Oringer had written for Roy Thinnes's cult-classic UFO series *The Invaders* (1967–1968).

The cast of *Intruders* included Richard Crenna, Mare Winningham,

Intruders (1992): The title characters go about their other-worldly work in an atmospheric shot from the miniseries.

Daphne Ashbrook, Susan Blakely, and Robert Mandan. Ben Vereen was nominated for an Emmy Award for his role as a mental patient. Robert Cobert composed the music and even slipped "Quentin's Theme" into a restaurant scene (as he also had done in *The Great Ice Rip-Off* 18 years earlier).

Although far from the massive scope of *War and Remembrance,* Curtis's new miniseries received positive reviews. *USA Today* called *Intruders* a "riveting" horror/mystery which is "a cross of *Close Encounters of the Third Kind, Rosemary's Baby, Mars Needs Women,* and any number of government-conspiracy flicks."[89] The *Washington Post* asserted, "It won't matter if you believe or not. You'll still be wowed."[90] *Tune in Tonight* wrote, "It's a likely favorite with viewers because of its tabloid-style subject matter — abduction by alien beings — and its classy treatment by a producer-director with a known talent for creating credible drama from essentially unbelievable material."[91] *Variety* added, "Scaremaster Dan Curtis applies his directorial skills to a two-part sci-fi adventure, and the first two hours are whiz-bang stuff ending with a sure-fire cliffhanger."[92]

While his made-for-television accomplishments were numerous, Dan Curtis made only four theatrical films, including *House of Dark Shadows* (1970), *Night of Dark Shadows* (1971), and *Burnt Offerings* (1976). His fourth and final feature, *Me and the Kid* (Orion, 1993), was a bittersweet experience for the director. Because of its uneven (but refreshing) mix of broad comedy, crime drama, and kids' adventure, *Me and the Kid* under-performed in theatres and greatly disappointed Curtis. He recalled,

> While I was doing *The Winds of War,* a fellow who worked with me, Joe Stern, came across this book called *Taking Gary Feldman,* by Stanley Cohen. He showed it to me, and I thought it was a good story although I felt certain things needed to be done to it. But we sold it to CBS, and they developed a screenplay while I was off doing the miniseries. Unfortunately, it never worked out — the option lapsed, and that was that. But I always remembered that story. It's really a problem finding material. It limits me as it limits everybody else. And I'm very tough on material — there's not a lot of stuff I like, particularly after I finished those two giant epics, *The Winds of War* and *War and Remembrance.* I mean, everything paled by comparison, and nothing appealed to me. It was awful; I was in a very depressed state. I thought, "I'll never find anything else I want to do." Then, I remembered the *Gary Feldman* script. It was a sweet little movie, a direct departure from the epics I'd been making [and a throwback to Curtis's warm, semi-autobiographical movies *When Every Day Was the Fourth of July* and *The Long Days of Summer*]. So I optioned it again and developed the screenplay — without talking to any studios. I just developed the material myself, and I thought I would try to put it together and make a deal. I took it around to a few places and met a lot of people who felt the central relationship needed to be developed more, but I said, "Hold the phone; I believe this works — I'll make it myself!" And that's what happened.[93]

Curtis spent four million dollars of his own money filming *Me and the Kid* in California, New York, and New Jersey from mid–October to early December 1992. Richard Tannenbaum assisted producer-director-writer Curtis with the script, and Robert Cobert supplied the background music (as well as a song, "Goin' to Mexico"). The cast was excellent — it included Danny Aiello, Joe Pantoliano, Cathy Moriarty, David Dukes, Anita Morris, Demond Wilson, Ben Stein, and Abe Vigoda — but the story, of a neglected rich boy who becomes involved in a small-time con artist's botched burglary and ends up befriending the crook and traveling with him, was difficult to sell. Curtis was aiming for a latter-day *The Kid* (1921) or *The Champ* (1931, 1979) — with elements of buddy movies, road movies, and his own 1974 *Great Ice Rip-Off* caper movie — but *Me and the Kid* became lost amid the many *Home Alone* (1990) imitations of the early 1990s. Perhaps the worst blow was that *Me and the Kid* (released on October 22, 1993) appeared at the same time as Clint Eastwood's much higher-profile film *A Perfect World* (1993), which itself was the story of a boy who accompanies a criminal (Kevin Costner) on his capers.

Despite favorable audience response at early screenings, *Me and the Kid* made no impression at the box office and vanished quickly. (By March 30, 1994, it was available on video.) The *Los Angeles Times* called the film "an amiable family entertainment for the undemanding, but it has the potential to be much more."[94] *Variety* noted young Alex Zuckerman's "unaffected acting,"[95] but the *Orange County Register* criticized the film's "weak" script and "major flaws in feasibility."[96] Granted, the beginning and the end of *Me and the Kid* could be considered weak or implausible, and a nevertheless very strong, involving middle could not counteract those flaws. The *Los Angeles Times* praised the "lovable duo" of Danny Aiello and Alex Zuckerman but lamented, "You really want their picture to be better."[97]

In an interview in the December 9, 1993 *Wire*, Dan Curtis blamed Orion Pictures for "opening and closing *Me and the Kid* in a week." He insisted, "The promotion was all wrong. It opened as a well-kept secret. Nobody came to see it. It broke my heart. I lost my tail on it. Never, never again will I finance a movie with my own money."[98] As *Me and the Kid* found a small cult audience on home video, Curtis put his noble experiment behind him and refocused his attention on television — and *Dark Shadows*.

Still yearning for a full-fledged revival of his Gothic serial, Curtis, in June 1993, toyed with the idea of making two *Dark Shadows* movies. However, no such movies materialized. In July, Curtis made plans to film a four-hour miniseries of Richard Matheson's Western novel *Journal of the Gun Years* for TNT. Sadly, in early 1994, he shelved his plans for this promising, change-of-pace Curtis/Matheson collaboration. June 2 of that year found Curtis reunited with Herman Wouk as they and members of Congress gathered at the Library of Congress to commemorate the fiftieth anniversary of D-Day. Clips from *War and Remembrance* were a part of the program.

Me and the Kid (1993): Danny Aiello (left, as Harry Banner) talks with director Dan Curtis on the set. *Me and the Kid* was screened at Tennessee State University in Nashville in April 2007.

In mid–1995, Curtis

considered remaking *The Night Stalker,* an idea which would prove to be another ten years away from fruition. On December 7, 1995 (Pearl Harbor Day), the *War* filmmaker was the guest speaker at a University of Southern California directing class. Finally, in the spring of 1996, Curtis traveled to Toronto to make another TV-movie — and another horror TV-movie at that. *Trilogy of Terror II* debuted on the USA Network on October 30, 1996, and starred Lysette Anthony (Angelique from the 1991 *Dark Shadows*) in three different roles in a trio of truly scary horror tales. "The Graveyard Rats" was Curtis and William F. Nolan's expanded, *noirish* adaptation of Henry Kuttner's classic 1936 *Weird Tales* story. "Bobby" was a shot-for-shot remake of Richard Matheson's script for the selfsame segment of 1977's *Dead of Night.* "He Who Kills," based by Curtis and Nolan on Matheson's 1969 "Prey" short story and 1975 "Amelia" TV adaptation, was both a sequel to and a close remake of Karen Black's unforgettable encounter with the Zuni fetish doll. In an interview in the November 1996 *Cinefantastique,* Curtis called it "scarier" than the original, "and it has more humor in it."[99] On December 31, the *New York Daily News* named *Trilogy of Terror II* as one of the best made-for-television movies of 1996.[100]

In 1996–1997, Curtis and Morgan Creek Productions planned a theatrical version of *The Night Stalker*— with a new, perhaps younger actor to play reporter Carl Kolchak. Nick Nolte expressed an interest in playing Kolchak but was never officially cast. On December 12, 1996, the headline on the front page of *The Hollywood Reporter* proclaimed, "Night Stalker on Prowl in Pic." However, in February 1997, Morgan Creek reneged on the deal, and Kolchak hibernated for another eight-and-one-half years until the short-lived ABC-TV remake in the fall of 2005.[101]

Curtis's next telefilm became the seventh-highest-rated *Hallmark Hall of Fame* presentation in history when it was watched by 20,920,000 viewers.[102] *The Love Letter* (CBS, February 1, 1998) was a critically acclaimed adaptation of time-travel master Jack Finney's short story about kindred spirits (Campbell Scott and Jennifer Jason Leigh) who exchange heartfelt letters across two centuries. The story first appeared in the August 1, 1959, edition of *The Saturday Evening Post.* In the updated film version, Scotty Corrigan lives in 1998 while the poet Elizabeth Whitcomb lives in 1864. He mails letters to her at an 1851-era U.S. Post Office still in use. She sends letters to him by leaving them in a secret compartment of the desk which each of them owns in her or his own time period. The time-travel gimmick serves to illuminate the more realistic concerns of seeking true love, overcoming life's obstacles, and coping with war (in Elizabeth's case, the Civil War). *Love Letter* scriptwriter James Henerson (*Love on a Rooftop, The Second Hundred Years*) won the Writers Guild of America award for the Best Long-Form Screenplay of 1998.[103]

Curtis directed the Hallmark movie in and around Richmond, Virginia, during the fall of 1997. He admitted that he had wanted to film Finney's time-travel romance for two decades. *The Love Letter* "is the most magical love story I've ever come across," he uncharacteristically gushed. Curtis explained,

> It transcends time and will enchant the audience. It reaches into your heart because it's about two people yearning for each other, separated by almost 150 years, who exist simultaneously and communicate through letters. Watching this movie is going to be the equiva-

lent of curling up in front of the fireplace on a winter's night with a wonderful, engaging romantic novel. You just know it's going to make you feel good, and that's what *The Love Letter* does. It tells us that romance is always possible in our lives — even though it may occur in very unusual ways![104]

USA Today observed, "Producer-director Curtis, who gingerly moved between time periods and parallel dimensions on the classic soap *Dark Shadows,* is up to his old tricks."[105] *Entertainment Weekly* awarded *The Love Letter* the grade of A- and added, "It's like that rarest of Hallmark cards: unabashedly romantic yet surprisingly light on cheese."[106] The *Christian Science Monitor* called *The Love Letter* "a delightful high romance; the movie spins a fantastic story of love that transcends time itself; beautifully acted and directed, it creates a world that is entirely engaging."[107] *Variety* praised the film's "well-executed script, based on a Jack Finney short story, that melds romance, fantasy, and quasi-time travel and is enhanced by endearing performances from its principals," including Scott, Leigh, Estelle Parsons, and Curtis mainstay David Dukes. According to *Variety,*

> Director Dan Curtis keeps the pace brisk, knowing when to move the tale along or to slow down for some weepy moments that are crucial but never indulgent. He is aided by Eric Van Haren Norman's camerawork, which uses the striking shades of autumn to backdrop the story and its emotional underpinnings while soaking in Jan Scott's lush production design. Bill Blunden's editing makes it all seamless. The only quibble is this Hallmark card should have been saved for airing closer to Valentine's Day [instead of 13 days prior to the date].[108]

Jennifer Jason Leigh declared, "I love Dan Curtis. With everything he's done — all those huge miniseries like *War and Remembrance*— I mean, he's a legend. But he's got a great young attitude and a really sweet heart. He's got this tough-guy exterior and this deep, gruff

The Love Letter (1998): Between *Somewhere in Time* and *The Lake House,* there is Dan Curtis's love letter to romantic fantasy. Campbell Scott and Jennifer Jason Leigh co-star in one of the highest-rated *Hallmark Hall of Fame* telefilms.

voice, but he really is a marshmallow."[109] Curtis's softer side did shine through in his sensitive direction of *The Love Letter.* Indeed, one wonders how *Somewhere in Time* (1980), Richard Matheson's gold-standard time-travel romance, would have been different if Dan Curtis, not Jeannot Szwarc (*The Devil's Daughter, Supergirl*), had directed it. Matheson named a *Somewhere in Time* character Professor Finney, after Jack Finney, and the 2000 South Korean film *Il Mare* (and its 2006 American remake *The Lake House*) appropriated Finney's plot of lovers separated by time but connected by their letters.

The Love Letter was Curtis's final film before a seven-year absence from the screen. On March 3, 1998, one month after CBS aired *The Love Letter,* Curtis received the Golden Laurel Award from the Producers Guild of America. On January 27, 1999, in Los Angeles, Curtis participated in the Museum of Television and Radio's seminar about film and television portrayals of the Holocaust from the 1950s to the 1990s. *War and Remembrance,* of course, held its own with *The Diary of Anne Frank* (1959) and *Schindler's List* (1993). On October 23, 2000, the Museum of Television and Radio honored Curtis, Karen Black, Robert Cobert, Richard Matheson, and William F. Nolan at its seminar, "Monster in the Box: Horror on Television" (or, more accurately, Dan Curtis's horror on television). The audience and the honorees watched *Trilogy of Terror* and then engaged in a question-and-answer session.

On March 8, 2001, Curtis once again appeared at the Museum of TV and Radio for what would be a once-in-a-lifetime gathering of *Dark Shadows* stars and fans. The Dark Shadows Festival fan conventions had been held around the country every year since 1983, but Curtis had never attended one. Finally he did participate in this momentous *Dark Shadows* thirty-fifth-anniversary reunion with Robert Cobert, Alexandra Moltke, Mitchell Ryan, Kate Jackson, David Selby, Nancy Barrett, John Karlen, director Lela Swift, and eight other *Dark Shadows* celebrities. It was the most highly and enthusiastically attended gathering in the museum's series of classic-TV reunion seminars. Surrounded by his cast, Dan Curtis marveled,

> The greatest fun in the world was hiring all of these people. I just hired people I liked. I couldn't tell if they could act or they couldn't. But I'll tell you something: they all learned. I've never seen anything like it. I remember when Katie [Jackson] came on, she could barely say her own name, but by the time she started to work in the story every day, she became great. *Everybody* became wonderful in this, and I would have a great time. I'd show up at this place [the *Dark Shadows* studio], and it felt like home. It was a big repertory company. In reality, that's what it was. The one thing I wanted to do and I never did — we just never got around to doing it — during the Christmas holidays, when there are no ratings, but we were booming along and I didn't want to waste the story that we had, I thought, why shouldn't we put the whole group together and for two weeks do Charles Dickens's *A Christmas Carol* with the *Dark Shadows* Players, and I really was going to do it. Each Christmas came along, and I never got to do it, and that's the one thing I regret.[110]

Later in 2001, Curtis considered making films about the Civil War, Franklin Delano Roosevelt's "Four Freedoms" speech, and the 1951 scandal involving the West Point football team, but none of these projects came to fruition. In the early 2000s, Norma Klein Curtis began showing signs of the Alzheimer's disease which (along with heart disease) would end her life in March 2006. Ironically, Curtis's next-to-last film was about a man's struggle with his wife's debilitating neurological disease.

But first *Dark Shadows* occupied the director's attention once again. Ever since the short-lived 1991 revival, Curtis had been seeking a way to reincarnate the show. He had considered a theatrical film, a nighttime TV series, a daytime series, an animated series, and even a Broadway musical (with music by Robert Cobert and Rupert Holmes). In early 2002, the Fox network considered making a new, nighttime *Dark Shadows* based on a script by Eric Bernt, writer of the 2000 films *Romeo Must Die* and *Highlander: Endgame*, but Fox eventually passed on the idea.[111]

Finally, in 2003, the WB network, which had enjoyed considerable success with its shows about vampires, super-heroes, and teenagers, greenlighted the pilot for a new, younger, hipper *Dark Shadows*. Executive producers Dan Curtis and John Wells (*E.R., The West Wing*) asked Rob Bowman, one of the directors of the 1991 series, to direct the lavish, six-million-dollar pilot film. The scriptwriter was Mark Verheiden, who had written for *Timecop* (1997–1998) and *Smallville* (debuted 2001).

Bowman bowed out of the project in order to direct *Elektra* (2005) and was replaced by P.J. Hogan (*My Best Friend's Wedding, Peter Pan*). The new, much younger Barnabas Collins was Alec Newman, while Marley Shelton played Victoria Winters and TV veteran Blair Brown portrayed Elizabeth Collins Stoddard. Most of the cast was younger than before, beautiful in the style of the WB, and for the first time multicultural. The original *Dark Shadows* had included only one Asian American and two African Americans in minor, short-term roles, and the 1991 remake had featured only Caucasian actors. For the 2004 *Dark Shadows,* Dr. Julia Hoffman was Asian American, Sheriff George Patterson was African American, and the young housekeeper "Sophia" (not the middle-aged Mrs. Johnson of the two previous series) was Latina. Curtis looked forward to a spot for his new show on the WB's fall 2004 schedule.

Dark Shadows (2004): After four dark-haired Victorias, Marley Shelton is the first blonde Victoria Winters. Alexander Gould is Vicki's charge, David Collins.

After a rough cut of the pilot (minus completed special effects, titles, or music score) was screened for WB executives, the network rejected it, and the unfinished pilot was never broadcast. Its only public exhibition has occurred at every Dark Shadows Festival fan convention since 2004. Without postproduction, the rough cut was never released on DVD. The WB later regretted its decision to shelve *Dark Shadows,* for the show's fall 2004 debut would have caught the wave of the similarly mystical and quirky *Lost* and *Desperate Housewives,* which premiered that fall, as well as *Medium* (which began in January 2005) and the *six* horror/sci-fi-themed TV series (including *Supernatural* and *Ghost Whisperer*) that debuted in the fall of 2005. Dan Curtis and replacement director P.J. Hogan had never quite gelled in their visions for *Dark Shadows,* and Curtis felt that a Rob Bowman-directed pilot (if not a Dan Curtis-directed one) would have stood a better chance of successfully reimagining *Dark Shadows* for the twenty-first century.

On April 22, 2004, Curtis made his final appearance at the Museum of Television and Radio for "*War, Shadows,* and *The Night Stalker:* A Conversation with Dan Curtis." Near the end of his career, Curtis was finally receiving the kind of recognition that his Gothic-horror projects and his *War* miniseries had always warranted. Interestingly, his final two films recalled the heartrending drama of his two semi-autobiographical TV-movies and the issue-oriented fare of *Mrs. R's Daughter* (1979). *Saving Milly* (CBS, March 13, 2005, and July 9, 2006) was based on political journalist Mort Kondracke's non-fiction best-seller of the same name. As adapted by Jeff Arch (*Sleepless in Seattle*), *Saving Milly* was the story of Kondracke's 38-year love affair with his activist wife Millicent "Milly" Martinez Kondracke (d. July 22, 2004), who was diagnosed with an especially severe form of Parkinson's disease. Bruce Greenwood and Madeleine Stowe played the long-suffering couple, and Stowe won an Imagen Award for Best Television Actress. Arch's emotional script was nominated for the Humanitas Prize.[112]

Curtis admitted that he was drawn to the project because Alzheimer's disease had touched his family and he wanted to raise the public's awareness of all debilitating neurological diseases. "I'm usually never happy to hear about people crying," Curtis told *USA Today.* "This time, I am. *Saving Milly* is not a disease-of-the-week movie. If we can get the word out there, without it being a lesson or homework, and tell a great, moving love story, a ten-handkerchief picture, then I'll do it."[113] He did.

The *New York Daily News* called *Saving Milly* "challenging," "well-acted," and "tender," as well as "part passionate romance, part advocacy piece, and definitely worth a look."[114] The Parents Television Council named it "the best TV show of the week."[115] *The Hollywood Reporter* called

Director Dan Curtis and actor/consultant Michael J. Fox smile on the set of *Saving Milly* (2005). Fox, who suffers from Parkinson's disease, appeared in a tag at the end of the film. *Saving Milly* has yet to be released on VHS or DVD.

Saving Milly "a beautifully acted, deeply moving film that manages to be at once inspirational and grueling."[116]

Two months later, Curtis was back on television with another hard-hitting topical work — and his swan song. *Our Fathers* (Showtime, May 21, 2005) was a fact-based examination of the Boston Catholic diocese's pedophile scandal as it was first exposed in 2000. Christopher Plummer portrayed Cardinal Bernard Law (and received Emmy and SAG Award nominations), and Ted Danson played Mitchell Garabedian, the real-life Boston attorney who represented some of the victims of alleged abuse by Boston-area priests. Brian Dennehy as Father Dominic Spagnolia also received an Emmy Award nomination. Also featured were Ellen Burstyn, Daniel Baldwin, Colin Fox, and Jan Rubes.

Curtis's film was based on the book *Our Fathers: The Secret Life of the Catholic Church in an Age of Scandal,* by *Newsweek* writer David France (himself a victim of alleged abuse by a priest). The screenplay by Thomas Michael Donnelly (*Quicksilver*) was nominated for a Writers Guild of America award for Best Long-Form Adapted Screenplay. The film attracted attention and ratings to Showtime.[117]

Curtis sought to make a non-sensational, balanced look at both the church and the victims. "It had everything that I thought would make a really riveting picture," he noted. "Then comes the difficulty of doing something that's as touchy as this. How do you do it? It's kind of simple in a strange way. You just tell the truth."[118] Indeed, *USA Today* observed, "Curtis never allows a trace of salaciousness to enter the film. He sets the tone without showing anything explicit."[119] Nevertheless, the *Boston Herald* conceded, "If your heart hasn't already been broken by the priest sex-abuse scandal, then Showtime's strong film *Our Fathers* will finish the job."[120]

The San Jose *Mercury News* proclaimed that *Our Fathers* was "everything most TV docudramas about recent events are *not:* thoughtful, restrained without sacrificing emotion, and with a clear ring of truth to it."[121] The *News* added, "The real emotional core is the way *Our Fathers* handles the effect the abuse had on the victims. Without being explicit, the film captures the horror these young men went through as their innocence, faith, and trust were ripped away."[122]

TV Guide's Matt Roush noted, "Dan Curtis knows all about *Dark Shadows,* and there are plenty to be found in the conspiracy of silence that is shattered in *Our Fathers,* a forceful and sorrowful docudrama."[123]

In the fall of 2005, ABC attempted a remake of its 1974–1975 series *Kolchak: The Night Stalker,* based on Dan Curtis and Richard Matheson's TV-movies *The Night Stalker* (1972) and *The Night Strangler* (1973). In this new series, titled simply *Night Stalker,* Stuart Townsend played a much younger, more upscale Carl Kolchak, who along with a team of crime reporters investigates paranormal events in southern California. A brief, almost subliminal clip of Darren McGavin as Kolchak appeared in the first episode (September 29, 2005), as did McGavin's trademark straw hat on the new Kolchak's coat rack. Also, the license plate of Kolchak's car was 197DMG2. There the similarities between the incarnations ended. The dark, humorless *Night Stalker* was much more like *The X-Files, CSI,* and everything else on 1990s/2000s television than the unique, seriocomic *Kolchak: The Night Stalker* of yore. *Entertainment Weekly* and

Variety summed up the lackluster series perfectly when the former wrote, "This remake of the 1970s cult classic [...] has an eerie, *X-Files* vibe,"[124] and the latter added, "It lacks the flavor of the original."[125]

Also, *Night Stalker* was too affluent and stylish to be like its predecessor, which had reveled in Kolchak's shabbiness. The remake lacked the original's wit, as well as (according to *Syndicated*) "heart, drama, and — most inexcusably — horror."[126] In November, ABC unceremoniously dropped the series after airing six of its ten episodes. Ironically the unaired eighth episode, "Into Night," promisingly evoked *The Night Stalker* (1972) in its story of a vampire-like killer, and the ninth and best episode, "Timeless," was practically a remake of *The Night Strangler* (1973) as an ageless woman commits murders in 1900, 1935, 1970, and 2005 in order to retain her youth. Those and all of the other episodes of *Night Stalker* finally aired on the Sci-Fi Channel in the summer and fall of 2006. Dan Curtis, who had not been associated with the 1974–1975 series, was involved with the 2005 effort as a consulting producer who merely offered some script suggestions.

On February 25, 2006, Darren McGavin, the original and definitive Kolchak, died at age 83 — a sad foreshadowing of two more imminent deaths. In November 2005, Dan Curtis was diagnosed with brain cancer. Norma Mae Klein Curtis, his wife of 54 years, was already in an advanced stage of Alzheimer's disease. Kathryn Leigh Scott — Maggie and Josette on *Dark Shadows* four decades earlier — remembered,

> My last memory of Dan is an afternoon spent in his garden not too long before he passed away. He was no longer the big, gruff lion who used to terrify us. His illness had weakened him. He could no longer speak, but he could enjoy his favorite dark chocolates I'd brought. We sat together paging through the beautiful coffee-table book Jim Pierson had put together on the occasion of Dan's seventy-fifth birthday. As we sat there in the afternoon sun, his hand would fall across the page, pointing to a particular actor or a scene from one of his films — horror, Westerns, dramas, romances, mysteries — all of them great stories, well told by a master storyteller. I am so grateful I had that precious time with Dan, to tell him how much he inspired me, encouraged me, gave me so many rare opportunities — and how much I appreciated all of it.[127]

On Tuesday, March 7, 2006, Norma died of complications from Alzheimer's and heart disease. Twenty days later — Monday, March 27, 2006 — Dan Curtis succumbed to brain cancer at his home in Brentwood, California. Cathy and Tracy Curtis were dealt the unimaginable blow of losing both of their parents in less than three weeks' time.

The funeral for Dan Curtis was held on Thursday, March 30, at Eden Memorial Park in Mission Hills, California. Rabbi Abraham Cooper conducted the service. Speakers at the funeral included Cathy Curtis, Tracy Curtis, Norma's physician and Alzheimer's researcher Dr. Jeffrey Cummings, producer Barbara Steele, and author Herman Wouk. Pallbearers were Daniel Blatt, Hart Bochner, John Karlen, David Kennedy, John McMahon, Jim Pierson, David Selby, and Robert Singer. In attendance were Robert Cobert, Roger Davis, Jerry Lacy, Lara Parker, Robert Rodan, Kathryn Leigh Scott, and James Storm (*Dark Shadows*); Karen Black (*Trilogy of Terror, Burnt Offerings*); Dean Jones (*When Every Day Was the Fourth of July, The Long Days of Summer,*

St. John in Exile); Lisa Eilbacher and Peter Graves (*The Winds of War*); Barry Bostwick and Jane Seymour (*War and Remembrance*); Bruce Greenwood (*Saving Milly*); Frank Spotnitz (*X-Files* and *Night Stalker* producer); and many others.[128]

Herman Wouk told the mourners that Dan Curtis was the only man who could have brought the truth of the Holocaust so unforgettably to life in his *War* miniseries. The other speakers remembered the director as driven, creative, indefatigable, sometimes impatient, often generous, always inspiring, and determined to succeed. His daughters shared reminiscences of their father and his exhortation to them never to give up and always to believe in themselves.[129]

On Saturday, May 13, 2006, approximately 100 people attended a memorial service for Curtis at the Directors Guild in Los Angeles. A tribute video, compiled by Tracy Curtis and Dark Shadows Festival chairman Jim Pierson, presented still pictures from Curtis's personal and professional life followed by clips from *Dark Shadows, The Night Stalker, Dracula, Melvin Purvis G-Man, Trilogy of Terror, When Every Day Was the Fourth of July, The Last Ride of the Dalton Gang, The Love Letter, Our Fathers,* and *Saving Milly.* Extensive clips from *The Winds of War* and *War and Remembrance* followed, as well as clips of Curtis on *Entertainment Tonight* (1983) and at the Emmy Awards (1989). Marcy Robin's *Shadowgram* #108 (June 2006) provided an in-depth report about the occasion.

In his remarks, Dan Curtis Productions executive Jim Pierson called Curtis "a world-class motivator, mentor, and creative genius" and "the ultimate fearless leader." Former ABC executive Brandon Stoddard, who had greenlighted *Dark Shadows,* cancelled *Dark Shadows,* and overseen Curtis's TV-movies and epic miniseries, called *The Winds of War* and *War and Remembrance* "the greatest achievement by one man in the history of TV or movies." Richard Matheson remembered Curtis's "creative fervor" and his eager acceptance of Matheson's last-minute changes to the script of *Dracula* (1974). Daniel Blatt recalled that in his 50-year-long friendship with Curtis, Blatt went from being Curtis's teenage golf caddy to a fellow producer (*The Howling, Cujo*), thanks to Curtis's mentoring of him and the director's "enormous largesse."

Dean Jones, who twice had played Curtis's TV father, revealed that for 30 years he and his wife Lory had enjoyed bi-weekly dinners with Norma and Dan Curtis until the Curtises had become too ill. Twenty years earlier, in 1986, Curtis had taken a very short break from making *War and Remembrance* to film Jones's internationally acclaimed one-man stage show, *St. John in Exile,* which was directed by Lory Basham Jones. After filming Dean Jones's *tour de force* before a live audience in Van Nuys, California, Curtis had called Jones's work "the best performance I've ever seen."

Robert Singer, like Blatt, began as Curtis's teenage caddy and became one of his associate producers (*Trilogy of Terror, Burnt Offerings*). "I'll never forget these words Dan said to me many years ago — 'Kid, I'm tired of yelling; *you* yell for a while.'" Singer added that Curtis's direction of the two *War* miniseries was "the most underrated feat in the history of television." Dan Curtis Productions executive David Kennedy, who had run the company after Curtis no longer could, said that his "second father" Dan Curtis had been on an "eternal quest for excellence" and had "a never-give-up spirit."[130] Earlier, Kennedy had declared in print that Curtis's "wondrous love affair with Norma" made "Romeo and Juliet pale in comparison,"[131] and at the memorial service Kennedy compared Dan Curtis to Hamlet's father and declared, "This was a man."[132]

Kathryn Leigh Scott spoke for her *Dark Shadows* castmates when she said, "Dan gave so many of us our very first jobs [...] a great, rare opportunity to experiment and get paid while learning on the job." She continued,

> Every day, Dan had us climbing out on a new limb, risking failure doing a live half hour on kinescope with tons of special effects and scant rehearsal. We'd race to change costumes during commercial breaks; doorknobs came off in our hands; sets collapsed; a candle flame blew out, but the room stayed bright as day; dead bodies moved; and on a stroll through the cemetery, your cape would drag Styrofoam tombstones in your wake. And this was an era long before "bloopers" were considered funny! We begged, we wept, we pleaded for a chance to redo the show before we lost air time to the four-o'clock news, but Dan would say, "Whad d'ya kidding me? It'll air once, and no one will ever see it again." How wrong he was! The show has [almost] never been off the air. Thanks to DVDs, you can watch *Dark Shadows* on your laptop in a Brazilian jungle — and yes, *Dark Shadows* actors still earn residuals. To Dan, we were family. He wouldn't let any of us go. If the character we were playing was killed off, he'd bring us back as another character. After work, he'd join us for drinks at the pub on the corner, and sometimes he'd take the whole gang to dinner. With *Dark Shadows* as his proving ground, Dan went on to produce and/or direct four motion pictures, 30 television films, four TV pilots, six series and miniseries, and his crowning achievements, 18 hours of *The Winds of War* and 29 hours of *War and Remembrance. Dark Shadows* actors continued to pop up regularly in his other productions over the years, and in the case of Bob Cobert, who composed the music for *Dark Shadows,* he went on to compose all of Dan's scores for 40 years. Many of us here today have 40 years' worth of wonderful memories of Dan. I will forever be indebted to him and will miss him — as we all will.[133]

Cobert, of course, was in attendance at the DGA memorial service, as were *Dark Shadows* actors Lara Parker, Christopher Pennock, Robert Rodan, and David Selby. Representing the 1991 *Dark Shadows* were actress-producer Barbara Steele, writer William Gray, and directors Paul Lynch and Armand Mastroianni. Other celebrities paying their respects included Ben Murphy (*The Winds of War*), Ian McShane (*War and Remembrance*), and Madeleine Stowe (*Saving Milly*). *The Winds of War* actress Ali McGraw sent a letter "admiring [Dan's] vision and superhuman energy."[134]

In 1980, film historian and theatrical agent David Del Valle had met Curtis through Barbara Steele, who was his client. Del Valle remembered, "I vividly recall sitting in a small screening room with Barbara and Dan watching the rushes of John Gielgud on his way to the gas chambers in *War and Remembrance.* When the lights went up, Dan stood up and raised his fist heavenward: 'Steven Spielberg, eat your heart out!'"[135]

That same night, Curtis had mused, "You know, when I die, even if this show wins a truckload of Emmys, they will end up saying, 'Dan Curtis, creator of daytime television's *Dark Shadows,* died today.'"[136] It was an observation that Curtis repeated, privately and publicly, several times. In March and April 2006, all of his many obituaries mentioned both *Dark Shadows* and the *War* miniseries, and most of them mentioned his many Gothic-horror projects and his professional and personal involvement with golf. The great producer-director himself had mused,

People have always said to me since I've finished *War and Remembrance,* "How are you going to top yourself?" That's crazy. I don't plan to try. There's nothing I can do to top myself. I will never completely recover from it. I'm not destroyed by it, but it's something that will live with me forever. It's always in my mind. The images and moments run through my mind all the time. It will never leave me — never, never. This is something I'll be proud of until the day I go.[137]

CHAPTER II

Curtis's Dream: *Dark Shadows*

"I can see what it is now," Dan Curtis once mused, that made ABC-TV's *Dark Shadows* (June 27, 1966–April 2, 1971) a cult classic and one of his greatest achievements. "As crazy and naïve as the whole thing was, I can see what it was that had the whole audience fascinated. There was a very enchanting quality about it. *Dark Shadows* is its own unique fairyland. It doesn't exist in the reality of today, and it doesn't care about war or other problems. *Dark Shadows* is like nothing else."[1]

Jonathan Frid called the show "a dark *Brigadoon*"[2] because the world outside Collinsport, Maine, did not seem to exist. Except for the sometimes outrageous late-sixties/early-seventies fashions (courtesy of Ohrbach's), *Dark Shadows* existed outside time and certainly outside the realm of the many social issues of the era. The war in Vietnam was never mentioned. (Only "putting a man on the moon" and "the younger generation's preoccupation with love" were mentioned once each.) However, *Dark Shadows* always managed to emerge during a time of war. The original series ran during the Vietnam War, the 1991 series unluckily coincided with the Persian Gulf War, and the 2004 unsold pilot came about during the G.W. Bush administration's War on Terror. *Dark Shadows* equals any Shirley Temple movie or Busby Berkeley musical in terms of offering pure escapism during troubled times.

Curtis called the original series "nickel-and-dime television at its best."[3] The cost of producing all five episodes per week was $70,000, not counting the actors' salaries. "I'm amazed that it still holds up," Curtis marveled. "There we were in a little rinky-dink studio the size of a two-lane bowling alley, and we had nothing. We had four sets — the Great Hall was about as big as a telephone booth — and there it was."[4] Actually, future Emmy Award-winning scenic designer Sy Tomashoff's sets of the Collinwood drawing room, the dilapidated Old House, the Blue Whale tavern, and Maggie Evans's house were the most elaborate that 1950s-1960s daytime serials had ever seen. Stuart Goodman's camera made them look bigger and richer, and Mel Handelsman's skillful lighting gave the shadowed sets the atmosphere of Universal horror movies, *film noir,* or (after the 1967 switch from black-and-white to color) the colorful costume dramas of Joan Bennett's Hollywood.

The unusual premise of *Dark Shadows* had come to golf-show producer Dan Curtis in a vivid, haunting dream one night in the summer of 1965. Curtis remembered that he awoke suddenly. "The bedroom was pitch-black, but I could see the figure in my dream clearly — as though I were watching a movie. I saw a girl with long dark hair. She was about 19, and she was reading a letter aboard a train and occasionally staring wistfully out the window."[5] Curtis perceived that the dream girl had been hired as a governess at an old house somewhere on the New England seacoast.

"Then, the train stopped in this dark, isolated town. The girl got off the train and started walking. Finally, she came to a huge, forbidding house. At the door, she lifted a huge brass knocker and gently tapped it three times. I heard a dog howl, and then — just as the door creaked open — I woke up!"[6] Apparently Curtis, who later mastered the daily cliffhanger on his *Dark Shadows* soap opera, himself *dreamed* in cliffhangers.

"The next morning," he continued, "I wasn't so sure. At breakfast, I told my wife about the dream. When I finished, sure enough, Norma looked at me with wide-eyed enthusiasm and said, 'Dan, that's a great idea for a TV show!' She pointed out that the dream had a Gothic flavor, something eerie and threatening."[7]

Much of the debut episode of *Dark Shadows* (seen on June 27, 1966) was a literal filming of Curtis's fateful dream. Writer Art Wallace fleshed out Curtis's dream for the show's first 13 weeks, and then eight other writers, most notably Gordon Russell, Sam Hall, and Ron Sproat, continued the story until 1971. Nevertheless, Curtis was the idea man behind the show. Lela Swift, who directed 580 of the 1225 episodes of *Dark Shadows,* agreed that "Dan was the creative mind behind it; the writers were working off of his ideas for the show."[8] Whatever concept or character that captivated Curtis was incorporated into the show. When Curtis became bored with a certain story, the storyline changed.

In its first ten months, *Dark Shadows* was a mysterious but tame soap opera with the flavor of the woman-in-jeopardy Gothic novels which were popular in the 1960s and 1970s. Novelists such as Dorothy Daniels, Dan "Marilyn" Ross, Phyllis A. Whitney, and Daoma Winston were filling bookstore shelves with their stories of young women working as governesses in seemingly haunted old, dark houses where their

Dark Shadows (1966–1971): Kathryn Leigh Scott (in a blonde wig as waitress Maggie Evans) and Alexandra Moltke (as future governess Victoria Winters) perform the "You're a jerk!" scene from episode number one, seen on Monday afternoon, June 27, 1966.

lives were in danger from some unseen force. Dan Ross went on to write 32 Paperback Library novels based on *Dark Shadows* itself and a half-dozen other vampire novels. However, what made for enthralling reading was *not* generating high-spirited (or highly-rated) television. By early 1967, *Dark Shadows* was facing a danger far worse than creaking doors: cancellation.

"When the show went on the air," Curtis observed, "it was the best-kept secret since Oak Ridge. Nobody was watching it."[9] In 1966 and 1967, only nine to ten million viewers (a paltry number, ratings-wise) were following the stories of the neurotic Collins family of Collinsport, Maine — a far cry from the record 16 to 18 million fans who watched the show in 1968, 1969, and early 1970.[10] What turned the show around was another Curtis innovation: a vampire.

Curtis's own daughters suggested that their father make *Dark Shadows* scarier. What had begun as an extra-mysterious soap opera only several steps beyond *The Edge of Night* or *The Secret Storm* soon became overtly supernatural. Curtis decided to have fun with *Dark Shadows* and push the envelope since he thought the show was going off the air anyway. Curtis had the writers add ghosts, and the ratings increased. Next came a phoenix who rose from her ashes and lived again every 100 years. Finally, in April 1967, Curtis and the writers added the character of Barnabas Collins, an eighteenth-century vampire freed from his chained coffin to terrorize twentieth-century Collinsport.

Curtis intended the Barnabas character to be a short-term villain who would kill a few characters and then himself be killed by a stake through the heart. However, Curtis soon realized that Barnabas's portrayer, Shakespearean actor Jonathan Frid, "brought a very Gothic, romantic quality to this role that I guess will live forever."[11] Audiences reacted passionately to the vampire Barnabas, as well as to the witch Angelique, the werewolf Quentin, and the endless stream of ghosts, sorcerers, gypsies, zombies, and mad doctors. Time travel added to the romantic exoticism of *Dark Shadows,* and in mid–1969, as the show was telling a complex tale set in the year 1897, *Dark Shadows* was the highest-rated network program on daytime television.[12] Curtis credited his show with allowing ABC to compete with NBC (*Another World, Concentration*) and CBS (*As the World Turns, Search for Tomorrow*) during the day. Watching *Dark Shadows* led viewers to ABC's other daytime offerings, including *The Dating Game, The New-lywed Game, One Life to Live,* and *Let's Make a Deal,* all of which began on ABC between 1965 and 1968.

"The idea was to bring a vampire on as a marauding, evil presence: a Dracula," Curtis reiterated. "There was no other intention. I went off to England to do *Dr. Jekyll and Mr. Hyde* [in 1967], and I said to cast a vampire. And they cast a vampire: they cast Jonathan Frid." Curtis continued,

Frid was a wonderful actor to work with. He had a particular quality; he had a haunting quality about him. He was very "period" to me; he wasn't contemporary. He somehow probably encompassed the kinds of shadings that made a Heathcliff or a Rochester or people like that attractive to women. Here's a guy who's supposed to be a vampire and supposed to terrorize people, but he started getting all this fan mail, and I realized there was something really wild going on here. We had to find a way to perpetuate a vampire — I couldn't kill him off now — and this is the way the love story started.[13]

Curtis's "love story" was Barnabas's doomed love for Josette DuPres, the eighteenth-century woman who kills herself when she learns that her beloved Barnabas is a vampire. Curtis realized that this somber love story had become central to the appeal and success of his show.

"The audience really cared about Barnabas," Curtis admitted, "and he became the reluctant vampire. Now, I know a lot of people have tried that since then, but you really cared about him. So we had to take him from the mode of being this horrifying terror to this guy you feel sorry for."[14]

Barnabas Collins reflected the ambivalent social consciousness and pop psychology of the 1960s in that he was not all bad or all good. The vampire was tragic and guilt-ridden, an idea previously implied in the Universal classics *Dracula's Daughter* (1936), *House of Frankenstein* (1944), and *House of Dracula* (1945). A decade before Anne Rice's *Interview with the Vampire* (1976), the complex, multi-faceted, Byronic vampire/anti-hero came of age in Barnabas Collins as the turbulent times posed the questions: should wrongdoers be seen as evil and punished, or be considered as victims and rehabilitated? Should Barnabas Collins be despised and staked, or pitied and cured? Is vampirism curable like other social diseases? Jonathan Frid often remarked, "I played Barnabas as an alcoholic. I didn't play 'the bite.' I played his problems. He was a guy with a hang-up."[15] As a result, millions of housewives, college students, and school children sympathized with Barnabas and followed his daily exploits. Dr. Julia Hoffman sought to find a cure for him while suffering herself from unrequited love for the vampire.

The convoluted storyline of *Dark Shadows* can be easily divided into segments which fans refer to as "pre–Barnabas," "1795," "1897," etc. Henry Jenkins, author of *Textual Poachers: Television Fans and Participatory Culture* (1992), points out that each segment "is reduced to a brief phrase, evoked for an audience which has already absorbed its local significance and fit it into the larger sense of the series's development."[16]

Dark Shadows (1966–1971): Jonathan Frid as Barnabas Collins and Grayson Hall as Dr. Julia Hoffman pose for a rare alternate take from their 1968 photo session.

The 1966–1967 **pre–Barnabas** episodes concern Victoria Winters's exploration of the secrets of her past and their possible link to the Collins family and the great house of Collinwood. In April **1967**, Barnabas Collins rises from his chained coffin, kidnaps Maggie Evans, and tries to make her over as his lost Josette. The **1795** time period (late 1967–early 1968) reveals Barnabas's life as a mortal and dramatizes the witch's curse that caused his vampirism. The **1968** time period involves the Dream Curse, the *Frankenstein*-like creations of Adam and Eve, Barnabas's temporary cure, and the introduction of the werewolf Chris Jennings. The extremely popular **1897** time period (March-November 1969) takes Barnabas (a vampire again) back in time to try to save the life of the werewolf Quentin Collins, whose curse is linked to that of Chris Jennings in the present time.

Dark Shadows takes a sci-fi turn with the **Leviathan** storyline (late 1969-early 1970), in which shapeless prehistoric entities possess Barnabas and other Collinses in order to regain their dominion over the earth. Next (April-July 1970), Barnabas and later Julia enter the world of **1970 Parallel Time**, an alternate universe in which the people of Collinsport look the same but lead vastly different lives because they have made different choices. Escaping a burning Collinwood in parallel time, Barnabas and Julia find themselves back in their own time band but in the future year of **1995** when Collinwood is in ruins and the Collins family is dead except for Quentin and Carolyn, who are insane. Barnabas and Julia return to the summer of **1970** and attempt to prevent the future destruction of Collinwood. In the autumn of 1970, their quest again leads them and later Professor Stokes through time, to **1840**, when the present-day threat to Collinwood originated with the powerful warlock Judah Zachery and his possession of Gerard Stiles, whose evil ghost haunts Collinwood in 1970 and has destroyed the house by 1995. Barnabas, Julia, and Stokes succeed in defeating Judah Zachery, and they return to the present time and find a peaceful, happy Collinwood.

Beginning in January 1971, the final three months of *Dark Shadows* divorce themselves completely from the regular characters' time band and tell a Gothic love story between Bramwell Collins and Catherine Harridge in **1841 Parallel Time**. The story ends happily for this alternate Collins family when *Dark Shadows* airs its final episode on Friday, April 2, 1971.

Even in its tamer pre–Barnabas days and certainly in its heyday of vampirism, witchcraft, time travel, lycanthropy, and Leviathans, *Dark Shadows* profited from emotional, convincing, and enthralling writing. Art Wallace, who had written for *Goodyear TV Playhouse* (1951–1960), plotted and scripted most of the first four months and 65 episodes of the series. He based some of the characters on those in "The House," one of his *Goodyear Playhouse* scripts (September 8, 1957). Wallace went on to write the made-for-TV movies *A Tattered Web* (1971) and *She Waits* (1972). Next, 1940s-era screenwriter Francis Swann (*Shine on Harvest Moon*) wrote three dozen episodes, and Ron Sproat (*Love of Life*), one of the show's major writers, turned out 214 scripts. Malcolm Marmorstein (*Peyton Place*) wrote 80 episodes, and Joe Caldwell (*Strange Paradise*) wrote 63.[17]

Beginning in the fall of 1968, Gordon Russell (*A Flame in the Wind*) and Sam Hall (*Adventures in Paradise*) became the head writers of *Dark Shadows*. Russell and Hall wrote 366 and 316 episodes, respectively. They later co-wrote *One Life to Live*. Ralph Ellis (*A Flame in the Wind*) scripted only two episodes in February 1969. In March 1969, theatrical press agent Violet Welles began writing for *Dark Shadows* and eventually wrote 84 shows. The writers took many of their story ideas from Curtis himself.[18]

Lela Swift, a director of *Studio One* (1948–1958), directed more episodes of *Dark Shadows* than anyone else — 580. They included the first and last episodes plus Curtis's one-shot nighttime *Dark Shadows*-style experiment *Dead of Night,* a.k.a. *A Darkness at Blaisedon* (ABC, August 26, 1969). Swift went on to direct *Ryan's Hope* (1975–1989). Five hundred sixty-eight of the rest of the 1225 episodes of *Dark Shadows* were directed by either Henry Kaplan (*All My Children*), John Sedwick (*The Edge of Night*), or Dan Curtis.[19]

After producing but not directing *Dark Shadows* and *The Strange Case of Dr. Jekyll and Mr. Hyde* (1968), Curtis decided to try his hand at directing. He remembered, "I was producing all the time, and then I finally got to the point where I said, 'This is crazy. I develop the projects; then, I bring in directors, and I tell them what to do.' And I said, 'Why don't I just cut out the middle-man, the director?'"[20]

Curtis learned the art of directing from Lela Swift, the Ida Lupino of television. Kathryn Leigh Scott, who began playing Maggie Evans on the first episode of *Dark Shadows,* called Swift "a remarkable, seasoned, award-winning woman director, who was a pioneer in the era of live television." Scott added,

> She was present for all initial casting and directed the premiere episode of *Dark Shadows.* Dan became her protégé. She stood by, mentoring Dan when he directed his first episodes of the show, and advised him on his first feature, *House of Dark Shadows.* Dan always had a director's eye and an excellent sense of story. He developed rapidly into a strong, innovative director with a keen sense of drama. He gained his own vision and, over time, became a powerhouse, directing a wide variety of material. There was nothing pretentious in his work. He was a straightforward, solid craftsman who always put story first.[21]

Every aspect of Curtis's post-golf-show career began with *Dark Shadows.* Curtis created the series, produced the show, guided the writers according to his plot ideas, and finally directed 21 of the 1225 episodes. As he directed these segments, mostly in the conventional soap-opera style, he experimented with a few distinctive techniques, including pans, dissolves, extreme close-ups, and unusual compositions such as shooting through Victoria's foreground noose or Quentin's foreground brandy snifter. The particular episodes which he chose to direct involved almost all of the elements that defined *Dark Shadows:* vampirism, witchcraft, time travel, possessed children, dreams, and séances. His first episodes, #457–461 (March 26–29 & April 1, 1968), proved to be some of the classic segments of his admitted favorite storyline of the series. Curtis recalled,

> I loved the section where we went back to the past [1795]. That was my favorite. We did it when I was desperate. I had run out of story material. So why don't we go into the past and see Barnabas before he was a vampire? We knew we'd have to create the whole legend of how he became a vampire and somehow get it to match the cocka-bally stuff we were saying in the present.[22]

In these pivotal 1795 episodes, Barnabas's mother Naomi Collins sees her undead son in his coffin and takes poison. After Naomi dies in his arms, Barnabas hunts down and kills Lieutenant Nathan Forbes, who had told Naomi where to find his coffin. Meanwhile, the unjustly convicted Victoria Winters goes to the gallows, but just before she perishes at the end of the hangman's noose, she is transported back to the present time and to the séance which originally sent her to 1795. These episodes foreshadow scenes which Curtis later staged much more grandly in his two *Dark Shadows* movies.

Nathan's attack on Barnabas with a crossbow and Victoria's public hanging act as prototypes for Jeff Clark's attack on Barnabas with a crossbow in *House of Dark Shadows* (1970) and Angelique's execution in *Night of Dark Shadows* (1971). The extremely emotional 1795 storyline involving Josette, Barnabas, Victoria, Peter, and the witch Angelique was one of the most popular storylines of the series. Curtis remarked,

> We always built our stories around "the love story across time," that yearning that Barnabas wants his true love from 200 years ago. We always found ways to go into the past and to bring them together and to separate them. As long as we stayed with that [storyline], the audience went nuts, and the moment we moved away from things like that, we had a problem.[23]

In late 1968, as *Dark Shadows* concluded a *Frankenstein* storyline and began a werewolf story and a *Turn of the Screw*-like plot, the show's ratings dipped very slightly. By this time, Barnabas had not been a vampire for eight months because the *Frankenstein* procedure had siphoned off the vampire curse. Curtis resolved to take the show back to 1796 for a week and to allow Barnabas, a vampire once again, to change history.

Curtis himself directed episodes #661–667 (January 6–10 & January 13–14, 1969), which included smoother, more dynamic remakes of the Nathan/Barnabas crossbow scene and Victoria's hanging. This time, Barnabas lets Nathan live in exchange for his signed confession to his perjury in Victoria's trial, and the aftermath of Victoria's hanging unfolds differently and allows for a happy ending for Victoria and Peter, now together forever in the past (until history is changed *once again* in the 1970 Leviathan storyline). Curtis even remade Willie Loomis's release of Barnabas from the chained coffin, a classic sequence which Lela Swift had directed for episode #210 (April 17, 1967) and which Curtis would shoot still again for *House of Dark Shadows* and the 1991 TV series.

Episodes #661–667, with their re-creations of previous events, are significant because they began Curtis's career-long trait of doubling. After directing these sequences two different times, he went on to make two *Dark Shadows* movies, two *Dead of Night* TV pilots, two *Night Stalker* movies, two *Trilogy of Terror* films, two Melvin Purvis adventures, two caper movies (*The Great Ice Rip-Off* and *Me and the Kid*), two semi-autobiographical family dramas, a second *Dark Shadows* series (plus an unsold third attempt), two versions of Richard Matheson's "Bobby," and, of course, two World War II miniseries. He enjoyed underscoring many of his successful works with a second, equally fine production. Although he made only one Western (*The Last Ride of the Dalton Gang*), he considered making a second (*Journal of the Gun Years*), and if he had lived longer, it is possible that he would have remade *Burnt Offerings* for the twenty-first century.

On *Dark Shadows*, Curtis presented the phoenix storyline twice (1966 and 1969) and a *Turn of the Screw*-like plotline twice (1968–1969 and mid–1970). He next chose to direct his show near the beginning of the first *Turn of the Screw* story, episodes #680–682 (January 31 & February 3–4, 1969), when the ghosts of Quentin Collins and Beth Chavez begin to possess the children, David Collins and Amy Jennings. Curtis named Quentin after Peter Quint, the ghost in Henry James's novel (one of Curtis's favorite books). In these episodes, Maggie Evans comes face to face with Quentin in a frightening sequence well directed by Curtis; she has a dream in which Quentin strangles her; and she, Barnabas, Professor Stokes, and Mrs. Johnson hold a séance to contact the spirit of a medium whom Quentin has killed. With these episodes, Curtis continued his trend of taking the director's chair himself for especially important episodes.

Two months later, after *Dark Shadows* had begun its highly successful storyline set in the year 1897, Curtis directed a trio of episodes about the return of Laura the phoenix. In shows #735–737 (April 18 & April 21–22, 1969), Laura extricates her children from Worthington Hall, the Reverend Gregory Trask's school, by setting it on fire. Trask's strict school is inspired by Dotheboys Hall in Charles Dickens's *Nicholas Nickleby*, Lowood School in Charlotte Brontë's *Jane Eyre*, and the severe, unnamed school in Edgar Allan Poe's "William Wilson." Then, Laura's enemy Quentin tries to destroy the phoenix by extinguishing the flame in her urn, the source of her power. Laura must pray to the Egyptian god Ra for continued life. In her talks at the 1991 and 2005 Dark Shadows Festivals, actress Diana Millay, who played Laura in 1966 and again in 1969, revealed that if *Dark Shadows* had continued past April 1971, she would have returned to the show for a third phoenix saga at the request of Dan Curtis.

Curtis directed *Dark Shadows* for the final three times in the summer of 1969. In episodes #806–807 and 811 (July 28–29 & August 4, 1969), set in 1897, young Jamison Collins is possessed by the spirit of Count Andreas Petofi, and a *Picture of Dorian Gray* storyline begins when the painter Charles Delaware Tate starts a portrait of Quentin. The changeable portrait will suffer the werewolf curse instead of Quentin, and it will make him immortal. The highlight is Curtis's direction of Quentin's dream about his dead wife Jenny and their babies.

As indicated by these allusions to the works of Charles Dickens, Charlotte Brontë, Edgar Allan Poe, Oscar Wilde, and Henry James, *Dark Shadows* freely adapted classic Gothic works throughout its five-year run. Curtis explained,

Dark Shadows (1966–1971): From left, Jonathan Frid as Barnabas Collins, David Selby as Quentin Collins, and David Henesy as Jamison Collins interact in a scene from the popular 1897 storyline (seen in mid–1969).

The reason we went to the classics as much we did — ripping off portions

of *Jane Eyre, Wuthering Heights,* or *The Turn of the Screw*—is that all stories are basically the same. These are great story elements, and we put our own spin on them. It's so difficult to think of a story that hasn't in some way been done, so why not go right to the gold mine where it all really lies? We never did *Turn of the Screw,* but we certainly took elements from *Turn of the Screw.* We did *Frankenstein*: we built our own monster. Some [stories] were more successful than others. But it's a great source, and since I loved all of that material, I had great fun in doing our own version of *Frankenstein.* I just kept picturing the old Frankenstein movies, with the electrodes and everything flashing, and the monster! It was great![24]

The *Frankenstein* plotline, which resulted in the creations of the scarred Adam and the beautiful Eve, occurred in 1968 after the 1795 saga and before the *Turn of the Screw* story which led into the 1897 time period. Robert Rodan, who played Adam, noted that many of his fan letters came from young children who sympathized with Adam's childlike innocence. "I was approaching it [the role of Adam] from a human perspective, not a monster perspective," Rodan explained.[25]

The great Gothic novels by Charlotte and Emily Brontë influenced several parts of the series. Curtis saw Victoria Winters as Jane Eyre, an orphan who grows up to be the governess in a house of secrets. During the 1897 saga, Collinwood governess Rachel Drummond also evokes *Jane Eyre* as an orphan who first is a student and then a teacher at Worthington Hall. The writers patterned the Reverend Gregory Trask after Mr. Brocklehurst, and they further evoked Charlotte Brontë's novel by introducing Quentin Collins's mad, violent wife Jenny, who is kept locked in the tower room of Collinwood. Like Rochester's otherized Jamaican wife Bertha, Jenny is regarded as an alien other because she is a Gypsy.

For the final three months of the series, *Dark Shadows* told a *Wuthering Heights*-inspired story which recast Jonathan Frid and Lara Parker. No longer the vampire and the witch, they became Bramwell and Catherine, star-crossed lovers at the Collinwood of 1841 Parallel Time. By this time, Frid no longer wished to play Barnabas, and Parker finally got her wish to portray the ingénue instead of the heavy. (In 1966, she had auditioned for the role of Victoria Winters.) Bramwell is a poor Collins relation who is ambitious and driven. Catherine Harridge is a lady who loves Bramwell yet marries his cousin Morgan Collins. Although the 1841 Parallel Time storyline involved a vicious ghost and a family lottery (inspired by Shirley Jackson's 1959 novel *The Lottery*), the plot complemented the pre–Barnabas episodes in its return to family dynamics, interpersonal relationships, and soap-operatic devices, such as Catherine's pregnancy, Melanie's secret parentage, and Daphne's terminal illness.

A strength of *Dark Shadows* is its uniqueness in the midst of such borrowings. The show's eclecticism resulted in its originality. Countless myths and stories found their way into the show, but their recombination and reinterpretation made for startling innovations, especially in 1960s daytime television. On *Dark Shadows,* every classic fantasy collided to make a heady *new* mixture. Curtis agreed:

It's that kind of fantasy that captures the imagination of an audience. That's what *Dark Shadows* was; it was always reaching to do these magical kinds of things. It was scary, it was tremendously romantic, and people who have tried to rip it off over the years have never been able to do it because they truly don't understand what it's about. *I* barely understand. I do — but barely.[26]

Curtis carried his *Dark Shadows* formula over to his adaptations of nineteenth-century Gothic novels. Adam and Eve, Quentin's changing portrait, numerous male and female vampires, and the possessed children of haunted Collinwood were his creative springboards to his acclaimed 1973–1974 productions of *Frankenstein, The Picture of Dorian Gray, Dracula,* and *The Turn of the Screw.* He made his Frankenstein creature gentle and sympathetic like Adam, and he fashioned his Dorian Gray after the decadent 1897 characters Aristede and Quentin, themselves extensions of Gray. Having helped to create the most culturally significant vampire since Dracula, Curtis then felt compelled to put his stamp on the oft-told Dracula story. For his and Richard Matheson's *Dracula* (1974), Curtis transferred his love story across time from *Dark Shadows* to *Dracula* and gave the vampire a reincarnated love.

Curtis's two *Turn of the Screw* scenarios on *Dark Shadows* featured a major difference from Henry James's novel. In the novel, both ghosts, Peter Quint and Miss Jessel, are evil. On *Dark Shadows,* Quentin and especially Gerard are malevolent, but Beth and especially Daphne are benevolent. In 1897, Beth is in love with the living Quentin, and in 1970, Daphne's ghost becomes a living human once again and falls in love with the same Quentin, kept alive and young by his *Dorian Gray* portrait. However, in Curtis's 1974 adaptation of *The Turn of the Screw,* both ghosts are their customary evil selves.

Because Curtis produced *The Strange Case of Dr. Jekyll and Mr. Hyde* (1968) soon after *Dark Shadows* began, that adaptation influenced *Dark Shadows* and not vice versa. Two years after *The Strange Case of Dr. Jekyll and Mr. Hyde* aired, Curtis and his writers presented a Jekyll-and-Hyde story on *Dark Shadows.* In 1970 Parallel Time, Dr. Cyrus Longworth is a timid, dedicated scientist who seeks, through chemical means, to bring out "all that is good in man." Like Dr. Jekyll, Cyrus achieves the opposite effect and turns himself into John Yaegar, a sadist who terrorizes Collinsport and abuses Buffie Harrington, a waitress. As in Robert Louis Stevenson's novel, Cyrus eventually transforms into Yaeger even without drinking his potion, and as in the Curtis-produced TV adaptation, the scientist is blackmailed by the druggist who supplies him with his chemicals. After Yaeger kills his blackmailer and kidnaps Maggie Evans Collins, Barnabas fights Yaegar to the death. In death, the brute changes back to Cyrus.

The 1970 Parallel Time storyline, situated after the Leviathan plotline and before Gerard and Daphne's haunting of Collinwood, also borrows from Daphne Du Maurier's 1938 novel *Rebecca.* The TV plot is the story of Quentin and his new bride Maggie's adjustment to living in the house where Quentin lived with his now-legendary first wife Angelique. The dead woman's many male admirers sing her praises — one, Bruno Hess, constantly plays Robert Cobert's song "Ode to Angelique" on the piano — and Miss Hoffman, the stern housekeeper, worships Angelique's memory and regards Maggie as an intruder. *Rebecca* is also a basis for *Night of Dark Shadows* (1971), another story of a new wife's struggle with a hostile housekeeper and a beautiful predecessor.

The stories of Edgar Allan Poe were also re-imagined during the course of *Dark*

Shadows. In 1795, Barnabas bricks up the Reverend Trask behind a wall, as in "The Cask of Amontillado," in retaliation for Trask's involvement in Victoria Winters's witchcraft trial (itself an elaborate homage to *The Crucible* by Arthur Miller and the show's twist on the standard soap-opera court trial). In 1840, Trask's son Lamar turns the tables and bricks up Barnabas in revenge for the elder Trask's death. In 1897, Quentin re-enacts "The Tell-Tale Heart" when he continues to hear his dead grandmother's heartbeat. Later in 1897, Aristede subjects Quentin to a torture styled after that in "The Pit and the Pendulum." Barnabas rescues Quentin before the swinging blade reaches him. In 1968, Elizabeth Collins Stoddard, cursed by a witch, endures a "Premature Burial" and finally must ring a bell in her coffin when she awakes from her trance.

During the 1970 Leviathan saga, Quentin Collins and Amanda Harris re-enact the ancient Greek myth of Orpheus and Eurydice in the underworld when they must find their way through a hellish realm. The Leviathan storyline is even more notable as a pseudo-sci-fi shift in tone for the Gothic serial. The story has elements of *Invasion of the Body Snatchers* (1954) by Jack Finney and *Rosemary's Baby* (1967) by Ira Levin, as well as Gene Fowler, Jr.'s 1958 film *I Married a Monster from Outer Space.*

Its chief influence, however, is the Cthulhu mythos of H.P. Lovecraft (1890–1937), the Edgar Allan Poe of the early twentieth century. In the TV storyline, the Leviathan creatures are the shapeless elder gods of earth, air, fire, and water, which ruled the earth before the rise of humankind. According to Stephen King, "The Elder Gods, Lovecraft told us, are out there, and their one desire is to somehow get back in — and there are lines of power accessible to them."[27] Similarly, the Leviathans seek to regain their dominance by possessing Barnabas, Elizabeth, David, Amy, and others. Also, one of the Leviathan creatures takes human form and in a matter of *weeks* grows from baby to boy to teenager to man (in the writers' send-up of how all children on soap operas grow up fast — but not *that* fast). Now a grown man, Jeb Hawkes makes plans to marry Carolyn Stoddard, who as a baby was sold to the Leviathans by her unscrupulous father in 1949.

Lovecraft's weird, chilling stories such as "The Call of Cthulhu" (1926), "The Dunwich Horror" (1928), and "The Shadow over Innsmouth" (1931) tell of such prehistoric entities seeking to reclaim dominion of the earth. In the late 1960s and early 1970s, Lovecraft's stories were enjoying a resurgence in print and other media. Several episodes of Rod Serling's *Night Gallery* (1969, 1970–1973) dealt with Lovecraftian themes or even adapted Lovecraft's stories (e.g. "Pickman's Model" and "Cool Air," two classic 1926 tales). The writers of *Dark Shadows* were capitalizing on this apparent interest in such arcane literature, but the Leviathan storyline proved to be a thematic misstep for the show and one from which it never recovered. According to *The World of Dark Shadows* publisher Kathleen Resch, "Fans tended to dislike the portrayal of Barnabas as the pawn of some greater power."[28] They proved to be much more interested in the archetypes of classic horror (the vampire Barnabas, the witch Angelique, the werewolf Quentin) than in an off-camera suggestion of a slimy, flying dragon able to take human form.

After the record-high ratings of the 1897 saga, the ratings began dropping significantly during the Leviathan story. The viewership fell from 18 million during the

1897 saga to 16 million during the Leviathan storyline and the 1970 Parallel Time period and finally to 12 million during the 1840 and 1841 Parallel Time plotlines before the show's April 1971 cancellation.[29] Ironically, the post–Leviathan storylines set in 1970 Parallel Time, 1995, 1840, and 1841 Parallel Time ranked with the 1795 epic as some of the greatest stories ever told on *Dark Shadows,* but after the extremely complicated, often unsatisfying Leviathan saga, fewer and fewer viewers were left to enjoy them.

At the peak of its popularity and long after, *Dark Shadows* inspired many imitations. In 1969, Curtis himself presented *Dead of Night,* a.k.a. *A Darkness at Blaisedon,* and Canadian television mimicked *Dark Shadows* in its 39-week-long syndicated daily serial *Strange Paradise,* a claustrophobic drama set on a Caribbean island where a tragic, Barnabas-like man played by Colin Fox keeps his dead wife's body frozen cryogenically. Voodoo, witchcraft, and ghostly possession also characterize *Strange Paradise,* which truly became another *Dark Shadows* less than halfway through its 1969–1970 run when *Dark Shadows* producer Robert Costello and *Dark Shadows* writers Ron Sproat and Joe Caldwell took over the show. They picked up the pace by moving the action off of the island and to a Collinwood-style manor house. (In 1996, Dan Curtis filmed part of *Trilogy of Terror II* at Casa Loma, one of the houses seen on *Strange Paradise,* and in 2005, Curtis directed Colin Fox in *Our Fathers.*)

In 1974, Canadian novelist Dan "Marilyn" Ross, author of 32 paperback novels based on *Dark Shadows,* wrote *The Vampire Contessa: From the Journal of Jeremy Quentain.* Ross based the romantic vampire-hero Jeremy Quentain on Barnabas and Quentin Collins. "He does not smile often, and he usually dresses in dark or drab suits," Ross wrote. "His hair is jet black and romantically wavy. Think of an ascetic Byron, and you have him."[30] Two years later, when *Interview with the Vampire* by Anne Rice was published in 1976, many *Dark Shadows* fans could not help but remember the May 11, 1970, episode (#1011) set in 1970 Parallel Time, in which the writer William H. Loomis conducts an interview with the vampire Barnabas Collins for Loomis's book, *The Life and Death of Barnabas Collins.*

A Darkness at Blaisedon (1969): Cal Bellini as Sajeed Rau and Kerwin Mathews as Jonathan Fletcher confront the supernatural in this unsold pilot, which features *Dark Shadows* personnel in front of the camera (Thayer David, Louis Edmonds) and behind it (Robert Cobert, Sam Hall, Lela Swift, Trevor Williams).

During the late 1960s and early 1970s, Anne Rice watched the CBS-TV soap operas *As the World Turns, The Edge of Night,* and *Love of Life,* so it is possible that Rice may have switched over to ABC at some point and been influenced by *Dark Shadows.* Referring only to the CBS serials, Katherine Ramsland, author of *Prism of the Night: A Biography of Anne Rice* (1992), reveals, "Friends were amazed at how Anne's mind absorbed these dramas and how she could recite intricate details of plot and character. The television shows failed to influence her fantasy life but gave her ideas with which to tinker for possible writing projects."[31] Anne Rice has acknowledged that Lambert Hillyer's 1936 film *Dracula's Daughter,* Richard Matheson's 1951 short story "Dress of White Silk," and Jack Smight's 1973 TV miniseries *Frankenstein: The True Story* did make impressions on her. "I was fascinated by all that," Rice said, "and I know that my writing was seminally influenced."[32]

Another *Dark Shadows*-influenced project appeared in 1986 when Aaron Spelling produced the telefilm *Dark Mansions* (ABC, August 23), an unsold pilot for a series about a young woman (Linda Purl) who comes to live in a forbidding old house where supernatural forces are at work. Like *Dark Shadows,* it featured a movie star (Joan Fontaine) as its matriarch, and it was shot at Greystone, the Beverly Hills mansion where the 1991 and 2004 *Dark Shadows* revivals were filmed (and where Curtis shot some scenes for his *War* miniseries). In 1987, Group W produced one episode of a proposed syndicated Gothic serial called *Salem's Children,* a story of witchcraft and time travel. In 1988, *Dark Shadows* writer Ron Sproat authored the musical play *Ravenswood,* set behind the scenes of a daytime soap opera about a vampire. That same year, John Lutz wrote *Shadowtown,* a novel about a murder on the set of a TV soap opera called *Shadowtown.* All of these productions owe a debt to *Dark Shadows* and its formulas of the mysterious mansion, the supernatural forces, and the tortured anti-hero.

In the years since *Dark Shadows,* the regular daytime soap operas have included supernatural or sci-fi elements in their usually more realistic stories. In its final months, *The Secret Storm* (1954–1974) told a story of ghosts and reincarnation. *As the World Turns* (debuted 1956) presented the story of a ghost in a castle and a family curse, and *Search for Tomorrow* (1951–1986) featured a boy with telekinetic powers. *Guiding Light* (1952–2009) had a "Dreaming Death" storyline patterned after the 1968 Dream Curse plot on *Dark Shadows,* and more recently the serial's 15,000th episode (September 7, 2006) took place in parallel time. In the two shows' final months, *The Doctors* (1963–1982) did a story about grave robbers who inadvertently released the plague, and *Another World* (1964–1999) featured an immortal who regarded a present-day woman as his reincarnated love. *Texas* (1980–1982) took some characters to a cave which had supernatural powers. *The Edge of Night* (1956–1984), written by the Edgar Award-winning author Henry Slesar (*The Thing at the Door,* "One Grave Too Many," *The Gray Flannel Shroud*), told the stories of a haunted house (actually a hoax) and a woman with real psychic powers. *Ryan's Hope* (1975–1989), directed by Lela Swift, mimicked the plots of *The Mummy* (1932) and *King Kong* (1933) and inherited the *Dark Shadows* mausoleum set. *One Life to Live* (debuted 1968) sent a character back in time to 1888 for an Old West adventure and then told the futuristic story of the underground city of Eterna. In the 1970s, the set of Angelique's room also turned up on *One Life to Live,* and in 2008 three characters went back in time to 1968. Several soap operas have presented "Premature Burial" scenarios, staged brainwashing plots, allowed real ghosts to visit characters, and sent people to heaven or hell. Most famously, the 1981 Luke-and-Laura storyline on *General Hospital* (debuted 1963) involved a villain who controlled the weather, and in 1995 the psychiatrist Dr. Marlena Evans of *Days of Our Lives* (debuted 1965) became possessed by the devil and underwent exorcism. These daytime dramas would not have taken risks and involved the supernatural in their stories without the success that *Dark Shadows* had found with such outlandish plotlines.

The NBC daytime serial *Passions* (1999–2007) presented supernatural themes including witchcraft, zombies, and demonology, often with a humorous bent. Just as the Maine of *Dark Shadows* and Stephen King is a supernatural hot spot and the Massachusetts of the 1690s was plagued by witchcraft, Harmony, New England, the setting of *Passions,* is a place where the line between life and death, normal and paranormal, is thin. Tabitha Lenox (played by Juliet Mills) is a centuries-old witch who in one February 2006 episode revealed that Barnabas Collins was one of her old boyfriends. *Passions* did several tie-ins with *Dark Shadows, Bewitched, Psycho,* and *Wicked,* and just like *Dark Shadows,* reruns of *Passions* aired on the Sci-Fi Channel. After leaving NBC in September 2007, *Passions* began a year-long afterlife on Direct TV.

Halfway through its run, ABC's *General Hospital* spin-off *Port Charles* (1997–2003) switched from medical drama to supernatural melodrama as the town of Port Charles was overrun by vampires (including one played by Rebecca Staab, who had played a vampire on the 1991 *Dark Shadows*). As the vampires battled for supremacy, an incarnated angel entered the fray. The dark, brooding *Port Charles* was riding the wave of the much more light-hearted supernatural hijinks of *Passions,* itself an imitation of both *Dark Shadows* (1966–1971) and *Mary Hartman, Mary Hartman* (1976–1978), two offbeat serials that were ahead of their time.

In the mid–2000s, the Fox TV network and the cable channels BBC America and Here! TV debuted supernatural serials which owe a debt to *Dark Shadows*. BBC America's *Hex* (2004–2007) is a cross between *Dark Shadows, Night of Dark Shadows, Charmed,* and Harry Potter. It is the story of witches, voodoo, ghosts, and ancestral portraits at an English private school. In an echo of *Night of Dark Shadows,* a woman is accused of witchcraft and hanged from a tree on the grounds. The short-lived Fox series *Point Pleasant* (2005) is the story of the appearance in a small town of a young woman (Elisabeth Harnois) who could be the daughter of Satan. She is watched by a man (Grant Show) who is immortal because of his pact with the devil. Here! TV's *Dante's Cove* (debuted 2005) is a cross between *Dark Shadows* and *Strange Paradise* in its story of an immortal warlock released from bondage on a tropical island. Like *Dark Shadows,* some of the plot of *Dante's Cove* takes place in the year 1840, and the characters of Ambrosius and Grace share a Barnabas/Angelique dynamic. Ken Knox, in *Los Angeles* magazine, actually called this sexy supernatural mystery a cross between *Melrose Place* (1992–1999) and *Dark Shadows* (1966–1971). Fred Olen Ray's *The Lair* (debuted 2007), Here! TV's spin-off of *Dante's Cove,* is a centuries-spanning vampire serial which has been compared to *Dark Shadows, Buffy the Vampire Slayer* (1997–2003), and telenovelas.

Perhaps the two most significant imitative outgrowths of *Dark Shadows* are Dan Curtis's own short-lived remakes of the Gothic serial in 1991 and 2004. One year after the NBC-TV nighttime series, Curtis, in his foreword to Jim Pierson's book, *Dark Shadows Resurrected* (1992), wrote,

> After a quarter of a century, no one is more surprised than I with the devotion that *Dark Shadows* still commands. I can't believe that it's been going on all these years. When the original daytime series ended in the spring of 1971 and we finished the second theatrical film shortly thereafter, I figured that *Dark Shadows* was a thing of the past.
>
> As the years passed, it became apparent that *Dark Shadows* was much more than just a fond memory. The undying fascination and loyalty for the series were astonishing, and in 1990 I found myself back in the dark corridors of Collinwood, producing a new incarnation of *Dark Shadows* for primetime, weekly television.
>
> I never intended to do *Dark Shadows* again, but the show refused to die, kept alive by legions of passionate fans. Although the new series was given a network life of only 12 episodes, I think we were able to recreate and reinvent the magic that first enthralled viewers so many years ago.[33]

As Curtis was preparing the new *Dark Shadows* in 1989 and 1990, he drew as much inspiration from *House of Dark Shadows* as he did from the television series. With an order first for just a pilot, then for six hours, and finally for 13 hours, the director knew that he would have to condense and streamline the 1967 Barnabas storyline and the 1795 epic, which together had taken a full year's worth of daily episodes to tell. Curtis realized that he, Sam Hall (on board for the new series), and the late Gordon Russell had already condensed the original Barnabas/Maggie story for *House of Dark Shadows*, so he patterned some of the four-million-dollar pilot (filmed March 19–April 11, 1990) after the film. Curtis and Hall co-wrote the series with eight other writers, including Hall's novelist son Matthew Hall (*The Art of Breaking Glass*) and *Beauty and the Beast* writers M.M. Shelly Moore and Linda Campanelli. Daphne Budd, the

Dark Shadows (1991): Ben Cross stars as Barnabas Collins in the NBC-TV prime-time version of Dan Curtis's Gothic serial.

Collinwood employee whom Barnabas attacks in her car at the beginning of the 1970 film, becomes Daphne Collins for the 1991 series. (Since she is a niece to both Roger Collins and Elizabeth Collins Stoddard, the Roger and Elizabeth of 1991 must have a brother somewhere.) Daphne Collins is attacked in her car by the vampire and then follows the path of the Carolyn Stoddard character in *House of Dark Shadows*. It is Daphne who becomes the vampire, and Curtis shoots her funeral, her undead appearance to young David Collins, and her staking by Professor Woodard very similarly to the corresponding scenes in *House of Dark Shadows*.

The new Barnabas Collins (played by Ben Cross) is more sinister and ferocious than Jonathan Frid's TV Barnabas, but not quite the rampaging evildoer of the 1970 movie. This Barnabas has a tortured, vulnerable, romantic side which allows him to fall in love with Victoria Winters, whom he sees as the reincarnation of Josette DuPres, and which causes him to seek a cure for his vampirism from Dr. Julia Hoffman. In the new series, Victoria, not Maggie, resembles Josette and captures Barnabas's heart. In a sign of the times, the new Maggie Evans is a New Age mystic who is having an affair with Roger Collins (something unthinkable on the original series). After the so-called Harmonic Convergence in the year 1987, devotees of mysticism believed that a new era had dawned, and their New Age beliefs received a great deal of attention in various media. In a logical step in the updating of *Dark Shadows*, Dan Curtis and his writers acknowledged the new religion by reshaping the Maggie character into a free-thinking, self-aware psychic.

Other considerable changes occur in the characters of Willie Loomis and the Reverend Trask. Jim Fyfe portrays Willie much more comically than even John Karlen did, and Roy Thinnes unwisely plays Trask as a foppish dandy instead of as the frightening, dangerous witch-finder that Jerry Lacy portrayed. Other surprises in Curtis's 13-hour remake of the 1967 and 1795 storylines are the death of Joe Haskell, the manner in which Barnabas becomes a vampire (Josette's doppelganger, not a bat, bites him), and Dr. Hoffman's possession by the spirit of the witch Angelique (played by Lysette Anthony, later the star of Curtis's 1996 telefilm *Trilogy of Terror II*).

After directing the pilot in the spring of 1990, Curtis directed episodes two, three, and four between July 23 and August 28, 1990. Between August 29 and December 5, four other directors, including Armand Mastroianni (*Tales from the Darkside*) and Mark Sobel (*Quantum Leap*), directed episodes five through twelve with a few retakes directed by Curtis. Mastroianni remembered, "The biggest challenge was to maintain a consistency and style in the amount of time we had to shoot it. The story and the textures were so rich. The legacy of the story swept you away like an old-fashioned novel."[34] Sobel added, "We worked on a television schedule, but the production value was that of a movie. We were never on schedule; it was a constant catch-up process. I now feel like I can do anything—*Dark Shadows* was the ultimate challenge. I've done an epic."[35]

"There's a compressed energy when everything is shot at a crisis level, which *Dark Shadows* was shot under," Barbara Steele remarked.[36] The series originally was slated for NBC's fall 1990 schedule—hence the hurry—but suddenly NBC delayed it until January. The Persian Gulf War dealt the series a deadly blow when both it and *Dark Shadows* began in the same week. If *Dark Shadows* had premiered and caught on in

September 1990, perhaps it could have withstood the January interruption. *Dark Shadows* began successfully with a 14.6 rating and a 23 share for the January 13–14, 1991 miniseries that launched the show, and it received positive, enthusiastic reviews.[37]

The *Fort Worth Star-Telegram* called the series "dark, slick, and expertly acted and executed" and "beautifully photographed."[38] *The Hollywood Reporter* complimented the show's "wonderful sets and stately surroundings."[39] *Variety* observed, "Fans will get a rush from the

Dark Shadows (1991): In the short-lived series, Roy Thinnes as Roger Collins, left, Joseph Gordon-Levitt as David Collins, and Joanna Going as Victoria Winters are involved in a never-resolved subplot about David's mother Laura.

new *Dark Shadows* because, in many ways, it's faithful to the original, and new viewers looking for something to sink their teeth into won't be disappointed, either. Ben Cross and Joanna Going are excellent."[40] The *Chicago Sun–Times* proclaimed, "This Gothic chiller is bound to enchant TV viewers who are swayed by a lovingly designed experiment in style and flavor [...]. The vampire's kiss is irresistible!"[41]

After the series's twelfth and final episode aired on March 22, 1991, the new *Dark Shadows* was rerun later on TNT and Sci-Fi. The lush, romantic, magical atmosphere of the show influenced the styles of the subsequent long-running TV series *Buffy the Vampire Slayer* (1997–2003), *Charmed* (1998–2006), and *Angel* (1999–2004). Additionally, the Fox network's brief 1996 series *Kindred: The Embraced* was a cross between *Dark Shadows* (1991), *The Godfather* (1972), and *Highlander* (1992–1998). It starred Mark Frankel as Julian Luna, a powerful, brooding vampire cut from Ben Cross's Barnabas mold.

Dark Shadows rose again, albeit slightly, in April 2004 when Dan Curtis co-produced a third incarnation, this time for the trendy WB network. As with the 1991 revival, Curtis used Greystone mansion in Beverly Hills as Collinwood. The 55-room mansion on 18 acres of land was built in 1928 by the oil millionaire Edward Doheny, who earlier in the 1920s had played a role in the Teapot Dome scandal. The city of Beverly Hills assumed ownership of Greystone in 1965, and since 1971 it has opened the grounds (but not the house) as a public park. Since 1964 Greystone has been seen in countless movies and TV shows, including *The Disorderly Orderly, Color Me Dead, All of Me, The Bodyguard, The Phantom, Batman and Robin, The Prestige, Spider-Man 3, There Will Be Blood, The Immortal, General Hospital, Murder She Wrote, The Flash, Gilmore Girls, Alias, The Winds of War, Intruders,* and *Dark Shadows.*

The script for the six-million-dollar pilot episode of the WB *Dark Shadows* was written by Mark Verheiden, who in the late 1990s and early 2000s had written for *Timecop* and *Smallville*. Verheiden prepared for the job by watching some 1967 episodes of *Dark Shadows,* the two movies, and all of the 1991 series. Although Dan Curtis wanted to re-create the 1967 Barnabas-out-of-the-coffin storyline and the 1795 saga, Verheiden desired a new approach, perhaps one focusing on young David Collins. His ideas brought him into conflict with both Curtis and the WB. "I hate it" is what Verheiden reported that Curtis said to him several times.[42]

Another idea Verheiden devised was Victoria's witnessing Collinsport locals engaging in an ancient Halloween ritual around a bonfire — "a dark *Brigadoon,*"[43] to be sure. Verheiden explained,

> I really wanted to set it in a different world, but that collided with what the network wanted. They were very concerned that it *not* be like a different place. They wanted it to feel like this was a town in "real Maine, USA." It was a valid request but a bit hard to make come together because on *Dark Shadows,* the characters *are* in kind of a strange place — it's just the nature of the Gothic.[44]

Finally, Verheiden crafted a script that once again launched *Dark Shadows* with the arrival via train of Victoria Winters and with Willie Loomis's release of Barnabas Collins (played by Alec Newman) from the chained coffin. This time Willie has a girlfriend, Kelly Greer, who is present at the unchaining and who becomes Barnabas's first victim. Verheiden was pleased and proud when Peter Roth, head of Warner Brothers, called him and said that the script was "the best he'd read all year."[45]

Dark Shadows (2004): Ivana Millicevic and Alec Newman portray Angelique and Barnabas in the unsold WB pilot.

The 41-minute pilot also introduced Roger Collins, intended to be the J.R. Ewing-like villain to Barnabas's hero; Elizabeth Collins Stoddard, played by Blair Brown; Carolyn Stoddard, Elizabeth's daughter; David Collins, Roger's son; Dr. Julia Hoffman; and several other Collinsport citizens. Curtis wanted to introduce even more characters in the pilot, but Verheiden protested that the script was overcrowded. Therefore there is no Professor Stokes or Professor Woodard character, and there is no Maggie Evans. There is, however, Angelique (played by Ivana Milicevic), who for the first time is introduced simultaneously with Barnabas and Victoria. The pilot's final, unfinished scene, in which Angelique crashes through the windshield of Victoria's car, would have had to be redone or even excised before it matched the more serious tone of the rest of the pilot.

A definite misstep was Blair Brown's wrong-headed portrayal of Elizabeth Collins Stoddard. Brown lacked the majesty of Joan Bennett and Jean Simmons, and she did further disservice to the character by playing her as wacky and scatterbrained. Her sit-com-like portrayal did not complement the more serious efforts by Martin Donovan and Alec Newman in their interpretations of Roger and Barnabas. In the early stages of the pilot, the Internet hummed with fans' wishes that Kathryn Leigh Scott, Marie Wallace, or Kate Jackson could have played Elizabeth. In fact, Scott, as well as Susan Sullivan, did audition for the role, but co-producer John Wells pushed for Blair Brown.

Because this was a WB television production, the young men and women were fashionably beautiful as required by the network's distinctive look. Willie Loomis and Joe Haskell could have been models, Victoria and Carolyn were extremely attractive, and even Barnabas and Julia had been made more youthful. The reduction in Barn-abas's age was actually a wise move because Jonathan Frid and Ben Cross (both in their early forties when they played Barnabas) had been too old for the part. Barnabas had become a vampire as a young man in his early twenties, so it is logical that he would have retained a more youthful appearance in un-death.

Last-minute replacement director P.J. Hogan, while able to helm an excellent version of *Peter Pan* in 2003, did not quite capture the essence of *Dark Shadows.* Mark Verheiden recalled that Hogan attempted a colorful, overly artistic, "Dario Argento/ *Suspiria* look" which Verheiden called "nerve-wracking because the Argento style can be emotionally distancing."[46] Argento is the stylish Italian director of *Deep Red* (1975), *Suspiria* (1977), *Inferno* (1980), *Opera* (1987), and *Trauma* (1993). Critic Mark Daw-idziak stated the situation more harshly when he observed in his talk at the 2005 Dark Shadows Festival that much of the pilot was "lighted like a French whorehouse." Adding to the weird effect was the musical temp track, which temporarily scored the pilot with cues from *Klute* (1971), *Deep Red* (1975), and *Jennifer Eight* (1992). Post-production work on the pilot never progressed to the point of adding or even commissioning Robert Cobert's all-important compositions.

Despite these drawbacks, the 2004 *Dark Shadows* displayed great promise for a contemporary reinvention of the series. Most of the cast, especially the young women, played their roles very well, and Alec Newman displayed the definite potential for developing into a strong, romantic Barnabas. Having portrayed Paul Atreides in two *Dune* miniseries (2000, 2003) for the Sci-Fi Channel and Victor Frankenstein in the Hallmark Channel's superb 2004 *Frankenstein* miniseries, Newman had proven that he could play a tortured soul.

Nevertheless, when Curtis and co-producer John Wells (*E.R., The West Wing*) screened the unfinished pilot for Warner Brothers executives in June 2004, the executives rejected it out of hand and expressed no interest in retooling it. In July, WB chairman Garth Ancier said, "We had a new director [Hogan] come in who was accomplished in movies but frankly didn't do a particularly good job, and the rest is history." Ancier added, "The script was terrific, [but] creatively, the end result did not come out the way we'd all hoped for."[47] The WB had driven a stake through the heart of the 2004 *Dark Shadows*. Lacking post-production, titles, and music, the pilot never was telecast or released on video or DVD. Its only public exhibitions have taken place at Dark Shadows Festival fan conventions.

Dan Curtis, although terribly disappointed, was philosophical. "*Dark Shadows* refuses to die," he declared. "I can never escape it. The new pilot didn't work out, but we're still looking at other possibilities. We've considered a stage version, and it would make a great feature film, so who knows what might happen next?"[48] Curtis went on to direct *Saving Milly* and *Our Fathers* in 2005, but his terminal illness and death prevented him from returning to his 40-year-old dream of the girl on the train yet again. In one of his final interviews, Curtis again said,

> I'll probably be remembered for *Dark Shadows* instead of the things that I really cared about, which were the great epics that I made [*The Last Ride of the Dalton Gang, The Winds of War, War and Remembrance*]. *Dark Shadows* will be the thing that'll be on my gravestone — but *I love Dark Shadows*. I guess it's terrific to have somehow created something that will live forever. It *will* live forever.[49]

Dark Shadows (ABC, June 27, 1966–April 2, 1971). Executive producer: Dan Curtis. Producers: Robert Costello, Peter Miner, Lela Swift. Associate producers: George DiCenzo, Sy Tomashoff. Directors: Dan Curtis, Lela Swift, Henry Kaplan, John Sedwick, Jack "Sean Dhu" Sullivan, Penberry Jones, Dennis Kane, John Weaver. Writers: Art Wallace, Sam Hall, Gordon Russell, Ron Sproat, Joe Caldwell, Malcolm Marmorstein, Francis Swann, Herb Ellis, Violet Welles. Music: Robert Cobert. Art directors: Sy Tomashoff, John Dapper. Makeup: Vincent Loscalzo, Dick Smith, Dennis Eger, Bert Roth.

Cast: Joan Bennett (Elizabeth Collins Stoddard/Naomi Collins), Jonathan Frid (Barnabas Collins/Bramwell Collins), Grayson Hall (Dr. Julia Hoffman), David Selby (Quentin Collins), Lara Parker (Angelique Bouchard/Catherine Harridge), Mitchell Ryan (Burke Devlin), Alexandra Moltke (Victoria Winters), Louis Edmonds (Roger Collins), Nancy Barrett (Carolyn Stoddard/Melanie Collins), David Henesy (David Collins/Jamison Collins), Kathryn Leigh Scott (Maggie Evans/Josette DuPres), Joel Crothers (Joe Haskell/Nathan Forbes), Clarice Blackburn (Mrs. Johnson), David Ford (Sam Evans), Thayer David (Professor Timothy Eliot Stokes/Count Andreas Petofi), Dana Elcar (Sheriff George Patterson), Diana Millay (Laura Collins), John Karlen (Willie Loomis), Dennis Patrick (Jason McGuire/Paul Stoddard), Robert Gerringer (Dr. Dave Woodard), Sharon Smyth (Sarah Collins), Jerry Lacy (Reverend Trask/Lamar Trask/Gregory Trask), Roger Davis (Peter Bradford/Jeff Clark/Charles Delaware Tate), Anthony George (Jeremiah Collins), Addison Powell (Dr. Eric Lang), Humbert Allen Astredo (Nicholas Blair), Robert Rodan (Adam), Marie Wallace (Eve/Jenny), Don Briscoe (Chris Jennings), Denise Nickerson (Amy Jennings), Terrayne Crawford (Beth Chavez), Michael Stroka (Aristede/Bruno), Christopher Pennock (Jebez Hawkes/Cyrus Longworth/John Yaeger), Donna McKechnie (Amanda Harris), Christopher Bernau (Phillip Todd), Geoffrey Scott (Schuyler Rumson), Donna Wandrey (Roxanne Drew), Kate Jackson (Daphne Harridge), James Storm (Gerard Stiles), Kathy Cody (Hallie Stokes), Lisa Richards (Sabrina Stuart), Elizabeth Eis (Buffie Harrington), Paula Laurence (Hannah Stokes), Virginia Vestoff (Samantha Collins), Keith Prentice (Morgan Collins), Michael McGuire (Judah Zachery), John Beal (Judge Vail), Conrad Bain (Mr. Wells), Marsha Mason (Audrey), Abe Vigoda (Ezra Braithwaite). 1225 episodes.

Dark Shadows (NBC, January 13–March 22, 1991). Executive producer: Dan Curtis. Producers: Steve Feke, Jon Boorstin, William Gray. Directors: Dan Curtis, Armand Mastroianni, Paul Lynch, Rob Bowman, Mark Sobel. Writers: Dan Curtis, Sam Hall, Matthew Hall, Steve Feke, Hall Powell,

Bill Taub, Jon Boorstin, M.M. Shelly Moore, Linda Campanelli, William Gray. Music: Robert Cobert. Directors of photography: Dietrich Lohmann, Chuy Elizondo. Production designers: Tony Cowley, Fred Harpman, Bryan Ryman. Makeup: Dee Monsano, Mony Monsano, Jack Petty.

Cast: Jean Simmons (Elizabeth Collins Stoddard), Ben Cross (Barnabas Collins), Barbara Steele (Dr. Julia Hoffman), Roy Thinnes (Roger Collins), Joanna Going (Victoria Winters), Lysette Anthony (Angelique), Jim Fyfe (Willie Loomis), Barbara Blackburn (Carolyn Stoddard), Michael Weiss (Joe Haskell), Ely Pouget (Maggie Evans), Joseph Gordon-Levitt (David Collins), Juliana McCarthy (Mrs. Johnson), Stefan Gierasch (Professor Woodard), Eddie Jones (Sam Evans), Michael Cavanaugh (Sheriff George Paterson), Veronica Lauren (Sarah Collins), Rebecca Staab (Daphne Collins), Adrian Paul (Jeremiah Collins), Wayne Tippit (Dr. Hyram Fisher), Charles Lane (Antique-Shop Proprietor). 12 episodes.

Dark Shadows (WB, filmed April 2004). Executive producers: Dan Curtis, John Wells. Producers: David Kennedy, Ed Milkovich, Andrew Stearn, Mark Verheiden. Associate producer: Jim Pierson. Director: P.J. Hogan (replacing Rob Bowman). Writer: Mark Verheiden. Music: none commissioned. Director of photography: Bobby Bukowski. Production designer: Kirk Petruccelli. Makeup: Todd McIntosh, Steven Anderson.

Cast: Blair Brown (Elizabeth Collins Stoddard), Alec Newman (Barnabas Collins), Kelly Hu (Dr. Julia Hoffman), Martin Donovan (Roger Collins), Marley Shelton (Victoria Winters), Ivana Milicevic (Angelique), Matt Czuchry (Willie Loomis), Jessica Chastain (Carolyn Stoddard), Alexander Gould (David Collins), Jason Shaw (Joe Haskell), Michael Roberts (Sheriff George Paterson), Alexis Thorpe (Kelly Greer), Jenna Dewan (Sophia Loomis), E.J. Callahan (Old Man on Train). One unfinished episode.

CHAPTER III

Big-Screen Shadows: *House of Dark Shadows* and *Night of Dark Shadows*

In 1969, when ABC-TV's *Dark Shadows* and its merchandising were at the peak of their popularity, Dan Curtis dreamed up another incarnation for his Gothic serial: a major motion picture. Curtis conceded,

> No one had ever done this before, but the show's such a big hit, so why don't we make a movie out of it? A soap opera turned into a movie! We did it, and the movie was a huge hit. We kept the show going at the same time. We juggled the scripts around. People would be brought out on buses and brought back to play on the show the next day. Those were unbelievable, wild days.[1]

ABC was not interested in financing the film version, so the tenacious Curtis finally convinced Metro-Goldwyn-Mayer to budget his movie at $750,000. Curtis intended to produce and direct. However, in order to secure the financial backing and the directorial assignment, Curtis had to place $300,000 of his own money in an escrow account to cover any budget overruns. None occurred; in fact, Curtis completed *House of Dark Shadows* under budget by $8000.

The August 13, 1969, issue of *Variety* announced the deal for the *Dark Shadows* movie.[2] Three decades later, Kathryn Leigh Scott mused, "No two people could be less alike than Dan Curtis and Mickey Rooney, but the spunk of Andy Hardy — 'Hey, guys, let's get together and put on a show in the barn!' — has a certain resonance when you realize that, eventually, the *Dark Shadows* movies were MGM productions."[3]

Sam Hall and Gordon Russell, the head writers of *Dark Shadows,* wrote a script whose title changed during post-production from simply *Dark Shadows* to the grander *House of Dark Shadows.* While daily episodes of the TV series continued to be taped at 433 West 53rd Street in Manhattan, Curtis filmed the movie (between March 23 and May 1, 1970) in upstate New York and Connecticut.

The Collinwood of *House of Dark Shadows* was Lyndhurst, the magnificent Gothic Revival mansion on the banks of the Hudson River in Tarrytown, New York. It was designed and built in 1838 by the famous nineteenth-century architect Alexander Jackson Davis. Earlier in the 1830s, Davis had designed the Indiana state capitol, the Federal Customs House in New York City, and several buildings on the campus of the University of Michigan.

Davis built Lyndhurst (first called "Knoll") as a country villa for William Paulding, a brigadier general in the War of 1812 and a mayor of New York in the 1820s. In 1864–1865, Davis doubled the size of the house for its second owner, George Merritt, a New York City merchant. Merritt renamed the mansion "Lyndenhurst" (soon "Lyndhurst") after the linden trees which he planted on the 67-acre estate.

Between 1880 and his death in 1892, Lyndhurst was the summer home of the railroad magnate Jay Gould, who controlled the Union Pacific Railroad, the New York Elevated Railway, and the Western Union Telegraph Company. Gould ran a spur line of his railroad behind the mansion on the riverbank. A huge portrait of Gould is seen in *House of Dark Shadows*, and Gould's railroad track is the scene of a fight to the death in *Night of Dark Shadows*. (In 1979, actor Scott Brady portrayed Jay Gould in a few scenes of Dan Curtis's Western epic, *The Last Ride of the Dalton Gang*.)

After Gould's death, Lyndhurst became the home of Gould's daughter Helen Gould Shepard and her family until her death in 1938. For the next 23 years, Gould's other daughter, Anna, Duchess of Talleyrand-Perigord, resided there. Upon her death in 1961, Lyndhurst passed to the National Trust for Historic Preservation. Nine years later, *House of Dark Shadows* became the first of several movies, including *The Worst Witch* (1986) and *Reversal of Fortune* (1990), to shoot scenes at Lyndhurst — all while daily tours of the house were still conducted.

MGM rented Lyndhurst for Curtis and his 55 actors and crew members for $35,000. Cinematographer Richard Shore remarked, "The location was amazing. You could never build sets like that for anywhere near $35,000."[4] Curtis filmed in most of the mansion's rooms and bedrooms, all laden with antiques and paintings, and he also utilized the estate's huge coach house (glimpsed in one 1966 episode of *Dark Shadows* itself), the barren greenhouse (for a scene cut from the film), and the empty, crumbling indoor swimming pool (for one of the most frightening scenes of the movie). Curtis and his cast and crew also filmed scenes at the Sleepy Hollow Cemetery down the street from Lyndhurst; in Scarborough, New York; and in Westport and Norwalk, Connecticut.

On March 23, 1970, at Sleepy Hollow Cemetery, Curtis filmed a funeral scene, complete with artificial rain provided by the Tarrytown Fire Department. Curtis's longtime art director Trevor Williams (*Pretty Baby*, *The Changeling*, the *Police Academy* movies), who died in February 2008, recalled one hindrance to the shoot:

> There was a gravediggers' strike going on at the time, so all these dead bodies to be buried were piling up in one of the buildings where we were shooting. The cemetery hired non-union labor to remove and bury them late in the day. While we were shooting, we kept getting interrupted by this procession of workers carrying corpses out. Dan finally had enough distractions and bellowed, "Can you do that later, please? It's not like they're going anywhere!"[5]

Another interruption reportedly came in the form of a *real* funeral being conducted in the cemetery that day. As Kathryn Leigh Scott remembered,

Dan glowered at the bereaved family arriving with their own casket. But Dan used the time well. While we all stood around waiting, Dan picked up the script and a pencil and started cutting lines from the 23rd Psalm because he said, "It's too [...] long," to which the assistant director [William Gerrity, Jr.] responded, "Great; now, he's editing God!"[6]

Every day on location of *House of Dark Shadows* was not such a circus. Curtis and the actors soon settled in at Lyndhurst, only an hour's drive from Manhattan, for the nine-hour work days. Curtis filmed only during the day; he used the day-for-night lensing technique for nighttime scenes in both movies. The cast used the basement of Lyndhurst for wardrobe and screening rooms, the souvenir shop for the makeup room, and the stable for a cafeteria. Kathryn Leigh Scott remarked, "We'd worked together so long as a close-knit group, isolated in our TV studio on 53rd Street. Filming on location at Lyndhurst seemed like a natural extension — we'd just taken our show on the road."[7]

House of Dark Shadows is a bloodier, more violent retelling of the TV show's 1967 storyline, in which Willie Loomis releases the eighteenth-century vampire Barnabas Collins from his chained coffin in the Collins mausoleum. Barnabas violently preys on the residents of Collinsport, Maine, and he mesmerizes Maggie Evans, who bears an uncanny resemblance to his lost 1790s love Josette DuPres. During the course of the film, Barnabas strangles several characters to death, cruelly beats Willie, and vampirizes his cousin Carolyn Stoddard, her uncle Roger Collins, and the Collinses' friend, Professor Timothy Eliot Stokes.

The *Dark Shadows* TV series spotlighted Gothic mystery and doomed romance over violence and body counts, so the gory mayhem of *House of Dark Shadows* was a

jarring shift in tone. However, *Dark Shadows* fans were accustomed to such shifts. Barnabas was the reluctant vampire on the TV show, a romantic hero in Dan "Marilyn" Ross's *Dark Shadows* novel series, almost a super-hero in Gold Key's comic-book series, a teen idol in *16* and *Tiger Beat,* and now a ruthless villain in *House of Dark Shadows*.

House of Dark Shadows (1970): Grayson Hall (left, as Dr. Julia Hoffman), Kathryn Leigh Scott (as Maggie Evans), Roger Davis (as Jeff Clark), Jonathan Frid (as Barnabas Collins), and Louis Edmonds (as Roger Collins) play a scene in the Lyndhurst drawing room early in the film.

Curtis, apparently influenced by Hammer Films and eager to top his tamer TV series, chose to depict Barnabas according to his original vision of the character — as another Dracula. For the past dozen years, England's Hammer film studio had been turning out bloody, sexy vampire movies — *Horror of Dracula* (1958), *Brides of Dracula* (1960), *Kiss of the Vampire* (1964), *Dracula—Prince of Darkness* (1965), and *Dracula Has Risen from the Grave* (1968)—as well as Frankenstein, werewolf, and mummy films. Each Hammer horror movie was filmed with Gothic atmosphere, in bloody Technicolor, in approximately one month, and for approximately one-half-million dollars or so—just like *House of Dark Shadows.*

Around the time of the September-November 1970 theatrical run of *House of Dark Shadows,* Hammer released *Taste the Blood of Dracula* (1970), *The Vampire Lovers* (1970), *Scars of Dracula* (1970), *Lust for a Vampire* (1971), and *Countess Dracula* (1971). Ruthless male vampires as played by Christopher Lee and Jonathan Frid and voluptuous female vampires as played by Ingrid Pitt and Nancy Barrett were very much in vogue. It is to the remarkable credit of Curtis's movie that *Cinefantastique* magazine (the *Time* or *Newsweek* of all things horror) wrote, "The seventies have begun with an inordinate number of vampire films, [and] *House of Dark Shadows* is the superior film of the crop— a fast-paced, harrowing thriller."[8] In later years, Curtis downplayed the possible Hammer influence on his vampire movie but acknowledged that the slow-motion graphic violence of Sam Peckinpah's *The Wild Bunch* (1969) did influence not only *House of Dark Shadows* but also his Melvin Purvis crime dramas (1974, 1975) and *The Last Ride of the Dalton Gang* (1979).

Jonathan Frid, who had patented the reluctant, conflicted vampire on *Dark Shadows,* now found himself playing a monster in *House of Dark Shadows.* Barnabas makes Willie his Renfield and Carolyn his slave. Lovesick Dr. Julia Hoffman attempts to cure him of his vampirism and give him a normal life, but she intentionally gives him an overdose of her serum when she realizes that he has chosen Maggie instead of her. Barnabas ages rapidly and displays Dick Smith's horrifying old-age makeup design. Smith recalled, "We decided to make Barnabas bald with a veined, mottled, liver-spotted head, which we basically improvised, on the set."[9] Smith reworked the Old Barnabas design for Dustin Hoffman in Arthur Penn's *Little Big Man* (1970). Later, Tobe Hooper's *The Texas Chainsaw Massacre* (1974) imitated Smith's makeup.

In return for her betrayal of him, Barnabas strangles Julia to death. Although in 1967 the TV Barnabas threatened Julia's life several times, he never would have gone through with such an atrocity. *House of Dark Shadows* demonstrates the diabolical trajectory the Barnabas character would have followed if Curtis had stuck to his original plan of "letting him bite and kill people for a cycle [13 weeks of soap-opera episodes] and then driving a stake through his heart."[10] Indeed, the film concludes in a lurid scene shot on May 1, 1970, at the Lockwood-Mathews Mansion in Norwalk, Connecticut, with the bloody running-through of Barnabas by the arrow from a crossbow. Barnabas's death occurs after Stokes has been shot through the heart, Roger has been impaled on a spear, and Carolyn has been staked in another of the film's most stunning sequences. Although most of the cast has been killed, *House of Dark Shadows* manages a traditional happy ending as Jeff Clark rescues his love interest Maggie from the bloodsucker. However, it is not Jeff who is the true hero of the film but poor, hapless Willie, who gives his life to destroy his master. This shattering sequence is scored to Robert Cobert's emotional "Death of Hyde" music cue from *The Strange Case of Dr. Jekyll and Mr. Hyde* (1968).

Cobert wanted to write original music for the film, but Curtis wanted to reuse the TV show music. "I fought Dan tooth and nail on that decision but ultimately lost. While the budget was part of Dan's concern, I sincerely feel that he wanted to use the existing music because the fans liked it and Dan thought they would enjoy hearing it in the film."[11]

Cobert was correct in his observation — the legions of *Dark Shadows* fans certainly did like the familiar music cues — and Curtis was correct in his decision to re-use those cues (actually Cobert's *Jekyll and Hyde* score which had been re-recorded and re-used on *Dark Shadows*). The music of *Dark Shadows* was just as much a character on the show as Barnabas or Elizabeth, and Curtis wanted the fans to have that familiar musical touchstone as a consolation to their forced adjustments to a new Collinwood (Lyndhurst), a new level of violence (gory bitings and stakings), and a somewhat new Barnabas (an out-and-out villain).

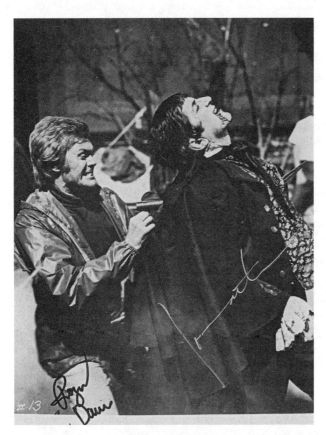

House of Dark Shadows (1970): Roger Davis (as Jeff Clark) impales Jonathan Frid (as Barnabas Collins) in the climactic scene filmed at the Lockwood Mathews Mansion in Norwalk, Connecticut.

Underneath the blood and gore, the heart of *House of Dark Shadows* is Barnabas's earnest search for identity and love in the modern world, a quest shared by Boris Karloff's Ardeth Bey before him (in *The Mummy*, 1932) and both Jack Palance's and Gary Oldman's Dracula after him (1974, 1992). With *Dark Shadows* (1966–1971), *The Strange Case of Dr. Jekyll and Mr. Hyde* (1968), and even *House of Dark Shadows* (1970), Dan Curtis establishes his pattern of allowing a degree of sympathy for the monster. The Barnabas of *House of Dark Shadows* is despicable, but he has definite reasons for his actions and (in this modern interpretation of vampirism) a scientific, pathological ailment which enslaves him.

As Dr. Julia Hoffman explains, "I've done a great amount of research on your victims. You carry a very destructive cell in your bloodstream. I've isolated it. I've been able to destroy it. I'm convinced this cell keeps you the way you are. That's right, Barnabas. I can eliminate it, and you'll be able to lead a perfectly normal life." Dr. Hoffman is engaging "the ongoing modern debate as to whether violent criminality is a behavior to be punished or a syndrome to be treated," a debate noted by Lyndon W. Joslin, author of the 1999 book *Count Dracula Goes to the Movies*.[12]

When this man of the 1790s is released into the world of 1970, he seeks to reconnect with who he was by introducing himself to his relatives (actually, his family's distant descendants), taking up residence in The Old House (the now-dilapidated ancestral home where he once lived), and making over Maggie into his long-lost bride-to-be Josette. He cannot help what he is or what he does — ever since "they put this curse on me," Barnabas cryptically explains to Willie. (Apparently there was no Angelique in this Barnabas's life; instead, the vague pronoun "they" suggests the Leviathans.) While Bram Stoker's Count Dracula wreaks havoc among the Harker, Westenra, and Holmwood families, Dan Curtis's Barnabas Collins, despite his atrocities, is more of a tragic figure because he victimizes his own family (as many of the vampires of folklore tend to do). Roger and Carolyn die, David is orphaned, and Elizabeth Collins Stoddard, in the sarcastic words of Roger Greenspun's *New York Times* review, "has the good fortune to settle into a catatonic state rather early on."[13]

In his negative review of *House of Dark Shadows* for the *Times,* Greenspun called the film "dreadful" and accused the movie of having "no subject except its special effects, which aren't very good, and its various shock sequences." However, Greenspun did note that "the film emphasizes the sinister rather than the benign aspect of much-tormented Barnabas Collins."[14] The *New York Post* complained that "the transfer to the large screen has magnified all the faults and foolishness" of the TV series.[15] In the *Chicago Sun–Times,* Roger Ebert dismissed the film with, "The problem these days is that no one believes in vampires."[16]

The aforementioned review in *Cinefantastique* was much more thoughtful and insightful. Frederick S. Clarke wrote,

> The screenplay by Sam Hall and Gordon Russell is highly inventive; however, credit for the film's unqualified success must go to director Dan Curtis, who previously had exhibited his skill in the genre by producing, incomparably, the finest version of Robert Louis Stevenson's *Dr. Jekyll and Mr. Hyde* on television several seasons ago. Curtis provides *House of Dark Shadows* with a stylistic flair indelibly his own, a restless, roving visual sense, never content in projecting a static image. Curtis directs Arthur Ornitz's excellent camerawork not at a scene but into it, through it, and around it with an hypnotically fluid ebb and flow of nightmarish montage.[17]

Donald F. Glut, author of *The Dracula Book* (1975), added, "Barnabas dies in one of the most vivid stakings ever recorded on film. The fast-paced, atmospheric, and graphic film proved that Curtis was capable of transforming a television soap opera into one of the finest horror films of the year."[18]

Horror movies are an acquired taste, so it is understandable that they would be more highly regarded in genre-sensitive appraisals than in mainstream-press reviews. Nevertheless, the majority of mainstream reviews of Curtis's subsequent adaptations of the classics and his supernatural movies of the week were quite favorable. With *House of Dark Shadows* and its follow-up, Curtis was still becoming acclimated to the director's chair. His greatest films, including *Dracula* (1974), *Trilogy of Terror* (1975), *Burnt Offerings* (1976), *When Every Day Was the Fourth of July* (1978), *The Last Ride of the Dalton Gang* (1979), and *The Love Letter* (1998), were ahead of him.

In 2004, Curtis said, "I looked at the feature film we made [*House of Dark Shadows*] and thought it held up amazingly well. It wasn't done like the soap. It was done like a very classy piece of film. It was the same premise, except we killed everybody, which you couldn't do on the show."[19] Despite the carnage — or perhaps because of it — *House of Dark Shadows* earned $1,836,000 for MGM in its first three months of release.[20] When MGM ordered a sequel, Curtis was faced with the happy problem of how to make a second *Dark Shadows* movie after such a bloodbath.

This time MGM approved a bigger budget of $900,000 for Curtis to film his and Sam Hall's script, first called *Dark Shadows II,* then *Curse of Dark Shadows,* and finally *Night of Dark Shadows.* Curtis began filming the movie at Lyndhurst on March 29, 1971, just five days after five of the movie's stars had taped the 1225th and final episode of *Dark Shadows.* For this feature Curtis filmed every scene on the Lyndhurst estate, including a car chase. Shooting stretched through April and until May 7, 1971.

After Jonathan Frid refused to play a risen Barnabas, Curtis abandoned his idea of another vampire movie and, with Sam Hall, crafted a psychological ghost story similar to the TV show's 1970 Parallel Time storyline, itself an homage to Daphne Du Maurier's 1938 novel *Rebecca. Night of Dark Shadows* also bears a strong resemblance to Roger Corman and Charles Beaumont's 1963 film *The Haunted Palace,* based on H.P. Lovecraft's 1927 story "The Case of Charles Dexter Ward." Both *The Haunted Palace* and *Night of Dark Shadows* involve the public execution of a witch, significant ancestral portraits, an attempted marital rape, a husband (Vincent Price, David Selby) influenced by a ghost, his anguished wife (Debra Paget, Kate Jackson) whom he endangers, and a sinister housekeeper (Lon Chaney, Jr., Grayson Hall) who exacerbates the problems. Also, as horror-film critic Tim Lucas points out, Grayson Hall's fate at the end of *Night of Dark Shadows* "is identical to the finale of Barbara Steele's possession vehicle, *An Angel for Satan* (1966)," directed by Camillo Mastrocinque.[21] Just as *Dark Shadows* borrowed classic devices, *Night of Dark Shadows* also turns eclecticism into originality.

Under the best of circumstances, *Night of Dark Shadows* faced an uphill battle. It was released four months after *Dark Shadows* had been cancelled, and it lacked the vampire angle that had defined the TV series. Furthermore, *Night of Dark Shadows* lost its soul on the cutting-room floor. As written and filmed, Curtis's follow-up to *House of Dark Shadows* would have been superior to that film and could have been at least a minor masterpiece of early-1970s horror cinema because of its numerous timely qualities (*déjà vu,* reincarnation, witchcraft, ghosts, and a downbeat ending). Instead, Curtis was forced, under a tight deadline, to cut his 129-minute film to 97 minutes. At the behest of the MPAA, the studio subsequently cut it even further to 93.5 minutes. What is left is a confusing, often unsatisfying narrative which nevertheless delivers enough atmosphere and impact for the *Boston Globe* to call the movie "a cut above the average" and "a horror film for people who don't really like horror films."[22]

Artist Quentin Collins and his wife Tracy move in to Quentin's inheritance, the Collinwood estate, which is sternly run by Carlotta Drake and handyman Gerard Stiles. Soon Quentin begins having dreams and visions of his lookalike ancestor, Charles Collins, also a painter, who lived at Collinwood in 1810. Quentin is especially drawn to Collinwood's mysterious tower room, where Charles had an affair with Angelique, his brother Gabriel's wife, before her public hanging for witchcraft. Angelique's spirit still haunts Collinwood, and Carlotta tells Quentin that he is the reincarnation of Charles Collins and the vessel through which Angelique and Charles's love will live again. Carlotta declares that she herself is the reincarnation of Sarah Castle, a young girl who lived at Collinwood in 1810 and who witnessed Angelique's unjust hanging.

As Quentin falls under the spell of the house and its beautiful ghost, he takes on the identity of his ancestor. He attempts to rape and later drown Tracy, whom he and Carlotta see as a threat to Angelique's plan for Quentin and Collinwood. Quentin, with the help of Tracy and their Gothic-novelist friends Claire and Alex Jenkins, attempts to resist his possession. The deaths of Gerard and Carlotta seem to vanquish the ghost, and the Collinses and the Jenkinses prepare to leave Collinwood forever. Then Quentin must go back into the house one last time to retrieve his canvases.

When Dan Curtis delivered his 129-minute opus to MGM chief James Aubrey, Aubrey demanded drastic cuts — and gave Curtis as little time as 11 hours to submit them! Aubrey, the so-called Smiling Cobra who at different times tyrannized MGM and CBS, was the basis for the ruthless television executive Robin Stone in Jacqueline Susann's 1969 novel *The Love Machine.* In his film career, Aubrey was accused of tampering with movies by Blake Edwards, Ken Russell, and Sam Peckinpah, as well as this one by Dan Curtis. Therefore, on a moment's notice, Curtis and an MGM staff editor were forced to eviscerate *Night of Dark Shadows* in order to please Aubrey.

As a result, several of Quentin's dream sequences are consolidated, thereby causing his pajamas to change from yellow to blue in the course of one night's sleep. The Jenkinses are edited out of some scenes, and much of Angelique's part is cut. As the film now stands, the audience does not know how Gerard and Carlotta are related (he is her nephew), why Tracy goes to the pool house (she had a dream about it), why

Night of Dark Shadows (1971): Lara Parker (as Angelique Collins) poses for David Selby (as Charles Collins) in a scene set in 1810.

Quentin/Charles tries to drown her there (Charles drowned his wife Laura in 1810), why Quentin/Charles limps (off-camera, he fell off his horse), or why Laura laughs during Angelique's funeral (Angelique's body is not really in the coffin but entombed with a still-living Charles in a secret room beneath Collinwood). The viewers also do not understand Reverend Strack's line about Angelique's "threats" (her spoken curse on her executioners is deleted, thereby making the earlier title *Curse of Dark Shadows* meaningless), and they see Carlotta re-hang Angelique's portrait when they never saw it removed in the first place. Most significantly, what would have been the film's most important and powerful scene — a séance conducted by Quentin, Tracy, Alex, and Claire and the revelation that Angelique was *not* a witch — does not appear in the movie and shortchanges the effect of the ending. Nevertheless, the final moments — when the audience learns the fates of the characters — still have the power to stun. According to Tim Lucas, "The material may be derivative, but it is consistently well-handled by writer-director Curtis, and the downbeat finale [...] is stimulating."[23]

When Aubrey viewed Curtis's hastily shortened film, he announced, "It's a tight little thriller." Curtis insisted, "But the film doesn't make sense any more!" Aubrey retorted, "With *your* audience, it doesn't matter!"[24] Aubrey made the common mistake of dismissing horror and sci-fi fans as indiscriminate geeks who consume any pabulum put before them, when in fact many genre fans are highly selective readers and viewers who bestow their undying loyalty only upon the best of the best, e.g. the novels and stories of Ray Bradbury and Richard Matheson, the films and television of Alfred Hitchcock and Dan Curtis, and such outstanding cult TV series as *The Twilight Zone* (1959–1964), *Star Trek* (1966–1969), *Buffy the Vampire Slayer* (1998–2003), and *Lost* (debuted 2004).

Understandably, some reviews of the truncated *Night of Dark Shadows* were lackluster. In the *New York Times,* A.H. Weiler pronounced the movie "a bore" but complimented the many atmospheric shots of Lyndhurst. Weiler wrote, "The attraction of this dour adventure is Lyndhurst, the Gothic Revival mansion, where the film was shot. Its many period rooms, paintings, and objects d'art are richly eye-filling. The somber story shot there, however, is strictly for the low-rent district."[25] Indeed, the titles of the two *Dark Shadows* films could be switched. The Barnabas movie is all about what happens at *night,* while the Quentin film lovingly shows off the bedrooms, stairways, second-floor gallery, and tower room of this Gothic *house* of dark shadows. The *Boston Globe* also noted the film's "visual beauty."[26]

The *San Francisco Examiner* observed, "Dan Curtis, who created the TV series, directed the film in a slow, languid style that contributes to the evocation of a menacing climate."[27] Sensing that important elements were missing from the film, Roger Ebert in the *Chicago Sun–Times* added, "Toward the end of the movie, not a lot goes on except for double takes, screams, and lots of bleeding."[28] Ebert realized that the film effectively builds, but the re-edited payoff is hasty and minimal.

Even Robert Cobert's eerie musical score suffers in the forced edit. Some of his cues end abruptly, and the scene that explains the frequent use of "Quentin's Theme" does not appear in the 93.5-minute cut. In a missing 1810 flashback, Angelique plays the unnamed melody on the piano and tells Charles that the music reminds her of him.

The lovers are interrupted by the appearance of Laura, Quentin's wife. The film uses several new recordings of "Quentin's Theme," as well as weird echo effects and some unnerving chase music played on strings and bongo drums.

The love theme from *Night of Dark Shadows* is one of Cobert's most haunting melodies. The tune originated as a piano solo in the final months of the TV series. For the film, Cobert follows a piano rendition of the love theme with a refrain played on harmonica and guitar, a novel combination for Cobert but appropriate to the film's early–1970s origins. Cobert re-used the love theme in *The Invasion of Carol Enders,* a late-night ABC *Wide World Mystery* drama (March 8, 1974) produced by Dan Curtis and directed by Burt Brinkerhoff (*Steambath, Come Die with Me*).

Laura's intrusion upon

Night of Dark Shadows (1971): Lara Parker (as Angelique) haunts a cemetery in this rare publicity shot for the film.

Quentin and Angelique at the piano is one of many scenes — approximately 25 percent of the finished film — that Aubrey forced Curtis to eliminate. Other missing scenes, as evidenced in Hall and Curtis's complete shooting script, are Quentin and Tracy's picnic, Quentin's removal of Angelique's portrait, several clarifying discussions, and the all-important séance. In 1989, I wrote and directed *The Night Before,* a play which reinstated many of the missing scenes and afforded the audience at that year's Dark Shadows Festival a seriocomic feel for what the complete *Night of Dark Shadows* might have been like. In 1997, film historian Darren Gross definitively reconstructed the film in the pages of *Video Watchdog* magazine.

Then in August 1999, Gross did what seemed impossible by finding the long-lost, one-and-only 129-minute color separations of *Night of Dark Shadows* in a film-storage vault in a Kansas City salt mine. Gross recalled, "Being able to finally see all the shots from this legendary [séance] sequence was such a thrilling revelation that I had to stifle any yelps of joy."[29] Now Gross and Dark Shadows Festival chairman Jim Pierson are spearheading an effort to reconstruct the film for a possible 2010 or 2011 DVD release. Because only 100 minutes of the soundtrack survive, all of the film's living stars have re-recorded their missing dialogue. "That was the hardest I've ever worked!" David Selby told me at the 2008 Dark Shadows Festival in Burbank, California. "We had the script, but we didn't know the *exact* words we'd said, so they brought in lip-reading specialists to help us match our dialogue to the picture." More than three dozen years after an unjustly truncated *Night of Dark Shadows* fell far short of its potential, the complete film may yet be appraised and appreciated by scholar, critic, and fan alike.

An interesting postscript is that in 1976, *Night of Dark Shadows* seemed to live again as Kate Jackson once again played the victimized wife of a man under a ghostly thrall in E.W. Swackhamer's made-for-TV movie *Death at Love House* (ABC, September 3). Both *Night of Dark Shadows* and its unofficial remake, *Death at Love House,* concern a possessed husband (David Selby, Robert Wagner) under the influence of his artist-forefather's past life, a beautiful ghost, and her portrait. Jackson plays the beleaguered wife in both films, and each film has a *Haunted Palace*-like sinister housekeeper (Grayson Hall, Sylvia Sidney). Both movies are filmed at historic homes (Lyndhurst in Tarrytown, the Harold Lloyd estate in Beverly Hills), but *Death at Love House* finally differs from its predecessor by eschewing the downbeat ending of *Night of Dark Shadows* for a typical Hollywood ending.

Horror-film critic Anthony Ambrogio points out that *Night of Dark Shadows* was riding the wave of a strong trend toward downbeat endings taking hold of films "from at least 1970 on" and probably even earlier. Ambrogio notes,

> One can gauge how widespread this trend became in a very short time by comparing the two *Dark Shadows* films. The first, *House of Dark Shadows* (1970), ends traditionally with the hero saving the heroine from the vampire Barnabas (Jonathan Frid). The second, *Night of Dark Shadows,* made only a year later, seems to end with hero Quentin Collins (David Selby) cured of his demonic possession. But, no, an epilogue is added in which he reverts to his "former self," and all the good characters are disposed of.[30]

After the stark, hopeless conclusion of *Bonnie and Clyde* in 1967, downbeat endings became all the rage in 1968 because of their use in three landmark American fantasy films. *Rosemary's Baby* ends with a mother resigning herself to raising a devil-child. *Planet of the Apes* climaxes with the sight of the Statue of Liberty in ruins. *Night of the Living Dead* ends when the hero, mistaken for a zombie, is shot to death. Then, in 1969, *They Shoot Horses, Don't They?* depicts assisted suicide; the hero of *The Witchmaker* perishes in quicksand; "Ratso" Rizzo expires on board a bus (*Midnight Cowboy*); James Bond's wife dies (*On Her Majesty's Secret Service*); and the members of *The Wild Bunch* die spectacularly in their bloody, slow-motion last stand.

By the early 1970s, downbeat endings were gaining even more ground, partially as a result of Americans' growing pessimism over the economy, the war in Vietnam, and the direction of the government. In *How Awful About Allan* (1970), the title character (played by Anthony Perkins) overcomes danger only to have his hysterical blindness return. In *The Return of Count Yorga* (1971), the heroine is unexpectedly vampirized by the hero. In *Frogs* (1972), the animals overrun the house and defeat humanity. In *The Devil's Daughter* (1973), co-starring Jonathan Frid, a woman is turned over to a cult of Satanists by someone who she thought was her friend but who actually is the Devil incarnate. *Chinatown* (1974) inflicts perhaps the most famous and devastating downbeat ending in movie history. The film ends with an innocent woman's death, a man's total disillusionment, and a young girl's delivery to her incestuous father/grand-father. *Race with the Devil,* co-starring Lara Parker, continued the trend in 1975 when (as in *Night of Dark Shadows*) two couples are literally surrounded by the forces of evil and cannot escape. Dan Curtis contributed another downbeat ending with *Burnt Offerings,* in 1976. That same year, who could forget the horrifying jolt at the end of *Carrie?* At least that twist is only a dream.

Just as Dan Curtis's films often reflected timeliness in the midst of their timelessness, *Night of Dark Shadows* exemplified to 1971 audiences the modern slant toward hopeless endings. The film made money for MGM — $1,400,000 — but $436,000 less than *House of Dark Shadows* had made in the same amount of time and not enough to justify making a third *Dark Shadows* movie.[31] Perhaps its downbeat ending, coupled with the confusing re-edits and the absence of vampires, contributed to its lesser performance at the box office. (Also, *Night of Dark Shadows,* unlike *House of Dark Shadows,* did not play in England or Japan.) Nevertheless, *House of Dark Shadows* and *Night of Dark Shadows* proved to be effective training grounds for Curtis, and a crystallization of his techniques in horror filmmaking. The low camera angles in the movies became his trademark. He repeated his shot sequences from the two movies' funeral scenes in the funeral scenes in *Dracula* (1974) and on the new *Dark Shadows* (1991), and he referenced Angelique's beckoning Carlotta to jump when he shot a similar scene for *The Turn of the Screw* (1974). After *Night of Dark Shadows,* he perfected his filming of a falling body in *Burnt Offerings* (1976) and *Curse of the Black Widow* (1977). His effective use of the beauty and mystery of Lyndhurst in both films (especially *Night of Dark Shadows*) began his pattern of infusing his films with a palpable sense of place, such as the Seattle Underground in *The Night Strangler* (1973). Curtis insisted,

People don't realize that it's far more difficult to do a horror picture well than a straight drama. That's why most supernatural pictures stink. They attract a lot of people who have no talent and don't know what the hell they're doing. Now, I'm telling you from experience. I know that the supernatural pictures I made were really good because I knew what the hell I was doing. It was

Night of Dark Shadows (1971): John Karlen (as Alex Jenkins) and Grayson Hall (as Carlotta Drake) perform a scene on the roof of the Lyndhurst mansion in Tarrytown, New York.

very, very difficult. Anybody can make a horror movie if you don't have to end it or make it clever. I got into the field because I love it. This sprang from a deep childhood fascination with the genre.[32]

Lara Parker, who wrote her M.F.A. thesis on horror literature and film, agreed:

When I look back over his many Gothic films, I can see that he always had an original vision, steeped in his love of the genre, with repeating motifs: obsession, its attendant guilt and madness, the power of dreams, evil children and housekeepers, graveyards and ghosts. What a privilege it was, seeing him bring these images to life.[33]

Those obsessions, dreams, evil children, and graveyards sprang to life in *Dracula, Burnt Offerings, The Turn of the Screw, Trilogy of Terror II,* and one dozen other memorable horror films crafted by Dan Curtis. As generally pleasing as *House of Dark Shadows* and *Night of Dark Shadows* were, Curtis was capable of much more, as he demonstrated in his remaining films, whether classic (*The Picture of Dorian Gray*) or modern classic (*The Night Strangler*).

House of Dark Shadows (MGM, 1970). Released September 1970. Producer: Dan Curtis. Director: Dan Curtis. Screenplay: Sam Hall and Gordon Russell. Music: Robert Cobert. Director of photography: Arthur Ornitz. Production designer: Trevor Williams. Makeup: Dick Smith and Robert Layden.

Cast: Jonathan Frid (Barnabas Collins), Grayson Hall (Dr. Julia Hoffman), Kathryn Leigh Scott (Maggie Evans), Joan Bennett (Elizabeth Collins Stoddard), Nancy Barrett (Carolyn Stoddard), Louis Edmonds (Roger Collins), John Karlen (Willie Loomis), Thayer David (Professor Timothy Eliot Stokes), Roger Davis (Jeff Clark), David Henesy (David Collins), Don Briscoe (Todd Blake Jennings), Dennis Patrick (Sheriff George Patterson), Barbara Cason (Mrs. Johnson), Lisa Richards (Daphne Budd), Jerry Lacy (Minister). 97 minutes. 30th anniversary screening (attended by *Dark Shadows* stars): Vista Theatre, Los Angeles, California, October 13, 2000.

Night of Dark Shadows (MGM, 1971). Released August 1971. Producer: Dan Curtis. Director: Dan Curtis. Screenplay: Sam Hall and Dan Curtis. Music: Robert Cobert. Director of photography: Richard Shore. Production designer: Trevor Williams. Makeup: Reginald Tackley. Technical Advisor: Hans Holzer.

Cast: David Selby (Quentin Collins/Charles Collins), Kate Jackson (Tracy Collins), Grayson Hall (Carlotta Drake), Lara Parker (Angelique Collins), Nancy Barrett (Claire Jenkins), John Karlen (Alex Jenkins), James Storm (Gerard Stiles), Christopher Pennock (Gabriel Collins), Diana Millay (Laura Collins), Thayer David (Reverend Strack), Clarice Blackburn (Mrs. Castle), Monica Rich (Sarah Castle). 93.5 minutes. 30th anniversary screening (attended by *Dark Shadows* stars): Vista Theatre, Los Angeles, California, October 25, 2001. 35th anniversary celebration (attended by *Dark Shadows* stars): Vista Theatre, Los Angeles, California, October 26, 2006.

CHAPTER IV

Curtis and the Classics: *The Strange Case of Dr. Jekyll and Mr. Hyde, Frankenstein, The Picture of Dorian Gray, Dracula,* and *The Turn of the Screw*

"When I was a kid," Dan Curtis reminisced, "I loved horror films. Any film that came out that was a horror film, I used to go to it."[1] Curtis loved the Universal monster movies: *Frankenstein* (1931), *Son of Frankenstein* (1939), *The Wolf Man* (1941), and especially *Dracula* (1931). "Bela Lugosi scared the hell out of me!" he recalled.[2] Beginning in 1967, Curtis populated ABC-TV's *Dark Shadows* (1966–1971) with similar vampires, werewolves, and man-made creatures, and between 1968 and 1974, he brought to television five respected adaptations of the classic Gothic-horror tales of Mary Shelley, Robert Louis Stevenson, Oscar Wilde, Bram Stoker, and Henry James. Thanks to Dan Curtis, Dr. Frankenstein, Dr. Jekyll, and other great literary characters were reincarnated for the modern TV audience and kept alive for the *Last House on the Left / Texas Chainsaw Massacre* generation of the early 1970s.

In 1967, around the time of the casting of Jonathan Frid as Barnabas Collins, Curtis took a break from *Dark Shadows* and began preparing a prestigious TV adaptation of Stevenson's 1886 novel, *The Strange Case of Dr. Jekyll and Mr. Hyde.* (Curtis and Stevenson share the curious trait that both *Dark Shadows* and *Jekyll and Hyde* came to their creators in vivid dreams.) The plan was for Rod Serling to write the script, Jason Robards to play Jekyll and Hyde, and Curtis to produce the drama in London. Suddenly both Serling's script and Robards's services became unavailable, and Curtis had to rethink the production. He hired Jack Palance to star and moved the taping back to New York near the *Dark Shadows* studio. Then a technicians' strike forced Curtis to move once again, this time to Toronto. Sets for the production had already been built in New York, but Curtis had to start all over with new sets in Canada.

Curtis had hired an accomplished director when he had been in London. Since

1960, Charles Jarrott had directed episodes of the BBC-TV series *Armchair Theatre,* *The Wednesday Play,* and *Haunted.* After *The Strange Case of Dr. Jekyll and Mr. Hyde,* Jarrott went on to direct the features *Anne of the Thousand Days* (1969); *Mary, Queen of Scots* (1971); *Lost Horizon* (1973); *The Dove* (1974); and *The Other Side of Midnight* (1977). Jarrott agreed to follow Curtis's production to New York and finally to Toronto. He and Curtis shot *Jekyll and Hyde* on videotape, not film. (Of Curtis's five adaptations of the classics, only *Dracula* (1974) was shot on film.)

The script writer for *The Strange Case of Dr. Jekyll and Mr. Hyde* was Ian McClellan Hunter, who had written some B-movies in the 1940s and more recently had scripted the TV series *The Adventures of Robin Hood* (1955–1958) and *The Defenders* (1961–1965). Hunter is best remembered for winning the Academy Award for the Best Motion-Picture Story of 1953 for his screenplay for William Wyler's *Roman Holiday.* Hunter was, in fact, only a front for the blacklisted Dalton Trumbo, the actual author of the screenplay. Hunter passed along some of his screenwriting fee to Trumbo, but neither he nor later his son, director Tim Hunter (*River's Edge*), ever gave the Oscar itself to Trumbo or his family. Finally in 1993 the Academy presented Trumbo's widow Cleo with a replacement Oscar.

At least Ian Hunter did better by *Dr. Jekyll and Mr. Hyde.* Hunter's script is one of the more nearly faithful adaptations of Stevenson's story, which has been filmed for movies and television more than 75 times, beginning in 1908. Of course a *completely* faithful filming has never materialized, for it would be devoid of women and probably of heterosexuality. According to critic Elaine Showalter, "While there have been over 70 films and television versions of *Dr. Jekyll and Mr. Hyde,* not one tells the story as Stevenson wrote it — that is, as a story about men."[3]

The Strange Case of Dr. Jekyll and Mr. Hyde (1968): Jack Palance, in Dick Smith's frightening makeup, portrays Mr. Hyde.

The dance-hall girls and female prostitutes who populate almost all of the screen adaptations of *The Strange Case of Dr. Jekyll and Mr. Hyde* are not found in Stevenson's novel. It is the story of the London solicitor Gabriel John Utterson, his cousin and dear friend Richard Enfield, and his secretary and confidant Mr. Guest. It is also the story of the prominent physician Dr. Henry Jekyll, his estranged but formerly close friend Dr. Hastie Lanyon, and his devoted butler Poole. This is a world of powerful men — doctors, lawyers, educators, even a member of Parliament — and women play little or no part in this world except as servants. Utterson and Enfield take a much-anticipated walk together every Sunday afternoon, and Dr. Jekyll often holds jovial dinner parties for the male intelligentsia of London. None of the men seem to have, need, or want women in their lives; instead, they find fulfillment in their important work and in each other's company.

Ian McClellan Hunter's script hints at this circumstance when Drs. Lanyon and Jekyll goad each other by pointing out that neither has a woman in his life, but both men quickly agree that their work makes their lives complete. What Stevenson's novel hints at more concretely — but still nebulously enough for polite reading society — is that these men make up London's hidden but quite organized homosexual community of the late nineteenth century and that Jekyll's alter-ego Mr. Edward Hyde represents the unbridled, socially taboo homosexual nature that these Victorian men must *hide*. In "Henry Jekyll's Full Statement of the Case," the tenth and final chapter of the novel, Jekyll never reveals the exact nature of his "irregularities" and his "profound duplicity of life," but he confesses that he "hid them with an almost morbid sense of shame."[4] In chapter nine, "Doctor Lanyon's Narrative," Jekyll's estranged friend is equally cryptic. "What he [Jekyll] told me in the next hour I cannot bring my mind to set on paper. I saw what I saw, I heard what I heard, and my soul sickened at it," Lanyon admits. "As for the moral turpitude that the man unveiled to me, even with tears of penitence, I cannot, even in memory, dwell on it without a start of horror."[5] Stevenson allows the reader to decide the exact nature of Henry Jekyll's questionable acts, which began in his youth and continued to the time of this confession and his death.

Almost all screen adaptations of *The Strange Case of Dr. Jekyll and Mr. Hyde* are based most heavily on these final two chapters, in which Jekyll's experiments and Hyde's misdeeds are revealed. The first eight chapters detail Utterson's investigation of the mystery surrounding Jekyll. Readers in 1886 did not realize that Jekyll and Hyde were the same man until the last two chapters, which provided the fantastical explanation. Only the 2004 Australian short film *The Strange Game of Hyde and Seek*, directed by Nathan Hill, approaches the story as Utterson's investigation and not chiefly as Jekyll's story. (Paolo Barzman's 2008 *Jekyll and Hyde* telefilm, set in present-day Boston, divides its time between Jekyll's activities and a female attorney's thorough investigation of Hyde's string of murders.)

Of course, a straightforward presentation of the events as Dr. Jekyll experiences them first-hand is a richer cinematic construction than Utterson's mere study of the events. Therefore, the Dr. Jekyll character, as played by James Cruze (1912), Lionel Barrymore (1920), Frederic March (1931), Spencer Tracy (1941), Boris Karloff (1953), Paul Massie (1960), Christopher Lee (1971), Udo Kier (1981), John Malkovich (1996), Tony Todd (2006), and more than 60 other actors, is almost always the protagonist, and Utterson, Lanyon, and especially Enfield are often not even included in the film.

Hunter's script for Curtis does include Enfield, Lanyon, and Utterson, although the latter's name is changed to George Devlin. While shifting the focus to Jekyll, the script, set in London in 1888, remains faithful to the tone of Stevenson's novel. Devlin looks into the matter of Hyde and (as Utterson does in the novel) quizzes Jekyll about him and asks if Hyde is blackmailing Jekyll. Jekyll and Lanyon's strained friendship plays a part, as does the faithfulness of Jekyll's butler Poole. The script also recreates the scene in which Poole summons Jekyll's solicitor to investigate Hyde's pathetic howling in Jekyll's laboratory while, in Stevenson's words in chapter eight, "the whole of the servants, men and women, stood huddled together like a flock of sheep" in their fright.[6] Although in the novel Hyde beats Sir Danvers Carew to death, in this version Hyde beats but does not kill Dr. Lanyon, and although in the novel Hyde changes back to Jekyll before Lanyon's eyes, here Hyde transforms in front of Devlin. The adaptation forgoes Jekyll's suicide for a more sensational climax, a deadly confrontation between Devlin and Hyde in the very room (the hospital amphitheatre) where the movie opens.

In the same vein as Gabriel Utterson's investigation of Edward Hyde's actions, this Henry Jekyll must investigate Mr. Hyde's actions of the night before because Jekyll, at first, has no knowledge of what Hyde has done. This search leads Jekyll to Tessie O'Toole's Music Hall, a necessary invention of scriptwriter Hunter's in order to inject heterosexuality and women's roles into the teleplay. Tessie is a stout, aging chanteuse and madame who warmly welcomes Dr. Jekyll and informs him that Mr. Hyde "took a real shine to" her employee Gwyneth Thomas, a "dancer" who also privately entertains men in the upstairs "dining rooms." Billie Whitelaw as Gwyneth serves the same purpose that Nita Naldi (1920), Miriam Hopkins (1931), Ingrid Bergman (1941), and countless other women before and after her do: to give Mr. Hyde a female object of desire. However, Hunter offers another subtle hint at Jekyll's "irregularities" when on two different occasions Gwyn offers Jekyll a "cure" for his (in her word) "shyness," which could connote sexual repression, impotence, or homosexuality. Not as subtle is Hunter's use in the script of the words "damn," "doxy," "orgy," "slut," and "trollop," terms still rather daring for 1960s television.

The Strange Case of Dr. Jekyll and Mr. Hyde debuted on the Canadian Broadcasting Corporation network (CBC) on January 3, 1968, and it first aired on the American Broadcasting Company network (ABC) on January 7. The production received overwhelmingly positive reviews. "It was incredibly gratifying," Dan Curtis remembered. "The reviews on that thing were absolutely incredible."[7] The *Baltimore Sun* raved,

Producer Dan Curtis (dressed in white) talks with actor Denholm Elliott (left) and director Charles Jarrott on the set of *The Strange Case of Dr. Jekyll and Mr. Hyde* (1968).

Dan Curtis, producer of *The Strange Case of Dr. Jekyll and Mr. Hyde*, introduced on ABC last Sunday, made good on all his promises. It was indeed a version of the Robert Louis Stevenson story never before seen in photoplay or television form; it adhered closely to the book; and the artistry of Dick Smith, master of makeup, did surpass anything seen in earlier transformations. What's more, the production, co-produced by the Canadian Broadcasting Corporation, surpassed the best version hitherto offered — the one in which Frederic March played the title role [and won an Oscar for it]. Jack Palance is the new champion in this difficult assignment, and he may hold the title for a long time.[8]

The Strange Case of Dr. Jekyll and Mr. Hyde (1968): Jack Palance (as Dr. Henry Jekyll) transforms into the fiendish Mr. Edward Hyde via Dick Smith's makeup.

The *Boston Globe* concurred: "Jack Palance, a rugged villain from way back, for my money was the best Jekyll-and-Hyde yet to come along."[9] The *Sacramento Union* added,

With its overpowering sense of time and place, the production proved immensely effective, all very dark and shadowy and Gothic — and scary. I bow to Dan Curtis and Charles Jarrott, producer and director, for framing the yarn so adeptly. Robert Cobert's music was properly spooky, too, alive with jabs of tense foreboding.[10]

The Strange Case of Dr. Jekyll and Mr. Hyde is scored with *Dark Shadows* music — in a way. Although *Dark Shadows* fans who watch the film today recognize almost every note of music as coming from the 1968–1971 years of the TV series, these music cues actually originated in this 1968 production. Cobert later re-recorded them for use on *Dark Shadows,* and these actual cues were used as the music score of *House of Dark Shadows* two years later. The heartbreaking, operatic music heard at Jekyll and Hyde's death is the same used at the staking of Barnabas Collins at the end of the 1970 film. (The cue was used yet again at the climaxes of Curtis's 1973 adaptations of *Frankenstein* and *The Picture of Dorian Gray*.) Most remarkably, the bouncy music-hall ditties which Cobert composed for the scenes at Tessie's place took on new life on the *Dark Shadows* TV series as "I'm Gonna Dance for You," associated with Nancy Barrett's Pansy Faye character, and "Quentin's Theme," the hit record and Grammy Award nominee forever associated with David Selby's several Quentin Collins characters on TV and in *Night of Dark Shadows* (1971). "When Dan told me there was a new spook [Quentin] coming on *Dark Shadows* and he needed a theme song," Cobert laughed, "I said, 'You remember what I wrote for Billie Whitelaw? You loved that! Use that!'"[11]

The Strange Case of Dr. Jekyll and Mr. Hyde was a prestigious entry into prime-time television producing for Dan Curtis. He, Jarrott, Hunter, and Palance had created a quality production which enjoyed several TV airings and later life on VHS and DVD. According to film critic Mark Dawidziak,

> Although often overlooked because it was done for the so-called "small screen" and shot on videotape, this Curtis gem is cherished by a fiercely devoted group of horror fans, Stevenson devotees, and TV scholars. The sheer brilliance of this *Dr. Jekyll and Mr. Hyde* demands special attention in any discussion of the Curtis career and accomplishments.[12]

The television academy took notice and bestowed four technical and two major Emmy Award nominations on *Dr. Jekyll and Mr. Hyde*. Tony Award-winning Welsh music-hall entertainer Tessie O'Shea was nominated for Outstanding Supporting Actress in a Drama or Special but lost to Barbara Anderson for *Ironside*. *Jekyll and Hyde* was nominated for Outstanding Dramatic Program of 1967–1968 but lost to *Elizabeth the Queen*, a *Hallmark Hall of Fame* drama co-starring Judith Anderson and Charlton Heston.[13] Despite losing all six awards, the Dan Curtis production took its place in television history as an early example of Curtis's brand of "ornately atmospheric horror," in the words of *The Hollywood Reporter*.[14]

Curtis's other four adaptations of the classics aired in 1973–1974, an extremely productive time period when the producer-director brought 13 of his productions to ABC, CBS, and NBC (11 of them to ABC). Except for *Dracula* (1974), these adaptations were shot on videotape for ABC's late-night *Wide World Mystery* series.

First was *Frankenstein* (ABC, January 16–17, 1973), which Curtis co-wrote with Sam Hall and Richard Landau. Hall had been one of the head writers of *Dark Shadows* and co-writer of the two subsequent movies. Landau had co-written *The Quatermass Xperiment*, a.k.a. *The Creeping Unknown* (1955), and *Frankenstein 1970* (a 1958 Boris Karloff movie), among other films and TV episodes.

Curtis chose one of his protégés to direct *Frankenstein*. Glenn Jordan had directed only five TV movies (1969–1972) before *Frankenstein*, but he went on to direct *Les Misérables* (TV-1978), *Mass Appeal* (1984), *O Pioneers!* (TV-1992), and two of the three *Sarah, Plain and Tall* telefilms for *Hallmark Hall of Fame*. Even though Curtis did not direct *Frankenstein*, he put his distinctive stamp on the production through his work on the script and his careful management of the *Dark Shadows / Jekyll and Hyde* look of the movie.

Radu Florescu, author of *In Search of Frankenstein* (1975), observed of this "really first-class" adaptation of Mary Shelley's 1818 novel that "for the very first time, an attempt was made to try and stay reasonably close to Mary Shelley's original conception of the monster." Florescu continued,

> With Robert Foxworth as Victor Frankenstein and Susan Strasberg as Elizabeth, Bo Svenson emerged as a literate, well-spoken, and sensitive monster. Although the plot once again had the creature created electrically rather than biologically, director Glenn Jordan adhered to Shelley's desire to have her monster seek a mate in order to pacify his destructive impulses. Admittedly, the intricate flashback mechanism of the novel was again shunted aside, but at least a sincerely admirable linkage between printed page and movie (or TV, in this case) screen was attempted.[15]

The practice of using electricity to bring the creature to life is a deeply entrenched tradition in film versions of *Frankenstein*. Of the more than 230 filmings since 1910, one dozen of them even used the same electrical equipment, built by Kenneth Strickfaden for Universal's 1931 classic. Mary Shelley's novel avoids any concrete description of exactly how Dr. Victor Frankenstein brings his creation to life, but the author implies that the process involves chemistry, alchemy, and electricity. In fact, in chapter five Dr. Frankenstein remarks, "I collected the instruments of life around me that I might infuse a spark of being into the lifeless thing that lay at my feet."[16] Film audiences expect some sort of galvanic process in the obligatory creation scene, and Curtis and Jordan's *Frankenstein* does not disappoint.

Horror-film critic Paul O'Flinn concedes, "There is no such thing as *Frankenstein*; there are only *Frankensteins* as the text is ceaselessly rewritten, reproduced, refilmed, and redesigned."[17] He adds that "the shift of medium" from novel to film demands that the screenwriters "must inevitably obliterate and replace" elements of the novel in order to make the work more visual and filmable,[18] a mandate which had necessitated a few cinematic changes to Curtis's *Jekyll and Hyde* production several years earlier.

Even after making such changes to their *Frankenstein,* writers Curtis, Hall, and Landau do succeed in remaining more nearly faithful to the spirit of Shelley's novel than previous movie versions. All of the major characters and plot threads are present and true to form except for Captain Robert Walton (and the framing device of Frankenstein's telling the story to him aboard his ship) and housekeeper Justine Moritz (and the subplot of her being wrongly accused and hanged for William's murder). Most of the action takes place in Ingolstadt, Germany — for budgetary reasons, this version eschews Frankenstein's travels around Europe and to England and the Orkney Islands — and the year is now 1856, more than a half-century after the novel's time setting. The

movie's primary focus is on Dr. Victor Frankenstein, the Creature, and Agatha DeLacey. Secondary focus is on Alphonse Frankenstein, Elizabeth Lavenza, and Dr. Henri Clerval, all of whom frequently question Frankenstein about his erratic, obsessive behavior.

For dramatic purposes, Dr. Frankenstein has two lab assistants, Hugo and Otto. Frankenstein uses the mortally wounded Hugo's heart as the creature's heart, and the creature later accidentally kills Otto by hugging him much too strongly

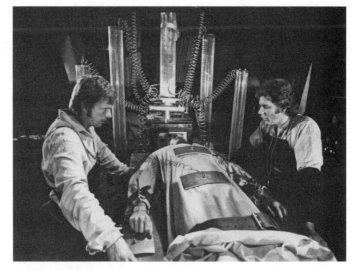

Frankenstein (1973): John Karlen (left, as Otto Roget) and Robert Foxworth (as Victor Frankenstein) prepare to bring Bo Svenson (as the Giant) to life. In a June 2006 DVD commentary, Foxworth said of *Frankenstein* producer Dan Curtis and his input, "As I recall, he got his two cents in!"

after Otto has thrown a ball with him and taught him the words "Otto" and "play." Dr. Frankenstein finds the puzzled creature standing over the dead man and begging him, "Otto, play?" This is the first of many instances of poignancy and sympathy for the monster. An important trait of many of Curtis's productions is a degree of sympathy for the evildoer—Barnabas Collins, Dr. Jekyll, the Night Strangler, Count Dracula, the crook Harry Banner in *Me and the Kid*, and one of the accused priests in *Our Fathers*. Curtis reflected, "I try to find an additional dimension to the monster. Sometimes, you actually end up feeling sorry for him. We certainly did that with Barnabas Collins and Dr. Jekyll."[19] Curtis, Hall, Landau, and director Jordan achieve the same effect with the Giant (as Bo Svenson's character is called).

Although, as Florescu notes, the storyline aboard Robert Walton's ship is not included in this version, Curtis and the scriptwriters do offer a rich portrayal of the DeLacey family, the French exiles who unknowingly become the creature's family after he hides in their shed for months and learns about language, history, friendship, and love by listening to them through the walls. Monsieur DeLacey, his grown children Felix and Agatha, and Felix's fiancée Safie play their same instructive roles from the novel, but with two changes. In this version Safie is Spanish, not Turkish, and it is Agatha, not her father, who is blind. Curtis and his co-writers did not want to try to top the famous monster-meets-blind-man scene in James Whale's *The Bride of Frankenstein* (1935)—or even want to remind viewers of that outlandish meeting—in the middle of their serious adaptation of Shelley's novel. Plus, allowing the Giant to interact with a young blind woman instead of an old blind man injects more pathos and even a hint of love interest into the movie. Furthermore, the Giant and Agatha's similar desire to have friends echoes Captain Robert Walton's selfsame desire for a friendly companion as expressed in his letters to his sister Margaret Walton Saville at the beginning of Shelley's novel—"I bitterly feel the want of a friend."[20]

Of the hundreds of actors who have portrayed the Frankenstein creature over the decades—Charles Ogle (1910), Umberto Guarracino (1921), Boris Karloff (1931), Lon Chaney, Jr. (1942), Christopher Lee (1957), Kiwi Kingston (1964), David Prowse (1970), David Warner (TV-1984), Robert De Niro (1994), Luke Goss (TV-2004), and many others—Bo Svenson is one of the most successful at infusing the monster with pathos. When he hears Agatha tell Safie that talking with someone is the best way to learn a language, the scarred Giant carves a face on a potato in the DeLaceys' shed and speaks to it. He later tells Agatha, "Sometimes, I wish the whole world was blind; then, everyone would be alike." Soon the DeLacey men and Safie return home and recoil from the Giant. In two other moments that humanize the creature, the Giant kills young William Frankenstein by accident when he tries to stop the boy from crying out to Elizabeth, and the Giant desires to "learn forgiveness" just before his death (scored to Robert Cobert's death-of-Jekyll/death-of-Barnabas music).

Cobert did not write a new score for *Frankenstein*; instead, he used his tried-and-true music cues from *Dark Shadows*, as well as two cues from *The Strange Case of Dr. Jekyll and Mr. Hyde*. By January 1973, the time of the *Frankenstein* telecast, almost two years had elapsed since *Dark Shadows* fans had heard Cobert's famous TV music cues anywhere except on their well-worn 1969 *Dark Shadows* soundtrack record album (as of 2008 still one of the top five best-selling TV soundtracks of all time). Cobert's distinctive brand of (in his words) "great spook music"[21] instantly marked a program as a Dan Curtis production, and loyal *Dark Shadows* / Dan Curtis devotees eagerly sought out any TV show that afforded them another example of Curtis and Cobert's work. Dan Curtis was always well aware of his fan base. In later years, he closely monitored (but never attended) the Shadowcon and Dark Shadows Festival fan conventions.

Frankenstein garnered more stellar reviews for Dan Curtis. Cecil Smith of the *Los Angeles Times* wrote, "*Frankenstein* is the best shot yet in ABC's ongoing war to woo the midnight audience. Despite a miniscule budget, [*Frankenstein*] is quite a handsome show, with huge, foreboding sets and a splendid array of special effects."[22] *Variety* called the production "extraordinary entertainment" and declared, "*Frankenstein* marks a decided step forward in late-night entertainment. It's really too good to relegate to the insomniacs."[23] Two years later, in his book *In Search of Frankenstein*, Radu Florescu paid Curtis the ultimate compliment when he wrote, "This 180-minute television film was probably the most faithful rendering the screen has yet seen."[24]

Unfortunately, *Frankenstein* did not receive the lasting recognition that it deserved because it aired late at night, was shot on videotape, and was quickly overshadowed by Jack Smight's *Frankenstein: The True Story* (NBC, November 30–December 1, 1973 & December 30–31, 1974) and Mel Brooks's *Young Frankenstein* (1974). The former, with its close relationship between Victor Frankenstein (Leonard Whiting) and his *handsome*, inquisitive creation (Michael Sarrazin), was one of Anne Rice's inspirations for her 1976 novel *Interview with the Vampire*. The latter, an uproarious spoof of Frankenstein movies, was one of Kenneth Branagh's inspirations as he filmed *Mary Shelley's Frankenstein* (1994), despite the two films' vast difference in tone. *Young Frankenstein*, of course, features a monster-meets-blind-man scene which has *never* been topped.

Five years before the *Los Angeles Times* published Dan Curtis's letter putting *War and Remembrance* (1988, 1989) and *Schindler's List* (1993) into perspective, the *Times* published another of Curtis's emphatic statements, this one about *Frankenstein*. In the November 30, 1992, edition, Curtis wrote,

> I read with interest the location piece filed from England by Jeff Kaye regarding TNT's *Frankenstein*. In it, Kaye says that "TNT is producing the most true-to-the-original-story version of *Frankenstein* that has ever been filmed." He further asks, "If the original story is so good, why hasn't anyone filmed it before?"
>
> The fact of the matter is that I produced a three-hour adaptation of Mary Shelley's classic work that ABC aired as part of its *Wide World of Mystery* late-night programming schedule in two parts on January 16–17, 1973. The production, starring Robert Foxworth as Dr. Frankenstein and Bo Svenson as the creature, received rave reviews and was highly rated.
>
> In fact, the *Los Angeles Times*'s television reporter, Cecil Smith, wrote glowingly of the production, the direction, the cast, and so forth. Smith pointed out that "major departures were made from the *Frankenstein* we knew and loved in James Whale's great 1931 movie.
>
> "Instead of the inarticulate, lumbering monster that Boris Karloff played so brilliantly, this adaptation, by producer Dan Curtis and writer Sam Hall, is truer to Mary Shelley's classic novel, in which Dr. Frankenstein produced in his laboratory a 'superhuman,' the strongest, most brilliant man on earth."
>
> Although I eagerly await this new production of Shelley's enormously rich literary mas-

terpiece, I feel compelled to recognize the extraordinary contributions of my colleagues to this earlier, groundbreaking television production. These include my co-adaptors, Sam Hall and Richard Landau; director, Glenn Jordan; music director, Robert Cobert; art director, Trevor Williams; and a wonderful cast, headed by Foxworth, Svenson, and Susan Strasberg.

Throughout my career, I have felt a deep kinship for this particular entertainment genre. Who knew that a show I created almost 30 years ago called *Dark Shadows* would become a major daytime cult hit?

Actually, it was only recently, while reviewing the press materials for the soon-to-be-released video library of my "scariest" productions, that I realized what a large percentage of my creative output has dealt with such matters as the occult, vampires, horror, and "things that go bump in the night."

The Strange Case of Dr. Jekyll and Mr. Hyde with Jack Palance (1968), Darren McGavin in *The Night Stalker* (1972), Lynn Redgrave in *The Turn of the Screw* (1974), and *Bram Stoker's Dracula* (1974), again with Palance, to name a few — all of my works in this field have in some way been informed and nourished by the literary and cinematic references that have preceded them. That's how a subject matter becomes a genre in the first place. I only wish Kaye had researched the television lineage of Mary Shelley's *Frankenstein* a little more assiduously.

Signed, DAN CURTIS[25]

Three months after *Frankenstein*, Curtis and Jordan returned to ABC's late-night *Wide World Mystery* with *The Picture of Dorian Gray* (April 23–24, 1973), written by John Tomerlin from the 1891 novel by Oscar Wilde. Tomerlin had written "Dark Legacy," the May 30, 1961, episode of *Boris Karloff's Thriller,* and "Number Twelve Looks Just Like You," the January 24, 1964, episode of *The Twilight Zone,* among other teleplays. Now he submitted to Curtis a *Dorian Gray* adaptation which *The Hollywood Reporter* noted "adheres closely to the original."[26]

The Picture of Dorian Gray (1973): Nigel Davenport (left, as Sir Harry Wotton), Shane Briant (as Dorian Gray), and John Karlen (as Alan Campbell) perform a scene together.

Curtis's *Dorian Gray* is more widely remembered than his *Frankenstein* because there have not been as many movie versions of Wilde's novel and because this *Dorian Gray* is considered one of the two best adaptations of the more than 30 treatments filmed since at least 1910. Although everyone from Wallace Reid (1913) to Jeremy Brett (TV-1961) to Helmut Berger (1970) to Belinda Bauer (TV-1983) to Stuart Townsend (2003) has played Dorian

Gray, the two most widely remembered portrayals are those by Hurd Hatfield in Albert Lewin's 1945 MGM feature and Shane Briant in Curtis's 1973 telefilm. Both the 1945 and 1973 adaptations take a few liberties with Wilde's text, but Curtis's production is the most faithful adaptation of *The Picture of Dorian Gray* ever filmed. Tomerlin's script retains many of Lord Henry Wotton and Dorian Gray's famous aphorisms about beauty, love, marriage, and temptation — and the movie is more revealing of Dorian Gray's pansexuality than the more discreet versions made in the 1910s, 1945, and the 1960s.

Whereas the action of Wilde's 1891 novel (an expansion of his novella published in the June 20, 1890, issue of *Lippincott's Monthly Magazine*) takes places over the course of 18 years, the events of this adaptation stretch from 1891 to 1911. The film begins with a Wildean epigraph — "Those who go beneath the surface do so at their peril" — just as Curtis's *Frankenstein* begins with an epigraph from *Paradise Lost*. *The Picture of Dorian Gray* does especially well in faithfully bringing to the screen the novel's first and second chapters (Basil and Henry's conversation about Dorian and the introduction of Dorian himself) and chapter 16 (Dorian's visit to the opium den and his confrontation with Sibyl's brother James). Artist Basil Hallward is suitably protective (and enamored) of young, blond, androgynously beautiful Dorian, and Lord Henry Wotton (*Harry* Wotton in this adaptation) is charismatically witty, seductive, and Svengaliesque toward this new object of his affection.

The script offers a more expansive depiction of Dorian's scandalous activities than do other adaptations. Dorian is seen gambling, smoking opium, cavorting with female prostitutes, and courting Sibyl Vane, whom he pressures into having sex with him. After he drops her, Sibyl kills herself (in this version by drowning herself, not by taking poison as in the novel). In a shocking scene that had to be reworked at the demand of the ABC censors, Dorian pays a prostitute extra to let him have sex with her unseen, underage daughter. Also, after Wotton influences him, Dorian counts homosexual gratification among his "new interests." For example, Wotton offers to share his "young friends" with Dorian; Gray flirts with a handsome young blond man at a party; and a rent boy is seen leaving Dorian's bedroom. Shane Briant explained,

> That was done to show Dorian's depravity though it's not actually suggested in Wilde's book. Both Glenn [Jordan] and I thought, if you're doing a show in 1973 and all Dorian does is go to bed with *women* — well, what's so depraved about that?! So he drinks a lot! So he smokes! So what? You had to do something that the audience considered depraved [at least, in 1973].[27]

In this adaptation, Dorian's relationship with Alan Campbell is more overtly homosexual. In the novel, Dorian summons Alan, a scientist, after Gray stabs Basil to death, and he demands that Campbell dispose of the corpse for him. Dorian persuades Alan to do his bidding by handing him a note on which Dorian has written Alan's ghastly secrets (undisclosed in the novel but assumed to be homosexual liaisons). In this adaptation, Dorian does not call for Alan when he bludgeons Basil to death — two disreputable Burke and Hare–type fellows take the body away — but Dorian does summon him when he stabs James Vane to death. (Tomerlin changes James's accidental death in the novel to murder in order to provide Dorian with yet another sin of commission.)

Callously lounging in his bed, Dorian now voices aloud a suggestion of Alan's secrets by calling the names of three men ("Brighton, Pembroke, Sir William Nolan"). Alan stops in his tracks and meekly agrees to do his estranged friend's grisly bidding. (Similarly, Basil, in an earlier re-enactment of Wilde's Chapter 12, has listed to Dorian three men whom Dorian has shamed.)

The movie's most considerable departure from Wilde's novel is a plot device that writer-director Albert Lewin first used in his 1945 version. In that film, Basil (played by Lowell Gilmore) has a young ward, Gladys, played as an adult by Donna Reed and invented as a latter-day love interest for Dorian Gray. Likewise, in Tomerlin's script, Basil has a niece, Beatrice, who as a five-year-old idolizes Dorian and who as a 25-year-old comes back into Dorian's life and becomes his fiancée. This plot device is a very effective way of showing the passage of time. Wotton has gone gray, Basil is long dead, and Beatrice has grown up — yet Dorian retains the beautiful, innocent countenance of a 20-year-old while Basil's portrait of Dorian depicts every debauch, excess, cruelty, sin, and murder committed by the Faustian playboy. Dorian exclaims that the hideous painting allows him "to read from the page of my own degradation."

Seventies-era movie-poster artist John Solie (*Soylent Green, Shaft's Big Score*) created six different portraits to trace the ruination of Dorian Gray's soul. Shane Briant revealed that he got to keep one of them (the beautiful one). Briant explained,

> On the last day, the prop man cut out the portrait — which was six feet long and four feet wide — and rolled it up and gave it to me, which was lovely. I went off to a party that Fionnula Flanagan was giving up in the [Hollywood] hills, and I left it in the back of the cab! I figured it was lost, [but] I rang up the cab company the next day, and they had it. So I still have it — but it hasn't changed! I used to stand in front of it and pray, "Please, I'm getting old! Isn't there something you can do?" But no, the picture is still as good as ever, and I'm getting old and wrinkled.[28]

The Picture of Dorian Gray, like Curtis's *Frankenstein*, was shot on videotape at the MGM Studios in Culver City, California. Briant remembered,

The Picture of Dorian Gray (1973): Shane Briant (left, as Dorian Gray), an unidentified extra, and John Karlen (as Alan Campbell) interact in Dorian's bedroom.

We had eight days of rehearsal, and then we shot it in four. We did a three-hour program from start to finish in 12 days, which must be some kind of a record! We were really going! We rehearsed in the Culver City studios — not the ones now, but on the old *Gone with the Wind* lot, and then we shot it with four videotape cameras. We went from start to finish almost in order, from eight in the morning until eight at night, non-stop. Dan Curtis is a very strong character, strong-willed and a hard taskmaster. If he says you shoot it in four days, you shoot it in four days![29]

While Lewin's MGM movie with Hurd Hatfield, Angela Lansbury, and George Sanders was Old Hollywood's gold-standard adaptation of *Dorian Gray,* Curtis's 1973 production became the definitive version for the modern era. *Variety* declared,

Oscar Wilde's world of entertainment (London, 1891), stylishly produced by Dan Curtis Productions, revives the horror tale with insights entirely in keeping with the theme of the original book. Hints of malevolence, sensuality, and decadence, all played out with fine restraint by exotic young actor Shane Briant, give the story freshness and suspense. Wilde knew what he was talking about, and Dan Curtis's production, handsomely mounted, handles the tale with respect and care. Everyone associated with this production deserves kudos.[30]

As produced by Curtis, the stories of Dr. Jekyll, Dr. Frankenstein, and Dorian Gray all point out man's dual nature. Jekyll, recognizing that man has the capacity for both good and evil, drinks his potion in the hope of bringing out the virtuous side of man — but he unleashes the monstrous side instead. Frankenstein and the Creature are two sides of the same coin. As a matter of fact, David Wickes's aforementioned adaptation for TNT (June 13, 1993) suggests that the monster (Randy Quaid) is the alter ego of Frankenstein (Patrick Bergin). Frankenstein creates a totally *innocent* monster who kills only after dreadful circumstances cause him to do so. The doctor begins as a knowledge-hungry student, and he turns *himself* into a monster because of his rejection of the creature, his depression, and his guilt. Dorian Gray constantly struggles with his feelings of righteousness and sinfulness, optimism and cynicism, heterosexuality and homosexuality, and hopefulness and hopelessness.

Dan Curtis's adaptations effectively capture these characters' dual natures through general fidelity to the texts, excellent performances, striking makeup (the satyr-like Hyde and the pitiful visage of the Giant), meaningful set design (Jekyll's bright, opulent townhouse and his dark, dingy laboratory), and, of course, Robert Cobert's music. Again for *Dorian Gray,* Cobert does not compose new music but oversees the skillful use of his *Dark Shadows* cues, including several versions of "Quentin's Theme," as well as two cues from *Jekyll and Hyde.* Cobert's emotional cue "Death of Hyde" has lived again at the deaths of Barnabas, Frankenstein and his creation, and now Dorian Gray. In Wilde's words,

When they entered, they found, hanging upon the wall, a splendid portrait of their master as they had last seen him, in all the wonder of his exquisite youth and beauty. Lying on the floor was a dead man, in evening dress, with a knife in his heart. He was withered, wrinkled, and loathsome of visage. It was not 'til they had examined the rings that they recognized who it was.[31]

The first of Dan Curtis's final two adaptations of the classics took him to Yugoslavia and England, where he directed his acclaimed version of *Dracula,* based on Bram Stoker's 1897 novel. The film, sometimes known as *Bram Stoker's Dracula* or *Dan Curtis's Dracula,* aired on CBS-TV on February 8, 1974 (and November 28, 1992). It was the fourth of six collaborations between Curtis and author Richard Matheson, who had written about vampires in such 1950s stories and novels as "Drink My Red Blood," "Dress of White Silk," and *I Am Legend*. Matheson's 1959 short story "No Such Thing as a Vampire" had been filmed for the April 19, 1968, premiere episode of BBC-TV's *Late-Night Horror*— one of the very first BBC productions filmed in color.

Matheson recalled that his and Curtis's *Dracula* aired in a two-hour timeslot. He added,

> [It] turned out quite well, I thought, but it was even better at the three hours originally shot. I wrote a script for three hours, and Dan shot a three-hour version, but the network would give us only two hours. So Dan had to edit it down. I would have loved to have seen it at three hours. It was the first one that tried to follow the book and the first one to use the Vlad the Impaler material. To this day, I think we came the closest.[32]

What Matheson includes in his adaptation *is* an accurate reproduction of Bram Stoker's novel, especially the novel's first four chapters relating Jonathan Harker's stay at Castle Dracula, the shipwreck of the *Demeter* (Chapter 7), Dracula's release of a wolf from the zoo (Chapter 11), Mina's drinking of Dracula's blood from an open wound (Chapter 21), and Van Helsing's hypnosis of Mina (Chapter 23). However, Matheson omits the characters of Quincey Morris (often absent from film adaptations), Dr. John Seward, and the mad R.M. Renfield. The adaptation works without the Seward/Renfield subplot as it focuses fully on Jonathan Harker, Mina Murray, Arthur Holmwood, Lucy Westenra, Mrs. Westenra, Dr. Abraham Van Helsing, and Count Dracula (played by Jack Palance).

Matheson, with input from Curtis, makes two significant changes, one of which makes this adaptation of *Dracula* so distinctive and influential. In the novel, Jonathan's opening storyline leaves him a prisoner of Castle Dracula and at the mercy of Dracula's three vampire brides at the end of Chapter 4. Four chapters later, Mina receives word that Jonathan is in a hospital in Budapest. Stoker never explains exactly how Harker managed to escape the castle. In Matheson's teleplay, Jonathan does *not* escape. When Arthur and Van Helsing arrive at Castle Dracula, they find that their friend has become a vampire.

Dracula (1974): Jack Palance stars as Bram Stoker's vampire creation.

The more important change is Matheson and Curtis's revisionist explanation of why Dracula comes to England in the first place. Stoker does not offer a reason until Chapter 24 when Van Helsing assumes that Dracula is "leaving his own barren land — barren of peoples — and coming to a new land where life of man teems 'til they are like the multitude of standing corn."[33] In other words, Dracula may as well relocate to the world's largest city (London) in order to have an endless supply of victims. Curtis insisted,

> Richard Matheson, who's a wonderful writer, and I adapted the Bram Stoker novel and brought to it something that wasn't in it. I ripped myself off. I took the *Dark Shadows* love story and put it in our *Dracula* because in the novel, Dracula leaves Transylvania and goes to England for no reason at all. Stoker says he's sucked virtually everybody dry down there, and he had to find new blood. We didn't do that. I always felt that was ridiculous, so we came up with the central love story to *Dracula* that never existed in the novel but that has since, I might add, been *copied* by other *Draculas,* the most recent one, for instance.[34]

Curtis referred to Francis Ford Coppola's *Bram Stoker's Dracula* (1992). However, the animated adventures *The Batman Versus Dracula* (2005) and *Highlander: The Search for Vengeance* (2006) also fit this description. So does one of the subplots of Fred Olen Ray's vampire serial *The Lair* (debuted 2007), Here! TV's spin-off of *Dante's Cove* (debuted 2005). Curtis added,

> In our movie, he [Dracula] saw a picture of a girl [Lucy] in the newspaper, and we established that she was the reincarnation of this woman he was in love with in the 1400s. She's in England, and he goes to England to get her back. It's a little *Dark Shadowy,* but it worked. It was perfect. That's why our *Dracula* was as good as it was. It brought to the monster a degree of sympathy. Instead of making him just this marauding vampire, he was a haunted figure. You really cared about him even though you were terrified of him. Jack [Palance] is extraordinary. Jack is the best Dracula there ever was. He was the most frightening Dracula that ever put on that cape.[35]

The *Los Angeles Times* agreed. "This two-hour version of the classic horror story made for television by Dan Curtis and offered tonight on CBS would chill the bones of a plaster saint. It's as flesh-crawling an experience as you've ever had."[36] The *Times* proclaimed, "If the late [Bela] Lugosi was the definitive Count Dracula, it's no longer true. It's now Jack Palance."[37]

In a 2000 DVD featurette,

Dracula (1974): Fiona Lewis as Lucy Westenra and Jack Palance as Count Dracula perform a fantasy sequence.

Palance, who died on November 10, 2006, at age 87, mused that Count Dracula was "the only character I ever played that frightened me even in the doing of it. But I never thought of the character as being evil. He was someone who was trapped in a situation." Palance added that with Curtis at the helm of the movie, "I knew it would be done very well and with great authenticity."[38] Donald F. Glut, author of *The Dracula Book* (1975), agreed: "The film surely ranks with the best movie adaptations of Stoker's *Dracula,* and it firmly established director Curtis and actor Palance among the genre's upper echelon."[39]

That newfound authenticity is the other hallmark of Curtis's *Dracula*—and the other ingredient which Coppola's 1992 blockbuster appropriated from its 1974 predecessor. Except for a few vague references in Mehmet Muktar's 1952 Turkish film *Drakula Istanbulda,* Curtis's *Dracula* is the first Dracula film to make the all-important connection between Count Dracula and the real-life Vlad the Impaler of the fifteenth century. Matheson's screenplay reflects the scholarship of the time in Raymond McNally and Radu Florescu's *In Search of Dracula* (1972) and its 1973 follow-up *Dracula: A Biography of Vlad the Impaler, 1431–1476.*

Twenty-first-century film audiences take for granted that the Dracula character is based on the real-life story of a ruthless warrior, but at the time of Curtis's *Dracula,* such an idea was just coming into the popular consciousness. Vlad Dracula, also known as Vlad Tepes, was born in Sighisoara (a.k.a. Schassburg), a village in Transylvania, in late 1430 or early 1431. His father Vlad Dracul had been prince of Wallachia and a member of the Order of the Dragon, a Christian brotherhood founded by King Sigismund I of Hungary in 1418 and dedicated to fighting the Turkish people. "Drac" is a Romanian word meaning "devil" or "dragon." Vlad Dracul's son was called Dracul*a,* or "son of the devil" or "son of the dragon." In later life, Vlad Dracula also was called "Tepes," which means "impaler," because of his penchant for skewering as many of his enemies as possible. Vlad had many of them, for he spent his life attacking the Turks and fighting to acquire and keep the throne of Wallachia. After putting to death 40,000 of his enemies (four times more than Ivan the Terrible), Vlad fell to an assassin in December 1476 or early January 1477.[40]

Some evidence of Count Dracula's having been patterned after Vlad Tepes exists in Bram Stoker's novel. In Chapter 3, Harker notes that Dracula sounds "like a king speaking"[41] when the Count talks knowingly of his family's "guarding of the frontier of Turkey-land."[42] Dracula declares,

Who was it but one of my own race who as Voivode crossed the Danube and beat the Turk on his own ground? This was a Dracula indeed! [ ] Was it not this Dracula, indeed, who inspired that other of his race who in a later age again and again brought his forces over the great river into Turkey-land; who, when he was beaten back, came again, and again, and again, though he had to come alone from the bloody field where his troops were being slaughtered, since he knew that he alone could ultimately triumph! They said that he thought only of himself. Bah! What good are peasants without a leader? Where ends the war without a brain and heart to conduct it? Again, when, after the battle of Mohacs, we threw off the Hungarian yoke, we of the Dracula blood were amongst their leaders, for our spirit would not brook that we were not free.[43]

Later, in Chapter 18, as Van Helsing is explaining the rules of vampirism to Mina and the others, he reports his own findings about Dracula's origins.

Thus, when we find the habitation of this man-that-was, we can confine him to his coffin and destroy him, if we obey what we know. But he is clever. I have asked my friend Arminius, of Buda-Peth University, to make his record; and, from all the means that are, he tells me of what he has been. He must, indeed, have been that Voivode Dracula who won his name against the Turk, over the great river on the very frontier of Turkey-land. If it be so, then he was no common man; for in that time, and for centuries after, he was spoken of as the cleverest and the most cunning, as well as the bravest of the sons of the "land beyond the forest." That mighty brain and that iron resolution went with him to his grave, and are even now arrayed against us. The Draculas were, says Arminius, a great and noble race, though now and again were scions who were held by their coevals to have had dealings with the Evil One. They learned his secrets in the Scholomance, amongst the mountains over Lake Hermanstadt, where the devil claims the tenth scholar as his due. In the records are such words as "stregoic"'—witch, "ordog," and "pokol"—Satan and hell; and in one manuscript, this very Dracula is spoken of as "wampyr," which we all understand too well.[44]

Van Helsing's "friend Arminius" is the real-life Hungarian historian Arminius Vambery, author of *Hungary in Ancient, Medieval, and Modern Times* (1886) and other books of history and travel. Bram Stoker met Vambery at the Beefsteak Room, behind the Lyceum Theatre, in 1890 when Stoker was 43 and Vambery was 58. (The restaurant is mentioned in *Masterpiece Theatre*'s 2007 reimagining of *Dracula*.) At the time that he met Vambery, Stoker had already begun to write *Dracula*, and it is possible that Vambery told Stoker stories of Vlad the Impaler—stories that the leading Hungarian scholar doubtless knew even though he himself never wrote about Vlad Tepes in any of his own books.[45] "The land beyond the forest" refers both to the literal translation of the word "transylvania" and to Emily Gerard Laszowska's 1888 book, *The Land Beyond the Forest: Facts, Figures, and Fancies from Transylvania,* which Stoker is known to have read when he was gathering information about the region.

The Scholomance is a legendary school of occult sciences and necromancy—a kind of antediluvian Hogwarts—where Count Dracula studied and perhaps where he lost his soul to the powers of darkness and became a vampire. (Stoker offers no concrete explanation as to how Dracula became undead centuries ago, but he strongly hints that sorcery was involved.) Students at the Scholomance are taught by a dragon and/or the devil how to affect the weather and how to transform themselves into animals.[46] Dracula's name suggests both "dragon" and "devil."

In Curtis and Matheson's groundbreaking film, Count Dracula is seen as a medieval warrior prince in two brief flashbacks and in an enormous painting. The nameplate below the painting of the kingly soldier on horseback even names him as "Vlad Tepes, Prince of Wallachia, 1475." In one scene, Dracula refers to himself as "me, who commanded armies hundreds of years before you were born." Indeed, in the summer of 1475, Vlad had regained the throne and then led armies to Serbia and Turkey.[47] Finally, after Van Helsing and Arthur succeed in destroying the vampire, an epigraph in red letters on the screen proclaims,

In the 15th Century, in the area of Hungary known as Transylvania, there lived a nobleman so fierce in battle that his troops gave him the name *Dracula*, which means devil. Soldier, statesman, alchemist, and warrior, so powerful a man was he that it was claimed he succeeded in overcoming even physical death. To this day, it has yet to be disproven.

Matheson's words echo Dr. Seward's diary entry in Chapter 23 of Stoker's novel:

> He was in life a most wonderful man. Soldier, statesman, and alchemist — which latter was the highest development of the science-knowledge of his time. He had a mighty brain, a learning beyond compare, and a heart that knew no fear and no remorse. He dared even to attend the Scholomance, and there was no branch of knowledge of his time that he did not essay. Well, in him, the brain powers survived the physical death.[48]

Robert Cobert wrote a majestic, martial fanfare for the former warrior prince, as well as a dynamic main-title theme in the key of C minor. Cobert added, "I wrote a love theme for *Dracula* that came from a music box. I did something modal, with a Romanian accent, the kind of music box that he might have had."[49] By "modal," Cobert meant something evocative of medieval church music.

The music was only one of many elements which made Curtis's *Dracula* an important addition to the more than 165 film adaptations of Bram Stoker's novel since 1920. Of all of the actors who have portrayed the vampire — Max Schreck (1922), Bela Lugosi (1931), John Carradine (1944), Francis Lederer (1958), Christopher Lee (1965), Frank Langella (1979), Duncan Regehr (1987), Gary Oldman (1992), Marc Warren (2007), and scores of others — Jack Palance brought unique ferocity to the role and pioneered Dracula's cinematic portrayal as Vlad the Impaler. Radu Florescu and Raymond McNally later noted Palance's portrayal of Vlad Dracula by declaring, "The best scene is where Dracula, upon finding that his long-lost love has been destroyed, groans like a wild animal as he smashes the funeral urns."[50] J. Gordon Melton, author of *The Vampire Book: The Encyclopedia of the Undead* (1994), added,

> Knowledge of the historical Dracula has had a marked influence on both Dracula movies and fiction. Two of the more important Dracula movies, *Dracula* (1974), starring Jack Palance, and *Bram Stoker's Dracula,* a recent [1992] production directed by Francis Ford Coppola, attempted to integrate the historical research on Vlad the Impaler into the story and used it as a rationale to make Dracula's actions more comprehensible.[51]

Dan Curtis confidently insisted that his, Matheson's, and Palance's film "is the best *Dracula* that was ever made! It was very erotic, without showing a hell of a lot, and very scary and done with a lot of classic style. We had a wonderful director of photography, Ossie Morris, and we shot it in England and Yugoslavia. It was a really good production."[52] *Variety* called it "a tribute to Palance, Curtis, and Matheson that it comes off as logically as it does." *Variety* continued,

> Curtis and Matheson, ignoring previous flourishes made out of Bram Stoker's Victorian novel, approach the tale with a fresh, realistic fashion, designed to chill. With Jack Palance turning in one of the finest performances of his career as the bloodthirsty nobleman, Matheson has brought out the essential elements of the story [...] Stoker, Sir Henry Irving's business manager as well as a novelist, would be delighted.[53]

One final adaptation of supernatural literature was to be produced and directed by Dan Curtis for his 1968–1974 quintet of classics. "While I was in England shooting *Dracula* and finishing *Dracula*," Curtis explained, "I was in pre-production on *Turn of the Screw*."[54] Another late-night two-parter for ABC-TV's *Wide World Mystery, The Turn of the Screw* aired on April 15–16, 1974. Adapting Henry James's 1898 novel was fantasy novelist William F. Nolan, who wrote or co-wrote ten scripts for Curtis. Before *The Turn of the Screw,* Nolan had written *The Norliss Tapes* (1973) and its never-produced sequel *The Return,* and he had co-written *Melvin Purvis, G-Man* (1974) with John Milius. Nolan called *The Turn of the Screw* "one of my best scripts."[55]

The Turn of the Screw was one of Dan Curtis's favorite ghost stories. The director admitted,

> A good deal of it went into *Dark Shadows.* I first saw it as *The Innocents* as a play in some regional theatre in New Jersey, and it scared the hell out of me. I was always fascinated by it. Right after I saw the play, I read James's *Turn of the Screw* and was even more fascinated by it. Then, I saw Jack Clayton's *The Innocents* [1961], which I thought was absolutely brilliant, and I was still in love with the story. I thought if I ever got the chance, I would love to do my own version of it.[56]

In Essex, England, Curtis chose Hennick House to embody the novel's Bly House. He cast Lynn Redgrave as the governess — named Miss Jane Cubberly in Nolan's script — and Megs Jenkins herself as Mrs. Grose. Jenkins had played Mrs. Grose in Clayton's 1961 film with Deborah Kerr and Michael Redgrave (Lynn Redgrave's father), and Curtis could visualize no actress in the role other than Jenkins. For Flora (age eight in the novel and nine in the script), Curtis cast Eva Griffith, who had just appeared with Elizabeth Taylor and Richard Burton in *Divorce His / Divorce Hers* (ABC, February 6–7, 1973).

The only casting problem was the role of Miles (ten in the novel but fourteen in Nolan's script). Curtis hired Mark Lester, the star of *Oliver!* (1968), and he and his castmates began the two-week rehearsal period. Very soon, Curtis, Redgrave, and Jenkins saw that the 15-year-old Lester was not succeeding in the part and would have to be replaced. "Mark Lester could not play Miles," Curtis admitted. "It was a tragedy. He couldn't walk and talk at the same time. He couldn't play an upper-class boy. As sad as it made me feel — and it really did hurt me — I had to let the kid go."[57] Lester's last-minute replacement was the red-haired, quirkily talented Jasper Jacob, a 14-year-old who had appeared with Curtis's *Dorian Gray / Dracula* star Nigel Davenport in the 1972 BBC-TV miniseries *The Edwardians.*

As with *Jekyll and Hyde, Frankenstein,* and *Dorian Gray,* Curtis shot *The Turn of the Screw* on videotape. He had to use the early–1970s-era big, bulky cameras that barely fit into the rooms of Hennick House and were controlled by a mobile unit in a truck outside. "We didn't have anything back then," Curtis remarked about technology, but by ordering a special camera and a special dolly from the United States he managed to give *The Turn of the Screw* "that low-angle look that I always feel brings more intimacy and texture to the picture."[58] Curtis enjoyed having a chance to perfect the soap-opera-style, live-on-tape, in-camera editing he had learned when he directed 21 episodes of *Dark Shadows* in the late 1960s. Additionally, nine short scenes were filmed, not videotaped, for logistical or technical reasons. This mixture of film and tape was not uncommon in British television productions of the seventies (e.g. *Doctor Who; Blake's 7; Upstairs, Downstairs*). There was even one filmed exterior scene in Curtis and Lela Swift's otherwise videotaped *Dead of Night: A Darkness at Blaisedon* in 1969. Robert Cobert scored *The Turn of the Screw* (1974) with eerie music cues from *Dark Shadows* and *Night of Dark Shadows.*

William F. Nolan remembered that adapting Henry James's enigmatic novella was "difficult in that I had to 'extend' the material from a novelette to a two-night miniseries. I wanted to retain the mood and period atmosphere and to remain faithful to James's concept and characters. Apparently, I pulled it off because the critical reception to my teleplay was very positive."[59]

Nolan does remain faithful to the events of James's novel, from the governess's first-person narration to the overall authenticity of the characters' speech patterns to much of James's exact dialogue. For example, Miss Cubberly asks Mrs. Grose if Miles has the ability "to contaminate" or "to corrupt," James's words in chapter two.[60] Both on the page and on the screen, Mrs. Grose replies, "Are you afraid he'll corrupt *you*?"[61] Later, Nolan reproduces the governess's angry words to Miss Jessel in the schoolroom — "You terrible, miserable woman!" (Chapter 15)[62] — as, "You vile, miserable woman!" Later still, Nolan retains the governess's expression from Chapter 21 that Mrs. Grose's witnessing Flora's foul language "so justifies me"[63] in the governess's assertion that the ghost of Miss Jessel possesses Flora just as the ghost of Peter Quint controls Miles. Mrs. Grose admits, "I believe."[64] Finally, in a moment of foreshadowing, Nolan has Miss Cubberly say, "The boy's life — literally, his *soul* — was in my hands."

Since this TV production is a ghost story written for a master horror producer-director, Nolan, of course, makes the ghosts real. Because cinema and television are such visual media, all of the governesses in the 20-plus filmings of *The Turn of the Screw* since 1957 — Ingrid Bergman (TV-1959), Deborah Kerr (1961), Lynn Redgrave (TV-1974), Magda Vasaryova (TV-1982), Valerie Bertinelli (TV-1995), Leelee Sobieski (2006), et al. — have encountered more or less real spectres. Benjamin Britten's 1954 opera and William Tuckett's 1999 ballet also present *The Turn of the Screw* as the ghost story that it is — at least on the surface.

The straightforward, so-called "apparitionist" interpretation of James's ambiguous novel is that the ghosts constitute a real supernatural threat to the children — as they certainly do in Curtis's quite literal interpretation of two *Turn of the Screw*-like scenarios on *Dark Shadows* (in 1968–1969 and mid–1970) when first the ghosts of Quentin and Beth and later the ghosts of Gerard and Daphne haunt the children. However, the "non-apparitionist" approach, most famously promoted by the early-twentieth-century critic Edmund Wilson, maintains that the ghosts exist only in the governess's hysterical mind and are a manifestation of the sexual repression of this naïve, 20-year-old daughter of an austere parson.[65]

In James's novel, when the governess meets with the handsome, dashing uncle of the children and he hires her to care for Flora and Miles (with no further input expected from him), the young woman becomes infatuated with this romantic figure. In Chapter 1, she gushes, "I'm rather easily carried away. I was carried away in London!"[66] It is possible that the governess's overactive imagination invents the ghosts and publicizes them to Mrs. Grose as a ploy to lure the children's uncle back to Bly House so that she can see him again.

In Chapter 3, which features the first appearance of Peter Quint, the governess is strolling alone through the gardens of Bly and dreamily wishing "suddenly to meet someone" (like the distant uncle) along the path. She wishes that "someone would appear there at the turn of a path and would stand before me and smile and approve."[67] As if on cue, Peter Quint materializes. In Chapter 15, when the governess considers leaving Bly, Miss Jessel makes her dramatic appearance in the schoolroom — only the governess sees her, of course — and the governess realizes that she must stay and fight for the souls of Flora and Miles. As the novel progresses, the governess becomes more and more dogmatic, shrill, and "pressing" (James's word) in her crusade to force Miles and Flora to admit that they see the ghosts. Neither ever admits such, and Mrs. Grose never sees what the governess sees. Finally, the governess's pressure on Flora makes the little girl ill, and Mrs. Grose leaves for London with Flora. At the climactic moment when the governess presses Miles to acknowledge Peter Quint's ghostly face at the window, all the boy does is enigmatically mention Miss Jessel and then say, "Peter Quint — you devil!"[68]

The Turn of the Screw (1974): Lynn Redgrave as the governess and Jasper Jacob as Miles pose for a somber shot from the two-part ABC *Wild World Mystery.* *The Turn of the Screw* was screened at Tennessee State University in Nashville in March 2007.

before he dies of fright and exhaustion in the governess's arms. In life, and now perhaps in death, Peter Quint certainly has behaved like a devil, but was poor Miles calling *him* a "devil" or saying "you devil" to his *current* tormentor, the governess? Each reader must decide for herself or himself.

However, Nolan's script plays like the horror/ghost story that movie-and-TV audiences most often perceive *The Turn of the Screw* to be. Nolan increases the number of fleeting appearances of Peter Quint and Miss Jessel, and he climaxes part one of the two-night production with a recreation of the governess's encounter with Quint on the stairs. In the novel, each ghost appears four times. Peter Quint materializes atop the tower (Chapter 3), at the window (Chapter 4), on the stairs (Chapter 9), and again at the window just before Miles's death (Chapter 24). Miss Jessel appears at the lake (Chapter 6), on the stairs (Chapter 10), in the schoolroom (Chapter 15), and again at the lake (Chapter 20). In Nolan's teleplay, Quint appears — always only to Jane Cubberly —

at the base of the parapet atop which *she* is perched, then at the window, in a cemetery, on the stairs, again at the base of the parapet (in a scene reminiscent of one in *Night of Dark Shadows*), and finally on the stairs (instead of at the window) for the climactic confrontation with Miss Cubberly and Miles.

Peter Quint makes one additional appearance in a dream sequence scored to nightmarish music from *Night of Dark Shadows*. In Miss Cubberly's dream, the governess allows Quint to make love to her. Here Nolan is implying the governess's sexual repression. Meanwhile, Miss Jessel makes her customary appearances at the lake (twice) and in the schoolroom (once), but Nolan also places her in the clock tower (near a trunk of Quint's belongings) and in the reflection of a mirror. Interestingly, Miss Cubberly sees Miss Jessel in the mirror in place of her own reflection, suggesting that Miss Cubberly and her "corrupt" predecessor may not be as different as she wishes to believe.

Nolan augments the events of the novella with extra scenes in keeping with the spirit and realism of James's work. There are scenes of Miss Cubberly and the children in the schoolroom and on the grounds, roles for the groomsman Luke and his young son Timothy, and a disturbing scene in which Miles and Flora, under the evil influence of Quint and Jessel, perform an unsettling theatrical for Miss Cubberly and Mrs. Grose. Flora plays Edvard Grieg's funeral march on the piano, and she and Miles recite the boy's morbid poem about death. In another invention, Nolan acknowledges the topical nature of Curtis's recent *Dracula* (1974) by having Miles say,

> Miss Cubberly, I've been reading a book about a prince in the fifteenth century in Transylvania who employed a unique method of punishment. When someone displeased him, he ordered him stripped naked and impaled on a stake. He would often eat his dinners surrounded by his victims. Nasty fellow withal, wouldn't you say?

Nolan and Curtis's only two major deviations from James's novel occur at the very beginning and the very end of this adaptation. In the first scene, the children's uncle Mr. Fredricks is played unsympathetically by an older actor (John Baron), and Miss Cubberly does not fall in love with him. Instead of a starry-eyed infatuation, Cubberly's reaction is frankly a much more realistic one, especially in the minds of late-twentieth-century audiences. Love is the last thing on this governess's mind; instead, she expresses outrage over Fredricks's callous, unfeeling desire to ditch his niece and nephew with a stranger and never to be bothered with their care again, other than sending money. Miss Cubberly takes the job because she realizes that Flora and Miles need someone to care for them — and because she can relate to the children's situation since she does not remember her late mother and her parson-father is stern and distant. Nolan subtly updates the governess's motivations for contemporary audiences.

In the final scene — since this is, after all, an actual ghost story — Nolan has Miles speak more definitively and declare, "Yes, yes, yes, damn you, woman! You want to hear me say it? *Peter Quint is here!*" In a 2002 interview, Dan Curtis spoke even more concretely of his and Nolan's ending of the story. The director mused, "Did the governess lose the boy to Peter Quint? Did she win? When he actually died, was his soul freed? What was the meaning of it? What did Henry James have in mind? I had my feelings about what happened, and I wanted to tell the story my way." Curtis continued,

I knew it was a fight between the governess and Peter Quint for the soul of the boy, and I wanted to show that at the end when the boy was all alone in the house with her and Quint came to confront the governess and the boy. I put the governess at the top of the stairs, the kid in the middle, and Quint down below trying to draw the boy to him. The governess was telling him to turn his back on him and come to her. Finally, the kid turned and ran up the stairs to her, and she grabbed hold of him and held the kid in her arms. Suddenly, she looked, and it was no longer the kid. It was Quint, and he grabbed her head and smashed his lips onto hers. She screamed and pushed him back and pushed Quint over the railing and went to look. The thunder crashed, and the lightning lit up the room. She looked down there, and instead of the "body" of the ghost of Quint, she saw the little, smashed body of Miles. She ran down the stairs, and she knelt over him, and she started to cry, and we slowly started to pull back, and that's the way we ended it. I believe that what that that meant was yes, the kid is gone — the kid is dead — but his soul is saved. He didn't end up with Quint and the evil, infamous Miss Jessel![69]

Lynn Redgrave had her own memories of *The Turn of the Screw.* She recalled,

Dan Curtis is a larger-than-life character with a smile so broad, so extraordinary, that when he says, "You must do this," you think, "But of course!" He brings such enthusiasm to his projects. Boy, did he really get involved in this — so involved in the Henry James story, in where the location would be, in the costuming, in the whole thing of how to show the spirits of Quint and Miss Jessel, who were possessing the young children. It was wonderful working with him. All sorts of peculiar things happened because it was the seventies and we were on location, but he always somehow made sure that everything ended up okay.[70]

Once again, Curtis's efforts to adapt nineteenth-century literature met with critical approval. The *Los Angeles Herald-Examiner* wrote, "The Henry James story can still exert a magnetic pull, as witness the two-parter that will be screened by ABC tonight. The Dan Curtis production — he directed also — bears the glossy token of its English make. The acting has the glisteningly fine finish of the English period film."[71] *Variety* added,

Dan Curtis traveled to England to produce and direct William F. Nolan's tele-adaptation of Henry James's chilling *Turn of the Screw*, two-parter late-night version. Curtis brings off several interesting touches, such as [Megs] Jenkins's explaining the evils of the house to Cubberly — without being heard [by the viewers]. Or the frightening appearances of Quint — and the insinuations of evil by the children as they half-mock Cubberly. It should hold late-night viewers who want their goosebumps served large.[72]

Dan Curtis's 1968 and 1973–1974 adaptations of five great books reinvigorated classic horror and great literary characters for a new generation of television viewers. The productions were literate, mostly faithful adaptations of the texts, but they also succeeded in entertaining and *frightening* millions of viewers who knew that they could always depend on Curtis, Matheson, Nolan, Cobert, and company to deliver scares and quality.

Curtis's impressive literary adaptations did not end with this nineteenth-century quintet. The director's career also included adaptations of twentieth-century literature by Stanley Cohen, Jack Finney, Henry Kuttner, Robert Marasco, Richard Matheson, Jeff Rice, and, of course, Herman Wouk. Curtis even brought non-fiction books to television in his adaptations of *Intruders* (1992), *Saving Milly* (2005), and *Our Fathers* (2005).

"It's always better to have a script based on a book," Curtis declared, "because the material's there. The story is what it's all about. If you've got a story to start with, then that's great. But if the story doesn't work, then that's where everybody falls down flat on his ass."[73]

The Strange Case of Dr. Jekyll and Mr. Hyde (CBC, January 3, 1968; ABC, January 7, 1968). Producer: Dan Curtis. Director: Charles Jarrott. Teleplay: Ian McClellan Hunter (based on the novel by Robert Louis Stevenson). Music: Robert Cobert. Videotape consultant: Ron Meraska. Art director: Trevor Williams. Makeup: Dick Smith.
  Cast: Jack Palance (Dr. Henry Jekyll/Mr. Edward Hyde), Denholm Elliott (George Devlin), Billie Whitelaw (Gwenyth Thomas), Tessie O'Shea (Tessie O'Toole), Leo Genn (Dr. Hastie Lanyon), Geoffrey Alexander (Richard Enfield), Torin Thatcher (Sir John Turnbull), Oscar Homolka (Stryker), Rex Sevenoaks (Dr. Wright), Jeanette Landis (Liz), Lisa Creighton (Billie), Liz Cole (Hattie). 120 minutes.

Frankenstein (ABC, January 16–17, 1973). Producer: Dan Curtis. Associate producer: Tim Steele. Director: Glenn Jordan. Teleplay: Dan Curtis, Sam Hall, and Richard Landau (based on the novel by Mary Shelley). Music: Robert Cobert. Technical director: Gordon Baird. Art director: Trevor Williams. Makeup: Mike Westmore.
  Cast: Robert Foxworth (Dr. Victor Frankenstein), Susan Strasberg (Elizabeth Lavenza), Bo Svenson (Giant), Heidi Vaughn (Agatha DeLacey), Philip Bourneuf (Alphonse Frankenstein), Robert Gentry (Dr. Henri Clerval), John Karlen (Otto Roget), George Morgan (Hugo), Jon Lormer (Charles DeLacey), Brian Avery (Felix DeLacey), Malila Saint-Duval (Safie), William Hansen (Professor Waldman), Willie Aames (William Frankenstein), Leif Garrett (Boy), Bobby Eilbacher (Boy), Edgar Justice (Mayor). 126 minutes.

The Picture of Dorian Gray (ABC, April 23–24, 1973). Producer: Dan Curtis. Associate producer: Tim Steele. Director: Glenn Jordan. Teleplay: John Tomerlin (based on the novel by Oscar Wilde). Music: Robert Cobert. Technical director: Gordon Baird. Art director: Trevor Williams. Makeup: Mike Westmore. Dorian Gray portraits: John Solie.
  Cast: Shane Briant (Dorian Gray), Nigel Davenport (Lord Harry Wotton), Charles Aidman (Basil Hallward), Linda Kelsey (Beatrice Hallward), Vanessa Howard (Sibyl Vane), Tom McCorry (James Vane), John Karlen (Alan Campbell), Brendan Dillon (Victor), Fionnula Flanagan (Felicia), Dixie Marquis (Madame DeFerrol), William Beckley (Syme), Kim Richards (young Beatrice). 111 minutes.

Dracula (CBS, February 8, 1974). Producer: Dan Curtis. Associate producer: Robert Singer. Director: Dan Curtis. Teleplay: Richard Matheson (based on the novel by Bram Stoker). Music: Robert Cobert. Director of photography: Oswald Morris. Production designer: Trevor Williams. Makeup: Paul Rabiger.
  Cast: Jack Palance (Count Dracula), Nigel Davenport (Dr. Abraham Van Helsing), Murray Brown (Jonathan Harker), Penelope Horner (Mina Murray), Simon Ward (Arthur Holmwood), Fiona Lewis (Lucy Westenra), Pamela Brown (Mrs. Westenra), Reg Lye (Zookeeper), Sarah Douglas (Bride), Barbara Lindley (Bride), Virginia Wetherall (Bride). 100 minutes. (Originally scheduled to air on CBS on October 12, 1973, *Dracula* was pre-empted by President Richard Nixon's speech concerning the resignation of Vice-President Spiro Agnew. *Dracula* finally aired 17 weeks later on February 8, 1974.)

The Turn of the Screw (ABC, April 15–16, 1974). Producer: Dan Curtis. Associate producer: Tim Steele. Director: Dan Curtis. Teleplay: William F. Nolan (based on the novel by Henry James). Music: Robert Cobert. Director of photography: Ben Colman. Art director: Trevor Williams. Makeup: Paul Rabiger.
  Cast: Lynn Redgrave (Miss Jane Cubberly), Megs Jenkins (Mrs. Grose), Jasper Jacob (Miles), Eva Griffith (Flora), John Baron (Mr. Fredricks), Anthony Langdon (Luke), Benedict Taylor (Timothy), James Laurenson (Peter Quint), Kathryn Leigh Scott (Miss Jessel). 118 minutes.

CHAPTER V

The Kolchak Papers: *The Night Stalker* and *The Night Strangler*

The vampire Barnabas Collins was not the only iconic and influential character that Dan Curtis brought to the television landscape. The vampire *hunter* Carl Kolchak, a has-been investigative reporter, made another huge impression on the American consciousness when one-third of all U.S. TV households watched *The Night Stalker,* an *ABC Tuesday Movie of the Week,* on January 12, 1972. The telefilm aired between two of ABC's few hits at the time, *The Mod Squad* and *Marcus Welby, M.D.,* and it earned a 33.2 rating and a 54 share, representing 75 million viewers.[1] It instantly knocked *Brian's Song* (ABC, November 30, 1971) from the top spot as the highest-rated TV-movie ever, and it remained the number-one TV-movie for years. It stayed in the top five for more than three decades[2] and as of late 2008 is the fifteenth-highest-rated TV-movie in history.[3]

The intrepid, often annoying reporter Carl Kolchak had his genesis in a 1970 unpublished novel, *The Kolchak Papers,* by former newspaperman Jeff Rice. In 1963, Rice had worked as a copyboy for the *Las Vegas Sun,* where he had met an eccentric, temperamental reporter named Alan Jarlson. In 1966, Rice returned to the *Sun,* this time as a reporter alongside Jarlson. Both writers toiled under a volatile editor who fired Rice 14 times between 1966 and 1968. Before he left the newspaper business for a public-relations career, Jeff Rice was named the state's most outstanding journalist by the Nevada State Press Association.

In his professional travels through the newspapers, casinos, hotels, and big businesses of Las Vegas, Rice developed the idea for a novel about Las Vegas, a newspaperman, and a vampire. Rice had hit upon an innovation in modern horror. He would tell the almost documentary-style story of a vampire in a modern-day, believable setting — Las Vegas, the ultimate haunt of people who come alive at night! — as seen through the eyes of a down-on-his-luck, overzealous reporter. Rice regarded it as *Dracula* meets *The Front Page.* Rice wrote the novel in mid–1970 and completed the manuscript on Halloween night — just before midnight.

Rice patterned Karel Michail Kolchak, known as Carl Kolchak, after an amalgam of himself and Alan Jarlson; his inspiration for Tony Vincenzo, Carl's irascible editor

113

in the novel, was the real-life *Las Vegas Sun* editor for whom Rice had worked. Rice did not have immediate luck in getting *The Kolchak Papers* published, but it did catch the eye of television.

ABC optioned Rice's property and began developing it as a movie of the week. The network hired Everett Chambers (*Johnny Staccato*) to produce and John Llewellyn Moxey (*The House That Would Not Die*) to direct. Adapting the novel for television was Richard Matheson, the great fantasy author whose vampire novel *I Am Legend* (1954) was the most important vampire novel between *Dracula* itself (1897) and *Salem's Lot* (1975) and *Interview with the Vampire* (1976). Stephen King, author of *Salem's Lot,* often declared that the author who influenced his writing the most was Matheson. "Books like *I Am Legend* were an inspiration to me," he said. King, who dedicated his 2006 zombie novel *Cell* to Richard Matheson, added,

> He was the first guy that I ever read who seemed to be doing something that H.P. Lovecraft wasn't doing. It wasn't Eastern Europe — the horror could be in the Seven-Eleven store down the block, or it could be just up the street. Something terrible could be going on even in a G.I. Bill-type ranch development near a college; it could be there as well. And to me, as a kid, that was a revelation; that was extremely exciting. He was putting the horror in places I could relate to.[4]

A decade before his involvement with *The Night Stalker,* Matheson had been busy writing 14 memorable episodes of *The Twilight Zone* (1959–1964) and a string of 1960–1964 Vincent Price films (*The Fall of the House of Usher, Master of the World, The Pit and the Pendulum, Tales of Terror, The Raven, The Comedy of Terrors*). By the early 1970s, Matheson was dividing his time between movies, novels, and television. Between 1971 and 1980, Matheson wrote 12 made-for-TV movies (six of them with Dan Curtis as producer and/or director). Matheson's teleplay of *Duel* (based on his short story, in turn based on an actual 1963 event), as seen on ABC on November 13, 1971, had helped begin a young *Night Gallery* director's climb to the top of his profession: *Duel* was directed by 23-year-old Steven Spielberg.

Matheson had high praise for the fondly remembered *Movie of the Week* of the 1970s. "I've had more satisfaction by far from the television film," he admitted. "I'd rather write features because you don't have to worry about commercials and they pay a heck of a lot more. But I've had more creative satisfaction from television films."[5] In addition to *Duel* and his six collaborations with Dan Curtis, Matheson wrote the memorable TV-movies *Dying Room Only* (ABC, September 18, 1973), from his 1953 mystery story; *The Morning After* (ABC, February 13, 1974), a realistic examination of alcoholism; *The Stranger Within* (ABC, October 1, 1974), from his 1953 science-fiction story; *The Strange Possession of Mrs. Oliver* (NBC, February 28 & July 24, 1977), another suspenseful vehicle for Karen Black in the tradition of *Trilogy of Terror*; and *The Martian Chronicles* (NBC, January 27–29, 1980), a six-hour adaptation of the classic 1946 novel by Matheson's friend Ray Bradbury. Ten years later, Matheson wrote the acclaimed telefilm *The Dreamer of Oz: The L. Frank Baum Story* (NBC, December 10, 1990) and thereby launched a decade-long trend of partially factual, partially fanciful films about the lives and works of genre artists ranging from Charlie Chaplin (*Chaplin*, 1992), William Castle (*Matinee*, 1993), and Edward D. Wood, Jr. (*Ed Wood*, 1994) to Robert E. Howard (*The Whole Wide World*, 1996), James Whale (*Gods and Monsters*, 1998), and F.W. Murnau and Max Schreck (*Shadow of the Vampire*, 2000).

An accomplished and award-winning novelist himself, Richard Matheson was duly impressed when he read Jeff Rice's unpublished work, *The Kolchak Papers*. "It was quite a complete novel," Matheson remembered. "Don't make any mistake about that." He added,

> The story was all there, the structure was there, and that's what got everybody excited. It was sort of a *cinema verite* vampire story. It seemed so realistic. I'm reading this story, and it sounds like something that really happened. That's what makes it so remarkable, and that feel did come from the book. If you watch the movie and read the book, you see that all the basic story steps are in the novel.[6]

Matheson's Writers Guild of America Award-winning adaptation of *The Kolchak Papers* is extremely faithful to the source material, with only a few changes. Sam, the most prominent female character in the novel, is a Las Vegas prostitute and merely one of Carl Kolchak's street informants. Matheson changed Sam to Gail, kept her profession (involving "working nights") vague as per ABC's wishes, and made her Kolchak's girlfriend. The Karel Kolchak of the novel is a Rumanian-American who grew up hearing and believing vampire legends told to him by his Rumanian cabinetmaker grandfather. Matheson objected,

> If he starts out [believing in vampires], where can you go from there? Jeff Rice made him a smart-ass reporter, so I made him more of a smart-ass reporter who *finally* has to believe it. The other major change I made was to pick up on the *Front Page* humor in the book and emphasize it even more. The realistic approach and the smart-alecky sense of humor are what give the story an edge, so I decided to play it more like *The Front Page*.[7]

Audiences since at least the 1930s had been familiar with stories of newspaper life. The movies *The Front Page* (1931), *It Happened One Night* (1934), and *Nothing Sacred* (1937) featured wisecracking reporters and their tempestuous relationships with their volatile editors. In the subsequent decades, the Superman mythos revolved around several crusading reporters and their hard-to-please editor, Perry White. Meanwhile, Ben Hecht and Charles MacArthur's play and film *The Front Page* was remade as *His Girl Friday* (1940), *The Front Page* (1974), and *Switching Channels* (1988). Reporter characters also starred in *Foreign Correspondent* (1940), *Citizen Kane* (1941), *Deadline USA* (1952), *The Day the Earth Caught Fire* (1961), *The Reporter* (CBS, 1964), *The Name of the Game* (NBC, 1968–1971), and later *The Andros Targets* (CBS, 1977).

Thus, even before *All the President's Men* (1976) and *Lou Grant* (CBS, 1977–1982), audiences of the early 1970s were familiar with the concepts of competitive newspaper life and a crusading reporter-hero — but Carl Kolchak was a different kind of anti-hero. Darren McGavin had warmed up for a Kolchak-like character by playing a down-on-his-luck, second-rate private eye in his 1968–1969 NBC-TV series *The Outsider*. The actor made Carl Kolchak his own by insisting that Kolchak was Polish-American, not Rumanian-American, and by changing the character's prescribed wardrobe of Bermuda shorts, Hawaiian shirt, and golf cap to the now-iconic seersucker suit, straw hat, and white tennis shoes. McGavin observed,

Apparently, somebody thought that [shorts] was the uniform for a newspaperman in Las Vegas. But there was a line in the script about him wanting to get back to New York, so I got this image of a New York newspaperman who had been fired in the summer of 1962 when he was wearing a seersucker suit, his straw hat, button-down Brooks Brothers shirt, and reporter's tie, and he hasn't bought any clothes since. Well, I knew that was the summer uniform of reporters in New York at that time, so that's how the wardrobe came about. I added the white tennis shoes, and that was Kolchak. It might have been totally at odds with what everybody else was wearing in Las Vegas, but he hasn't bought any new clothes since then. You need goals for character, and Kolchak's goal is to get back to the big time. He always wanted to get back to New York and work on the *Daily News*.[8]

Instead, the hapless Kolchak of *The Night Stalker* finds himself toiling away at the *Las Vegas Daily News* under the oppressive thumb of editor Tony Vincenzo. Simon Oakland's contentious Vincenzo proved to be a powerful foil for McGavin's obnoxious Kolchak.

Just before the film's August 23–September 10, 1971, shooting schedule began, the picture gained a new producer: Dan Curtis. Original producer Everett Chambers left the project to produce his friend Peter Falk's new show *Columbo* (1971–1977), so ABC executive Barry Diller hired Curtis, fresh from *Night of Dark Shadows*, as his replacement. Curtis only produced and did not direct *The Night Stalker* because John Llewellyn Moxey had already been hired to direct. Nevertheless, as always, Curtis had a strong hand in the overall shaping, writing, direction, and feel of the project. Curtis remembered Rice's novel and Matheson's script as "a great story — so traditional yet so modern — and it had a sense of humor! It was a great premise waiting to be made into a great movie."[9]

The Night Stalker (1972): Darren McGavin stars unforgettably as Carl Kolchak.

However, Curtis hesitated to join the Rice/Matheson/Moxey endeavor because of the involvement of Matheson. Curtis maintained,

I thought Matheson was a bloody genius. I always wanted to work with him. So how could I *not* be sold by the combination of Jeff Rice's story and a screenplay by Dick Matheson? He's just a sensational writer, but I knew he didn't like me because of an offer I made on one of his books. He thought the offer was insulting, so I told Diller, "Matheson hates me," and I told him why. And Diller just said, "I don't care."[10]

Richard Matheson concurred that he had reservations about Curtis. Matheson explained,

> I didn't know that Curtis was going to do it. I had an antipathy towards Curtis from the beginning because when my war novel *The Beardless Warriors* came out, someone made a blind bid of $10,000 for the movie rights, which I turned down in a rage. It was ridiculously low. Then, I found out it was Curtis. So when I first met him at ABC, I was very cold to him. I didn't realize at the time that I was risking my life. He had such a temper that he could have leaped across the room and torn my throat out! And he might have if he hadn't respected my work so much. That was my main "in" with him although we did share a bizarre sense of humor. He just respected my work so much that he decided he wouldn't kill me.[11]

Indeed, Hollywood lore has Curtis lunging over a table at MGM's James Aubrey when Aubrey demanded drastic cuts in *Night of Dark Shadows* (1971). Curtis continued the story by remembering that Matheson was indeed a tough nut to crack upon their first meeting. Curtis recalled,

> Oh, yeah. Here's this bookish, reserved guy. So I figure I'll break the ice, and I tell him I think he's just the best writer in the whole world. And he just looks at me — nothing. He hardly talks to me. But as we go over notes for the script, he gradually loosens up. I think he liked some of my ideas and saw that I knew what I was talking about. And we went on to do a bunch of other things after that. I have nothing but respect for Dick. He's a wonderful writer with a wonderful, creative imagination — an imagination that worked beautifully with the kind of crazy stuff I was doing back then.[12]

The "crazy stuff" to which Curtis was referring turned out to be two Kolchak movies (1972, 1973), *Scream of the Wolf* (1974), *Dracula* (1974), *Trilogy of Terror* (1975), and *Dead of Night* (1977), all Curtis/Matheson collaborations.

If Curtis himself could not direct *The Night Stalker,* the film was in good hands with the British director Moxey. Before he relocated to America and the TV-movie market, Moxey had directed several 1964–1968 episodes of *The Saint* and *The Avengers* and such British features as *The City of the Dead* (a.k.a. *Horror Hotel* [1960], starring Christopher Lee), *The Face of a Stranger* (1964), *Strangler's Web* (1965), and *Circus of Fear* (a.k.a. *Psycho-Circus* [1967], again starring Lee). In 1969–1971 in the United States, just before beginning *The Night Stalker,* Moxey had helmed five episodes of *Mission: Impossible* and the TV-movies *San Francisco International, The House That Would Not Die, The Last Child,* and *A Taste of Evil.* In 1973–1976, after his Kolchak assignment, Moxey went on to direct *Genesis II, The Strange and Deadly Occurrence, Conspiracy of Terror,* and *Charlie's Angels.* Finally, he directed numerous late-1980s episodes of *Murder, She Wrote.* Moxey recalled,

> Actually, I was going to work with Dan on something else. One day, this story was there, and we were all excited about it. I read the Jeff Rice book on the beach, and I was pleased. I read Richard Matheson's screenplay, and I was more pleased. I always thought it was going to be a very special piece. The fun of it was the mixing of the humor and the horror. There was a lot of that in Jeff Rice's book. That was very much a part of the original concept.

Everybody understood that and elaborated on it—Richard Matheson's script, Darren's portrayal, the driving force of Dan Curtis as producer, my direction. There was a great deal of evolution, but we often referred back to the book.[13]

Moxey remembered that Curtis was very much a presence on the set but did not interfere. "He was very full of helpful hints. [*The Night Stalker*] had a very good script and an innovative and clever storyline [...] with well-drawn characters and a great cast. [Curtis] was the prime mover in bringing these first-rate people together, and everybody fit his particular role perfectly." Moxey remembered the stunt team as "wonderful" and the fight scenes as "still exciting today. [*The Night Stalker*] was very well publicized by ABC, and the promotion was well handled. There was a certain titillation about there being a vampire in Las Vegas. It tickled the imagination to read about it, and when people started watching, they stuck with it"[14]—to the tune of a record-high TV-movie viewership.

The success of the first Kolchak adventure is due not to critics, who barely previewed or reviewed it outside of Los Angeles, but to the tantalizing ABC promos telecast in early January 1972 and to the viewers who made it such a huge hit. *The New York Times* did not review *The Night Stalker* although it described the film in its TV listings as, "Newsman fights censorship, from his editor and the police, trying to prove that Las Vegas is being terrorized by a vampire."[15] In just those few words, the *Times* at least had hit upon what a multi-faceted movie *The Night Stalker* is. The refreshing mixture of humor, horror, newspapers, and *film noir* can be viewed as a reporter-fights-vampire thriller movie or as a reporter-fights-*censorship* message film.

The *film-noir* motif and the censorship theme make themselves known immediately when the movie opens on a lone man, down on his luck and inhabiting a seedy rented room. Like many *film-noir* anti-heroes before him, Carl Kolchak begins to narrate the film, albeit via a pre-recorded audiocassette tape—definitely a modern touch since cassette tapes were still somewhat new in 1971–1972. ABC's working title of the film had been *The Kolchak Tapes*. The reporter begins,

> Chapter One. This is the story behind one of the greatest manhunts in history. Maybe you read about it, or rather what they *let* you read about it, probably in some minor item buried somewhere in a back page. However, what happened in that city between May 16 and May 28 of this year was so incredible that to this day the facts have been suppressed in a massive effort to save certain political careers from disaster and law-enforcement officials from embarrassment. This will be the last time I will ever discuss these events with anyone, so when you have finished this bizarre account, judge for yourself its believability and then try to tell yourself, wherever you may be, "It couldn't happen here."

Kolchak concludes the film with those same final four words. Matheson, Moxey, and Curtis were struck by the "so traditional yet so modern" nature of Rice's story, and they successfully imbued the TV-movie with that double-edged sensibility. *The Night Stalker* has the feel of docudrama or, as Matheson characterized it, *cinema verite*. The film details an entire city government's investigation, along with one determined reporter's investigation, of the crimes of a real vampire. The movie showcases the inner workings of the Las Vegas Police Department, the district attorney's office, and the *Las Vegas Daily News* as all of those agencies face this outlandish threat. Even the Las Vegas coroner's office becomes involved via an unsettling autopsy scene from the point of view of the corpse. (At Matheson and Curtis's suggestion, Moxey's camera looks *up* at the medical examiners as they point their scalpels downward). Also, what could be more modern and *real* than the sight of a vampire driving a rented car?

Kolchak humanizes the vampire's victims— Las Vegas showgirls and cocktail waitresses walking alone at night — by listing in his narration the dead

The Night Stalker (1972): Darren McGavin (as Carl Kolchak) tries the patience of Simon Oakland (as Kolchak's irascible editor Tony Vincenzo).

women's names, ages, occupations, weights, dates and times of the attacks, and other vital statistics. These cold, hard facts add to the modern, clinical feel of the proceedings, as does the press conference which Kolchak attends and disrupts. Back in the newsroom, Kolchak's altercations with his volatile editor Tony Vincenzo set a serio-comic tone which lasts through all 22 original adventures of Carl Kolchak (*The Night Stalker, The Night Strangler,* and 20 episodes of *Kolchak: The Night Stalker*).

Another innovative technique is that *The Night Stalker* is not the story of a vampire *per se*, as is the case in such films as *Nosferatu* (1922), *Dracula* (1931), *Horror of Dracula* (1958), and *House of Dark Shadows* (1970). *The Night Stalker* (1972) is the story of a reporter — a regular type of guy — and the vampire is a secondary character. Plus the all-too-real notions of cover-ups and corruption are just as much the monsters of the story as is the vampire Janos Skorzeny. Kolchak defeats Skorzeny (played by Barry Atwater), but he cannot vanquish censorship or suppression of the facts.

The film has the ring of truth because it takes place in such a realistic setting, a modern American city. Whereas classic Gothic horror often derives its chills from castles, graveyards, and laboratories, modern horror often takes place in the ordinary here-and-now. *Psycho* (1960), *Rosemary's Baby* (1968), *The Exorcist* (1973), *Halloween* (1978), *Poltergeist* (1982), and *The Sixth Sense* (1999) are terrifying because their events could happen next door at any minute. Likewise, the events of *Jaws* (1975) or *Open Water* (2004) could happen on one's next trip to the ocean.

While *The Night Stalker* demonstrates what would happen if a vampire showed up in a real city like Las Vegas, the film also has a traditional side that ties it to classic horror. After all, the story is a vampire melodrama that climaxes in that most classic of vampires' lairs — an old, dark house — in this case, a dilapidated home the vampire

Janos Skorzeny has rented on an otherwise ordinary street on the outskirts of Las Vegas. The house, actually located near Echo Park in Los Angeles, was seen again in *When Every Day Was the Fourth of July* (1978).

All of the classic vampire trappings are present: Skorzeny's coffin (even with the added detail of the bloodsucker's native soil inside the casket); Kolchak's explanation of the rules of vampirism; Carl's crucifix, hammer, and mallet; the sunlight that stuns Skorzeny; and the obligatory staking scene. However, another reality check is that after Kolchak dispatches the vampire, he faces murder charges and must flee Las Vegas! Deciding that a vampire is "bad for business," the city officials have closed ranks, covered up the truth, and either paid off or run off everyone involved, including Kolchak. Again, this is what would probably really happen if a vampire invaded Las Vegas and threatened the status quo.

Another impressive touch is Robert Cobert's double-edged music — "detective jazz," as Cobert himself called it.[16] A detective show set to jazz music is nothing new — it dates back to Henry Mancini and his music for *Peter Gunn* (1958–1961) — but scoring a horror movie with "detective jazz" *is* something innovative. Cobert's theme for Carl Kolchak is a modern mixture of jazz and early-1970s funk while his background music accompanying the vampire's attacks on women and battles with police evokes a classic scary-movie sound, full of shimmering strings, shocking brass, and unnerving xylophones.

"It was spooky stuff," Cobert explained, "but it wasn't a *Dark Shadows* type of spooky. I mean, it was Las Vegas in 1971. That's the whole point. You need something that is spooky but contemporary — something with an edge to it."[17] This dichotomy of modern jazziness versus classic frightfulness perfectly captures the hybrid nature of *The Night Stalker*: realistic, scary; funny, shocking; irreverent, morbid; clinical, supernatural. At some points in *The Night Stalker*, Cobert overlays his horror chords onto his jazz beat for the ultimate effect. Later in 1972, composer Gene Page followed Robert Cobert's lead with a funky/scary score for *Blacula*. Michael Vickers did the same for the Hammer film *Dracula AD 1972*.

For many reasons, viewers who tuned in Carl Kolchak on that January 1972 night realized that they were watching something fresh and new. This writer-investigates-murders premise — a kind of *Murder, He Wrote* — would inspire a spin-off TV series and two future Dan Curtis movies (*The Norliss Tapes* and *Scream of the Wolf*) — as well as the tenacious reporter character played by Jack Colvin on *The Incredible Hulk* (1977–1982) and the paranormal paranoia of *The X-Files* (1993–2002) — but first the smash success of the Edgar Award-winning *Night Stalker* led immediately to *The Night Strangler* exactly one year later.

After the first film's amazing success, ABC clamored for a sequel, and this time, Curtis produced *and* directed Matheson's script. Darren McGavin and Simon Oakland reprised their roles of Kolchak and Vincenzo, now unluckily paired on the staff of the Seattle *Daily Chronicle*. Matheson noted, "We were still keyed up and in tune with the characters, and we had fun doing it. It was Dan's first directing job in a TV film, so he really poured himself into it to show what he could do. I added even more humor to it than we had in the first one."[18]

In the script, Vincenzo calls Kolchak someone who "looks like he just came from a road-company performance of *The Front Page*." Kolchak, in his narration, characterizes Vincenzo as "a bilious grouch." This time out, Kolchak and Vincenzo's noisy quarrels reach a fever pitch of bluster and comic timing. At one point, Kolchak breaks the glass window of Vincenzo's office — something novelist Jeff Rice actually saw *Las Vegas Sun* reporter Alan Jarlson do and which Rice documented in *The Kolchak Papers*. Indeed, for this second script Matheson adapted several incidents (the broken window, a sketch artist who draws a picture of the killer) and characters (a newspaper publisher, a college professor) from *The Kolchak Papers*, thereby building on what both he and Rice had written before.

Matheson's greatest dilemma in writing the sequel was deciding on what monster to use. What could top a vampire in present-day Las Vegas? Matheson decided that Jack the Ripper in present-day Seattle was the answer. The only problem was Matheson's friend Robert Bloch, the great *Weird Tales* writer and horror novelist.

Just as Jack Finney was a master of time-travel fiction, Robert Bloch was a specialist in all things Ripper. The author of the 1943 short story "Yours Truly, Jack the Ripper," Bloch often wrote stories and novels about the Ripper or Ripper-like killers with split personalities ("Enoch," "Lucy Comes to Stay," *American Gothic, Psycho*). Even his 1967 *Star Trek* script, "Wolf in the Fold," concerns a malevolent Ripper-like spirit which possesses people and forces them to kill (a plot appropriated by two 2006 episodes of *Medium*). Matheson did not want to step on Bloch's toes by using Jack the Ripper, so he telephoned Bloch and mentioned his idea of Kolchak meets the Ripper.

"I asked him if it would bother him," Matheson explained. "I could tell that it would — something about the tone in his voice. So I didn't do it."[19] Instead, Matheson and Curtis devised a different kind of legendary killer.

"Yeah, we worked our tails off on that story," Curtis remembered. "You know, a good sequel is hard to do. If you don't have a story that's strong enough, why do it? But with Richard Matheson, you're dealing with one of the best people in the business, period. I knew we were in good hands."[20]

Matheson was known for taking inspiration for his stories from real life. He wrote *The Shrinking Man* (1956), the story of the diminishing man trapped and forgotten in his basement, while he was living in his brother's basement. In 1971, he saw a photograph of the turn-of-the-century actress Maude Adams in a playhouse in Virginia City, Nevada, while he was on vacation with his wife and children. The enigmatic picture inspired him to write *Bid Time Return* (1975, later the 1980 film *Somewhere in Time*). That same momentous 1971 vacation included a visit to Las Vegas to watch John Moxey filming *The Night Stalker* along the world-famous Strip. Now Matheson recalled his family's 1970 vacation to Seattle and their tour of the Seattle Underground.

After the great Seattle Fire burned 31 city blocks on June 6, 1889, residents very rapidly rebuilt the downtown area — much faster than city officials implemented their plan to use landfills to raise Seattle's altitude to fend off encroaching high tides. Between extant buildings, the city built new streets as much as 36 feet higher than the ground floors of the buildings. Now, what used to be first- and second-floor windows looked out onto soil, debris, brick, or nothing, and the second or third stories of buildings became the new ground floors. Over time, Seattle forgot this eerie world of sub-base-ments as life went on high above. The underground floors were condemned in 1907 and abandoned (except for unsavory activities) until 1965 when entrepreneur Bill Spei-del began his popular Seattle Underground Tour, which starts in a restored 1890s saloon in Pioneer Square and winds its way through three blocks of subterranean labyrinths. Speidel and the saloon are glimpsed in *The Night Strangler.*

Matheson decided that the Seattle Underground would be the lair of the film's killer, a Civil War surgeon who has prolonged his life by concocting an elixir of longevity. Lest he revert to his actual age (as Barnabas Collins does in *House of Dark Shadows*), Dr. Richard Malcolm (played by Richard Anderson) must replenish his elixir with the fresh blood of young women every 21 years. Therefore, Seattle has suffered a spate of unsolved murders for 18-day periods in 1889, 1910, 1931, 1952, and now the present day of 1973. Thus, Carl Kolchak is back on the trail of a supernatural menace.

Matheson's original title for the sequel to *The Night Stalker* was *The Time Killer*, but ABC preferred the more famil-iar *The Night Strangler*. Dan Curtis filmed the movie over 12 days in Seattle and Los Angeles. The producer-director captured the local flavor of the Emerald City by showcasing Pioneer Square, the Seattle Under-ground, the Space Needle, and the city's monorail system. For decades afterwards, Seattle Underground tour guides still pointed out a loveseat prop used in *The Night Strangler* and dis-carded there. After *The Night Strangler*, the Seattle Under-ground was the setting for a 1975 episode of the cartoon series *Scooby-Doo*.

One unfortunate error in the film is that old newspapers from 1910, 1931, and 1952 report weird murders in "Pioneer Square," but that part of Seattle was not renamed Pioneer Square until 1970. Its actual name had

The Night Strangler (1973): Darren McGavin as Kolchak and Richard Anderson as Malcolm appear in a rare shot on the set of Dr. Malcolm's laboratory.

been Skid Row, a reference to the logging industry and how timber travels down water-filled tracks and *skids* to a stop at the bottom. Because Seattle's Skid Row was a disreputable part of town, the term "skid row" caught on as the name of any city's seedy area.

The Night Strangler (ABC, January 16, 1973) opens with Carl Kolchak's wry narration: "This is the story behind the most incredible series of murders ever to occur in the city of Seattle, Washington. You never read about them in your local newspapers or heard about them on your local radio or television station. Why? Because the facts were watered down, torn apart, and reassembled — in a word, falsified." Once again, an underlying theme is the people's right to know, and Kolchak is a noble crusader for that privilege.

This time, Carl's leading lady, though not his girlfriend, is belly dancer Louise Harper, who helps Kolchak locate Dr. Richard Malcolm in his underground laboratory. Jo Ann Pflug plays Louise with a mixture of intelligence and wackiness. Adding to the seriocomic feel of the film is the supporting cast of fondly remembered character actors: Wally Cox as an archivist, Al Lewis as a vagrant, Margaret Hamilton as a professor, and John Carradine as the *Daily Chronicle* publisher who orders Kolchak and Vincenzo out of town after he suppresses Kolchak's exclusive story of the 144-year-old murderer Malcolm. Instead, the noncommittal headline reads, KILLER FOUND — IDENTITY UNKNOWN.

It was with these two Kolchak movies that Dan Curtis began his practice of casting his personal-favorite character actors whom he remembered from classic movies and early television (a method directors Joe Dante and Fred Olen Ray used after Curtis). Curtis cast Elisha Cook, Jr. and Kent Smith in *The Night Stalker*, Carradine and the others in *The Night Strangler*, Hurd Hatfield in *The Norliss Tapes*, Clint Walker in *Scream of the Wolf*, Dale Robertson as *Melvin Purvis G-Man*, Gig Young in *The Great Ice Rip-Off*, June Allyson and Sid Caesar in *Curse of the Black Widow*, and dozens of familiar faces in the two *War* miniseries. Curtis explained,

All of these cameos came from my memory of movies when I was a kid. I remembered Scott Brady from years ago, and I got him to play the cop in *The Night Strangler*. He was so happy to play the cop, and I would say to him, "Hang

The Night Strangler **(1973): Darren McGavin as Kolchak and Al Lewis as "Tramp" pose for ABC publicity.**

around the set, Scott, and if there's anything else I can think of to stick you into, I'll do it." And he did it. He was always there for pick-up scenes in the picture because he would do anything just to be in the picture. I kept Scott around, and from that point on, Scott Brady became a part of my stock company. I used him in a million pictures. I loved him; he was great.[21]

Brady was the brother of Lawrence Tierney and a veteran of *film-noir* thrillers and early-TV anthology series. He went on to work with Curtis in *The Kansas City Massacre* (1975), *When Every Day Was the Fourth of July* (1978), *The Last Ride of the Dalton Gang* (1979), *Supertrain* (1979), and *The Winds of War* (1983). One year after *The Winds of War,* Joe Dante cast Brady in *Gremlins* (1984).

Dark Shadows actor Thayer David had remarked, "Dan Curtis, our producer, has the idea that people like to see a stock company of actors."[22] Having used David and the same repertory company of New York actors on *Dark Shadows* and in the two *Dark Shadows* theatrical films, Curtis continued his stock-company approach in his Hollywood productions. Just as Orson Welles before him, Robert Altman alongside him, and Joe Dante after him had done, Curtis populated many of his ensemble casts with the same proven, dependable actors. Dozens of actors made two movies with the director. Peter Graves, Jack Palance, and Dale Robertson each appeared in three Dan Curtis productions. George DiCenzo, David Dukes, Don Megowan, and Harris Yulin each appeared in four projects. Both Mills Watson and Orin Cannon appeared in five productions, and Scott Brady appeared in six. Curtis never forgot his *Dark Shadows* actors, either. Kathryn Leigh Scott worked with Curtis four more times, James Storm five more times, and John Karlen a record 13 more times after *Dark Shadows.* In his talk at the 2005 Dark Shadows Festival, Karlen quipped, "Dan knew a good actor when he saw one!" Horror-film critic Jonathan Lampley added,

It seems to me that the Curtis stock company suggested an organic world — a sort of "Earth-Curtis" — that adds a layer of familiarity to the proceedings and thus a degree of verisimilitude which is particularly useful in making fantasy films believable. Some younger directors (Tim Burton, Quentin Tarantino) seem to do the same thing.[23]

This time, many more critics sat up and took notice of *The Night Strangler* (viewed by 35 million TV households) and recognized a good movie when they saw one. The critics also noticed and commended the traditional/modern, scary/funny duality of *The Night Strangler,* a hallmark carried over from *The Night Stalker.* Kevin Thomas of the *Los Angeles Times* congratulated the sequel's "well-developed, amusing premise that places an old-style monster in a modern-day world coupled with genuine scariness, colorful characters, and sharp dialogue." Thomas continued,

Dan Curtis, creator of the long-running horror serial *Dark Shadows,* has directed zestfully as well as produced, and once again Richard Matheson, working from characters created by Jeff Rice, has come through with a lively script. McGavin is terrific, and so is Simon Oakland, [both] well supported by delectable Jo Ann Pflug.[24]

Howard Thompson of the *New York Times* wrote, "This made-for-TV thriller is a yeasty surprise, blending laughs, local color, and real chills."[25] *The Hollywood Reporter* concurred that *The Night Strangler* "achieves its purpose: it is flat-out scary as hell."[26]

Indeed, the newsroom hilarity, the Seattle travelogue, and the horrific climax in Malcolm's underground lair, full of cobwebs, test tubes, and rotting corpses, combine to deliver a realistic horror adventure equal to its groundbreaking predecessor.

Director Joe Dante (*Matinee*) observed, "I was a big fan of *The Night Stalker*, particularly the first two movies, and the second one, *The Night Strangler*, was surprisingly strong — much better than any sequel has a right to be. There were a lot of neat things going on in that,"[27] including the character actors' scenes, the newsroom bickering, the Underground tour, the belly-dancing scenes (somewhat risqué for 1973 television), Dr. Malcolm's aging via makeup by William Tuttle, Curtis's taut direction (an outgrowth of his two recent *Dark Shadows* movies) and the murder scenes ("staged," according to critic Howard Thompson, "with deep-freeze taste").[28] The movie even has a hint of lesbianism, played for laughs, as the quite mannish Wilma Krankheimer (Virginia Peters) jealously guards the beautiful belly dancer Charisma Beauty (Nina Wayne).

It is extremely rare that a movie sequel surpasses the original — Sam Raimi's *Spider-Man 2* (2004), Dante's own *Gremlins 2* (1990), Irvin Kershner's *The Empire Strikes Back* (1980), and Curtis's own *Kansas City Massacre* (1975) are arguable examples — but a case could be made that *The Night Strangler* (1973) is even better than *The Night Stalker* (1972). Of course, the sequel's now-familiar premise — tenacious reporter uncovers a supernatural threat, no one believes him, he vanquishes the threat, his story is suppressed, and he gets thrown out of town — is an intentional exact copy of the first movie's startlingly fresh scenario, but the fact that Kolchak and Vincenzo now have the history of the first movie behind them makes *The Night Strangler* even richer and more meaningful, especially in the scenes in which Kolchak discusses the Skorzeny matter with Vincenzo or Louise. Everything that was in the first movie, almost like a prototype, is fully developed in the second movie and ratcheted up a few notches. Kolchak's quarrels with Vincenzo are more boisterous, the humor is broader, the plot is more intricate, and Robert Cobert's "detective jazz" is even more aggressive in its use of saxophones and percussion for the upbeat theme, strings and vibraphone for scary interludes, and trumpets and muted trombone for weird effects. Cobert called his score "a combination of jazz and longhair music, with really wild harmonies."[29]

Most importantly, this killer is a much more well-defined character than the vampire was. Curtis noted,

> In most of my horror films, I try to find an additional dimension to the monster. Sometimes, you actually end up feeling sorry for him. We certainly did that with Barnabas Collins and Dr. Jekyll. In *Dracula*, I invented this whole past for him so you could see this once-great warrior. Now, that really wasn't possible for Janos Skorzeny, mostly because he doesn't talk and he's not on camera that much. And he's not the central character in *The Night Stalker*. Kolchak is. But that *was* more of a possibility with Richard Anderson's character. Let's see what makes him tick.[30]

Viewers learn Dr. Richard Malcolm's history, his motivations for his deeds, his ironic opinion of his own actions ("What's a few lives compared to immortality, Mr. Kolchak?"), and his hopes and dreams. After Kolchak destroys the last of his serum, Malcolm asks a poignant, "Why?" before he takes his own life.

Dan Curtis firmly believed that the two Kolchak movies hold up "perfectly" after more than three dozen years because of "the great storytelling." He insisted, "Great horror is all about story, and I will take this with me for the rest of my life: I've never come across a better story than *The Night Stalker*."[31] In 2004, Curtis lamented,

> Back in the 1970s, when the first television movies were being made, it was *fun* because the way you made a television movie in those days — the way you got one sold — was totally different than it is today. Today, the movie has to be "meaningful," it has to be "socially significant," it has to be filled with stars, it has to have — you name it. Come on! I get sick of the whole game, and everybody plays that game. To try to sell a television movie today is the most impossible thing in the world. The first thing they say to you is, "Well, we like the idea, but there's nothing *special* about it." It has to be "an event." Or, "How can we *sell* this picture? We wouldn't know how to *sell* this picture to the audience." In those days, the way it worked was I would go in to Michael Eisner and say, "Hey, Mike, I've got a great idea." I tell him a little story. He says, "Hey, that sounds great! Let's do it!" There weren't nine people that you met with; we would just *do it*. I had gotten in the habit of *every* script that we developed *got made*. I'd never heard of developing a script and then *not* getting it made. Today, scripts are developed and redeveloped and redeveloped some more and developed until they end up as absolute garbage! In those days, we had fun — *The Great Ice Rip-Off*, *The Norliss Tapes* — any kind of crazy little movie that we came up with — and you got these different stories. Quirky little stories, fun stories — they didn't have to be "an event." They just had to be entertaining, fun, good, scary, dramatic, whatever, and we made 'em fast, and we made 'em cheap, and it was a great period of time.[32]

Indeed, on the night of January 16, 1973, ABC belonged to Dan Curtis. *The Night Strangler* aired in prime-time, and after the local news, the first part of Curtis's two-night adaptation of *Frankenstein* followed. Just one month later, this time on NBC, Curtis was back on prime-time television with another "quirky little story" called *The Norliss Tapes*.

The Night Stalker (ABC, January 11, 1972). Producer: Dan Curtis. Director: John Llewellyn Moxey. Teleplay: Richard Matheson (based on an unpublished novel by Jeff Rice). Music: Robert Cobert. Director of photography: Michael Hugo. Art direction: Trevor Williams. Makeup: Jerry Cash.

Cast: Darren McGavin (Carl Kolchak), Simon Oakland (Tony Vincenzo), Carol Lynley (Gail Foster), Ralph Meeker (FBI Agent Bernie Jenks), Claude Akins (Sheriff Butcher), Charles McGraw (Chief Edward Masterson), Kent Smith (DA Thomas Paine), Larry Linville (Dr. Robert Makurji), Elisha Cook, Jr. (Mickey Crawford), Barry Atwater (Janos Skorzeny). 74 minutes.

The Night Strangler (ABC, January 16, 1973). Producer: Dan Curtis. Director: Dan Curtis. Teleplay: Richard Matheson (based on characters created by Jeff Rice). Music: Robert Cobert. Director of photography: Robert Hauser. Art direction: Trevor Williams. Makeup: William J. Tuttle.

Cast: Darren McGavin (Carl Kolchak), Simon Oakland (Tony Vincenzo), Jo Ann Pflug (Louise Harper), George DiCenzo (Tour Guide), Nina Wayne (Charisma Beauty), Virginia Peters (Wilma Krankheimer), Scott Brady (Captain Schubert), John Carradine (Llewellyn Crossbinder), Wally Cox (Mr. Berry), Al Lewis (Tramp), Margaret Hamilton (Professor Crabwell), Ivor Francis (Dr. Webb), Richard Anderson (Dr. Richard Malcolm). 74 minutes (later expanded to 90 minutes).

CHAPTER VI

In the *Night Stalker* Vein: *The Norliss Tapes* and *Scream of the Wolf*

After lightning struck twice with *The Night Stalker* and *The Night Strangler*, ABC and Dan Curtis wanted a third adventure for Carl Kolchak. Richard Matheson, busy with other writing projects, asked for help with the script from his friend and fellow fantasy author William F. Nolan (*Space for Hire, The Black Mask Boys, Logan's Run* and its sequels). Matheson and Nolan collaborated on an ill-fated teleplay called *The Night Killers*. Matheson revealed,

> It was set in Hawaii, and it was dandy, really dandy. I don't know why they didn't go ahead with it. It was a neat premise for the time. Key politicians were being killed off and replaced by look-alike androids. That was the basic idea. It was very fresh in 1973, but it has been used interminably since. It was a very funny, very fast script, and I tried to talk Dan into making it a number of times.[1]

Although Matheson, Nolan, and Curtis liked the script, Darren McGavin did not. The third Kolchak movie went into limbo at the same time that ABC and McGavin planned a weekly Kolchak series. Ultimately, Kolchak returned in the Friday-night series *Kolchak: The Night Stalker* (1974–1975), but Curtis and Matheson declined to participate. "Sure, they approached me about doing it," Curtis recalled. "I thought it was a bad idea. I didn't see how it could be done [week after week]."[2] The first of the 20 *Kolchak* episodes (ABC, September 13, 1974) pitted Kolchak against Jack the Ripper, an idea Matheson had rejected for *The Night Strangler*.

Just one month after *The Night Strangler* aired, NBC debuted its own Kolchakian character in *The Norliss Tapes* (NBC, February 21, 1973), a telefilm directed by Curtis and written by Nolan, who had met Curtis in June 1972 through his friend Matheson. In addition to his 1960s–1970s *Logan's Run* novels, Sam Space novels, and countless tales of science fiction, fantasy, and horror, William F. Nolan was the author of *How to Write Horror Fiction* and biographies of Charles Beaumont, Ray Bradbury, Max Brand, and Ernest Hemingway. Nolan's biography of Dashiell Hammett won the 1970 Edgar Award from the Mystery Writers of America.

Like Matheson, Nolan was an ideal collaborator for Curtis. "We have chemistry,"

Nolan confessed. "We operate on the same wavelength. Think alike. Laugh at the same stuff. Curtis can be thorny and doesn't get along with everybody, but he respects me, and I respect him, so we seem to hit it off."[3] After *The Norliss Tapes,* Nolan wrote or co-wrote *Melvin Purvis G-Man, The Turn of the Screw, Trilogy of Terror, The Kansas City Massacre, Burnt Offerings* (all 1974–1976), and *Trilogy of Terror II* (1996) for Curtis. For other directors, he co-wrote the 1975 TV-movie *Sky Heist* and the 1985 telefilm *Bridge Across Time,* another Jack the Ripper movie, later rebroadcast as *Arizona Ripper.*

Nolan adapted *The Norliss Tapes* from a story idea by novelist Fred Mustard Stewart (*The Mephisto Waltz, Six Weeks, Ellis Island*). "It had something to do with a walking dead man," Nolan recalled. "Beyond that, everything in the teleplay is mine. I wrote it without any references whatever to the Stewart story."[4] *The Norliss Tapes,* recalling the original title of the first Kolchak movie (*The Kolchak Tapes*), was the pilot for a series about a writer investigating the paranormal. Telecast on the heels of *The Night Strangler,* the film captivated the Kolchak fans who caught it, and it made a lasting impression — for decades a mythic one because *The Norliss Tapes* was never available on VHS and did not come to DVD until October 2006.

Roy Thinnes, already a cult favorite for his starring roles in the short-lived TV series *The Long Hot Summer* (1965–1966), *The Invaders* (1967–1968), and *The Psychiatrist* (1971), portrays David Norliss, a brooding author who writes books debunking the occult — "fake mediums, phony astrologers," and the like. However, Norliss is in crisis because his latest investigations have brought him face to face with supernatural forces all too real. He demands a meeting at his home with his editor Sanford Evans (Don Porter), but before the editor arrives, Norliss has vanished. All that is left is a stack of audiocassette tapes containing Norliss's narrations of the paranormal events he has witnessed. If *The Norliss Tapes* had become a weekly series, the lost protagonist might never have been seen in the present time — only in flashbacks dramatizing the events of each new cassette tape Evans plays.

In the pilot adventure, filmed in San Francisco, Carmel, and Monterey, Evans listens as Norliss's taped voice reveals how he aids Ellen Cort (Angie Dickinson), who is convinced that her recently deceased sculptor husband James (Nick Dimitri, in Fred Phillips's ghoulish gray makeup) has returned from the dead and is terrorizing

The Norliss Tapes (1973): Roy Thinnes (as David Norliss) poses for NBC publicity for the telefilm originally titled *Demon.*

Monterey. At one point, Norliss narrates a *Night Stalker*-esque scene in which a young woman, walking alone at night, is murdered. Claude Akins, who played Kolchak's adversary Sheriff Butcher in *The Night Stalker,* returns to portray Sheriff Hartley, a similar skeptic who blocks Norliss's investigation and who tells his men, "I'm putting a lid on this one." Clearly, Curtis and Nolan are mining the same Kolchakian vein.

Just as Las Vegas and especially Seattle were characters in their own right in the Kolchak movies, *The Norliss Tapes* creates a definite sense of place through Curtis's use of San Francisco scenery, a dramatic Pacific Coast highway bridge, and Carmel/Monterey local color. Watching a Dan Curtis movie inspires many viewers to want to visit Lyndhurst in Tarrytown, New York (*House of Dark Shadows, Night of Dark Shadows*); Las Vegas (*The Night Stalker*); Seattle (*The Night Strangler*); Monterey/Carmel (*The Norliss Tapes*); Yugoslavia (*Dracula, The Winds of War*); or Dunsmuir House in Oakland, California (*Burnt Offerings*) because they feel almost as if they have already been there. (Curtis's travelogue approach is in high gear in *The Great Ice Rip-Off* as the cross-country bus makes stops in Seattle, San Francisco, Carmel, Los Angeles, San Clemente, and San Diego.)

Another similarity between the Norliss and Kolchak movies is that the undead Cort's victims have lost blood. The terminally ill artist, who "was involved with the supernatural," made a pact with the dark gods that after his death he would return to life every night after sunset in order to sculpt a body for the demon Sargoth to inhabit. Norliss tells Ellen, "The clay mixture is 40 percent human blood." The zombified Cort has been draining women's blood to mix with his clay. That blood ultimately is his undoing, for just as Cort brings Sargoth to life, Norliss traps both creatures inside "a blood circle" and sets it on fire.

The film ends abruptly and unnervingly as Evans finishes listening to the tape and loads the cassette marked **2.** The first few words of a new narrative by the missing writer begin at the fade-out. These are the Norliss tapes left behind by a man now lost to the world of the occult. William F. Nolan added, "As a sequel to *The Norliss Tapes,* I

The Norliss Tapes (1973): NBC publicity for the TV-movie shows Bob Schott (as Sargoth) menacing Nick Dimitri (as James Cort).

wrote *The Return* for Dan, in which David Norliss moves through time to encounter his boyhood self. It was paid for but never scripted or produced due to a Writers Guild strike that killed the Norliss series."[5]

Still attuned to Kolchakian concerns, the critics took notice of *The Norliss Tapes*. *The Hollywood Reporter* wrote, "The movie is a lot of fun, with a new twist on the old vampire story."[6] *Variety* offered, "Curtis directed film with an eye to tension, and that he manages. The idea behind Nolan's script has validity, with its open dependency on the supernatural. The basic thrust, to scare, is what counts, and there Nolan, Curtis, Thinnes, and company succeed."[7]

The *Miami News* opined, "This program confirms one basic television truth: excellence in execution can be more important than mere originality [...] The professional, technical, and acting job reflected in *The Norliss Tapes* is a tribute to all those involved in its production."[8]

"People still talk about *The Norliss Tapes* all these years later," marveled Roy Thinnes, who worked with Curtis again on *Supertrain* (1979) and the 1991 *Dark Shadows*.[9] In a 2002 interview, Curtis laughed, "*Norliss* was supposed to be a pilot for a series. I just left everyone up in the air. When they didn't pick it up as a series, I laughed my ass off. What do I think happened to him? I have no idea."[10]

The Norliss Tapes, originally titled *Demon*, was definitely a product of its time — and not just as an imitator of *The Night Stalker*. Granted, the film was another mortal-investigates-the-supernatural drama, a TV trend which had begun in 1969 with the Guy Endore–inspired TV-movie *Fear No Evil* and Dan Curtis's own pilot *Dead of Night*, a.k.a. *A Darkness at Blaisedon*. Such 1970–1973 telefilms as *Ritual of Evil, Sweet Sweet Rachel, Moon of the Wolf, Gargoyles,* and *Baffled!* followed, as well as the 1972 ABC-TV series *The Sixth Sense*. After *The Norliss Tapes* and *Kolchak: The Night Stalker,* 1977 was another peak year for paranormal investigators in the TV-movies *Spectre, Good Against Evil, The Possessed,* and *The World of Darkness* and its 1978 sequel *The World Beyond.* Each owes a debt to the psychic investigators depicted in *The Haunting of Hill House* by Shirley Jackson (1959) and *Hell House* by Richard Matheson (1971).

This raft of similarly-themed TV presentations was a symptom of a larger trend: a late–1960s/early-1970s fascination with the occult, demonology, and the supernatural.[11] Between 1967 and 1977, readers made best-sellers out of such horror novels as *Rosemary's Baby* by Ira Levin, *When Michael Calls* by John Farris, *The Mephisto Waltz* by Fred Mustard Stewart, *The Green Man* by Kingsley Amis, *Hell House* by Matheson, *The Exorcist* by William Peter Blatty, *The Other* by Thomas Tryon, *Burnt Offerings* by Robert Marasco, *The Reincarnation of Peter Proud* by Max Ehrlich, *Salem's Lot* by Stephen King, *Interview with the Vampire* by Anne Rice, and *The Shining* also by King. Also popular in those same years were supposedly non-fiction works such as *The Satanic Bible* by Anton LaVey, *Real Hauntings: True American Ghost Stories* by Hans Holzer, *The Complete Art of Witchcraft* by Sybil Leek, *More Lives than One?* by Jeffrey Iverson, *Test Your ESP* by Martin Ebon, and *The Amityville Horror: A True Story* by Jay Anson. Plus, self-help books concerning astrology, numerology, self-hypnosis, transcendental meditation, ESP, and reincarnation flooded bookstore shelves. In the immediate aftermath of the sexual revolution, the Summer of Love, and the "God Is Dead" fad, some people were searching for mystical alternatives to organized Judeo-Christian religion. Horror fiction, metaphysics, and scary movies seemed to fill their needs. According to John Javna, author of the 1985 book *Cult TV*, "The sixties witnessed an increased interest in witchcraft and the occult. It was a pop phenomenon. *Time* and *Newsweek* did major stories on it, for example. *Dark Shadows* was the most successful mainstream exploitation of this fad."[12]

The Norliss Tapes also evokes the works of H.P. Lovecraft (prehistoric elder gods seeking to regain their power on earth, as in "The Call of Cthulhu" [1926] and "The Dunwich Horror" [1928]) and Dennis Wheatley (circles imbued with supernatural power, as in *The Devil Rides Out* [1935] *and The Devil and All His Works* [1971]). The film even invokes Egyptian mythology in Madame Jechiel's speech about Osiris and magic scarabs. Since interest in mysticism was at a peak in the late 1960s and early 1970s, these various occult themes were attractive to television audiences. Viewers had responded positively to the two Kolchak capers, and now they embraced Norliss's similar adventure with some of that same enthusiasm.

However, *The Norliss Tapes* is not merely a carbon copy of *The Night Stalker*. Two differences between the Kolchak movies and *The Norliss Tapes* are the leading men's performances and Robert Cobert's background music. Thinnes's Norliss is more laconic and respectable than McGavin's hyperkinetic, disreputable Kolchak, and Thinnes's portrayal of Norliss's shattered state just before his disappearance (what other horrors has he witnessed, and what made him vanish?) is as quietly frightening as the ghoulish Cort's rampages are bombastically scary. In *The Norliss Tapes*, composer Cobert eschews "detective jazz" for a more traditional horror score of strings, piano, staccato brass, xylophone, and bass clarinet, not unlike his *Dark Shadows* music cues. Shrill clarinets and urgent snare drums play an especially dire music cue.

All three films deliver thrills via wild encounters with the monsters. Just as scenes of the killers' battles with police are highlights of the Kolchak movies, the unforgettable moment in *The Norliss Tapes* is the scene in which Norliss intentionally hits the undead Cort several times with his car. Again, the traditional-versus-modern motif is apparent in *The Norliss Tapes* in that there are suitably creepy scenes set in a mausoleum and a tunnel — and shots of Cort's body in his coffin — yet this age-old terror is affecting another modern-day setting and is documented on audiotape by an anti-hero who apparently has *lost* his fight against the forces of evil. Screenwriter Nolan's innovative blending of zombie, vampire, golem, and Egyptian lore is a modern touch as is the film's nod to the demonology and downbeat endings so popular in early-1970s literature and film.

Perhaps the most significant difference between the Kolchak and Norliss vehicles is the total lack of humor in the latter film. While the Kolchak movies offer laughs along with frights, *The Norliss Tapes* is utterly serious and somber — perhaps too much so for mainstream audiences, who could not easily relate to or care about an absentee protagonist who delivers melancholy pre-recorded narratives from somewhere in his own, supernatural lost weekend. Kolchak and his formula are active while Norliss and his formula are passive. However, each excels in depicting a lone outsider as a crusader against societal evil. Kolchak and Norliss can be seen as metaphors for medieval reli-

gious reformers, post-war *film-noir* loners, or 1970s-era anti–Establishment maver-
icks — another broad sweep from traditional to modern to ultra-mod.

Dan Curtis exploited his own writer-investigates-murders sub-genre one last time
in *Scream of the Wolf* (ABC, January 16, 1974), telecast one year to the day after *The
Night Strangler*. Richard Matheson once again wrote the teleplay, this time from the
1969 short story, "The Hunter," by David Case, author of *Fengriffin* (1970). This movie's
picturesque setting is Malibu, California, where John Weatherby (Peter Graves) has
traded his big-game-hunting days for a more leisurely life as a men's-adventure novelist. Weatherby's girlfriend is Sandy (Jo Ann Pflug, playing a totally different type than
her wacky Louise in *The Night Strangler*). Living near Weatherby is his old friend Byron
Douglas (Clint Walker), a troubled, reclusive big-game hunter.

The strangely nonchalant Byron is more concerned with hunting, arm-wrestling,
and other manly pursuits than with the series of brutal, wolfen murders happening
around town. In a change from the Kolchak adventures, all but one of the six victims
are male. Sheriff Bell (Philip Carey) asks for Weatherby's help in the investigation after
Byron gives Bell the brush-off. "The tracks go from four feet to two feet to nothing,
period!" a baffled Weatherby observes — almost as if the wolf-like creature begins walking upright and gains enough human-like sentience to begin covering his tracks.

In a change from Claude Akins's skeptical-sheriff characterization, Sheriff Bell is
just as eager to solve the mystery — whatever it turns out to be — as Weatherby, who
begins to wonder if an actual werewolf is stalking the woods. In a nod to the two *Night
Stalker* movies, Bell and city officials hold a press conference, which a heckling reporter
not unlike Carl Kolchak disrupts. However, in another switch the local newspaper
freely prints the headline, "WEREWOLF" KILLER STILL AT LARGE. This is one
of Matheson's clever red
herrings to lull the audience into the belief that a
real werewolf is the cul-
prit.

Curtis films the mur-
ders with his usual quick
takes, low angles, and dark
shadows, as well as quite a
few zoom shots (popular
in genre filmmaking at the
time). Robert Cobert sup-
plies suitably tense, eerie
background music (plus a
funky main title). The
most memorable scene in
Scream of the Wolf is a
staple of the 1970s-era
woman-in-jeopardy TV-
movie. The creature's

Scream of the Wolf (1974): Phil Carey (left, as Sheriff Bell),
JoAnn Pflug (as Sandy), and Peter Graves (as John) discuss
the "werewolf" killings.

frenzied chase of Sandy through her house is a precursor to Curtis and Matheson's perfection of that scenario one year later in Karen Black's tour-de-force dash through her apartment with the Zuni fetish doll literally on her heels in *Trilogy of Terror*. Sandy survives the attack but is convinced that Byron, who was bitten by a wolf in Canada, is to blame. The hunter's only response is, "In a way, these killings may be of benefit to everybody."

Matheson has a few more twists in store in this underrated, almost-forgotten telefilm now relegated to public-domain DVDs. Weatherby finds a mangled corpse wearing Byron's clothes and believes the sixth and final victim to be his old friend. However, the dead man actually is Byron's mysterious live-in manservant Grant (Don Megowan), until now a possible suspect as the wolfman. Ultimately, Weatherby finds Byron alive and learns that the hunter has been turning a vicious, trained attack dog on the victims and then adding his own decorative touches to suggest weird footprints and werewolf attacks. "I gave him a little help with windshields and doors," the insane Byron boasts.

Byron's twisted motivation for the killings is his strange, almost lovesick obsession with Weatherby, his old hunting buddy. Byron resents how John's writing career and his girlfriend Sandy have softened him, "emasculated" him, and distracted him from the two men's glory days of hunting together and conquering their prey. In terms of berating John's professional and personal choices, Byron is Dr. Praetorius to John's Dr. Frankenstein in *The Bride of Frankenstein* (1935). Now, Byron forces John to hunt the attack dog and Byron himself— or else Byron will claim John as his kill.

Here, *Scream of the Wolf* evokes a literary cornerstone as it takes a page from Richard Connell's "The Most Dangerous Game," one of the most famous short stories in American literature. Written in 1924, this human-hunts-human story has been filmed at least once in each decade from the 1930s to the 1980s (as *The Most Dangerous Game, A Game of Death, Run for the Sun, Bloodlust, The Woman Hunt, Savages, Slave Girls from Beyond Infinity, Deadly Prey, Lethal Woman,* et al.). In television plotting, the scenario is an oft-used

Scream of the Wolf (1974): Clint Walker (as Byron) reveals his plan to hunt Peter Graves (as John) in Dan Curtis and Richard Matheson's updating of "The Most Dangerous Game." At Dan Curtis's memorial service, Matheson remarked, "Dan's firebrand temper was never directed at me."

stand-by (along with having to land an airplane, going on a game show, becoming trapped somewhere, winning the Big Game, etc.). Television series from *The Man from U.N.C.L.E.* (1964–1968) and *The Incredible Hulk* (1977–1982) to *Hart to Hart* (1979–1984) and *Falcon Crest* (1981–1990) have featured episodes in which crazed hunters hunt the leading characters. More recently, the hostile actions of The Others on *Lost* (debuted 2004) suggest Connell's people-hunting-people idea.

Thus, at the same time that *Scream of the Wolf* deviates from the newly minted Kolchak/Norliss tradition of actual supernatural menaces, it embraces one of the most traditional, old-chestnut stories. Then, the classic-horror scenario of the rampaging werewolf gives way to a more modern twist: it is a hoax (as in *Diabolique* [1955], *House on Haunted Hill* [1958], and *The Village* [2004], which go against the Gothic-horror tradition). The all-too-human adversaries, John and Byron, must fight each other to the death as in Connell's classic story of the hounds of Zaroff.

As if the film's wolfen attacks are not disturbing enough, another unnerving element — for 1974 audiences, at least — is the homosexual undercurrent in Byron and John's relationship. Clint Walker, the macho star of *Cheyenne* (1955–1963), plays against type as a hypermasculine heavy who met his future manservant Grant "in a bar" where they "arm-wrestled" each other. Byron resents how John has drifted away from him, and Sandy dislikes Byron's attention to John and does not want John to spend time with him. When Byron challenges John to a one-minute game of arm-wrestling, Byron asks, "Can't you even hold me for a minute now?" Instead of mixing horror and humor as before, Matheson modernizes this horror tale with innuendo and poignance. This time, Byron is the lonely outsider, and he finds the investigative writer and the intrepid sheriff opposing *him*. The film's alien other was expected to be a Dan Curtis-brand werewolf, but the otherized figure turns out to be much more realistic and common-place. Even in an *ABC Movie of the Week* programmer like this, Matheson's writing and Curtis's direction craft several layers of meaning. *Scream of the Wolf* can be viewed as a werewolf thriller, a mystery/crime drama hinging on a hoax, or even a film about relationships. Byron's elaborate artifice with the killings symbolizes a more personal masquerade he must maintain. One year later, Curtis, Matheson, and Nolan explored psychosexual themes again in their 1975 triumph *Trilogy of Terror*.

Peter Graves, who went on to work with Dan Curtis in both *War* miniseries, remembered,

> His directing style was his marvelous imagination because he knew exactly what he wanted to see on the screen and how to achieve it. If he got it nicely and quietly, that was wonderful, but if he didn't, he got it noisily — and he had a short fuse. But it was wonderful because if he blew it, it was for a very good purpose, and the whole pictures and the actors came out better for that happening.[13]

Graves realized that whether Curtis was working on a relatively minor movie of the week or on one of the greatest epics in television history, the director demanded perfection — and got it.

The Norliss Tapes (NBC, February 21, 1973). Executive producer: Charles Fries. Producer: Dan Curtis. Director: Dan Curtis. Teleplay: William F. Nolan (from a story by Fred Mustard Stewart). Music: Robert Cobert. Director of photography: Ben Colman. Art direction: Trevor Williams. Makeup: Fred Phillips.

Cast: Roy Thinnes (David Norliss), Don Porter (Sanford Evans), Claude Akins (Sheriff Tom Hartley), Angie Dickinson (Ellen Sterns Cort), Nick Dimitri (James Cort), Hurd Hatfield (Charles Langdon), Vonetta McGee (Madame Jechiel), Michele Carey (Marsha Sterns), Bob Schott (Sargoth). 72 minutes.

Scream of the Wolf (ABC, January 16, 1974). Executive producer: Charles Fries. Producer: Dan Curtis. Director: Dan Curtis. Teleplay: Richard Matheson (from a story by David Case). Music: Robert Cobert. Director of photography: Paul Lohmann. Art direction: Walter Simon. Makeup: Mike Westmore.

Cast: Peter Graves (John Weatherby), Clint Walker (Byron Douglas), Jo Ann Pflug (Sandy), Philip Carey (Sheriff Vernon Bell), Don Megowan (Grant), Brian Richards (Deputy Charlie Crane), Bill Baldwin (Reporter). 74 minutes.

CHAPTER VII

A Trilogy of Trilogies of Terror:
Trilogy of Terror, Dead of Night, and *Trilogy of Terror II*

The stories of Richard Matheson were well represented on CBS-TV's landmark anthology series *The Twilight Zone* (1959–1964). Rod Serling adapted two of Matheson's short stories, Matheson himself adapted six of his tales, and he wrote eight scripts original to *The Twilight Zone* (including "Nick of Time" starring William Shatner, "The Invaders" starring Agnes Moorehead, and "Once Upon a Time" starring Buster Keaton). In 1971 and 1972, Matheson wrote adaptations of his stories "The Funeral" (starring Werner Klemperer) and "The Big Surprise" (starring John Carradine) for NBC-TV's *Night Gallery,* as well. Several years later, Dan Curtis filmed a half-dozen of Matheson's stories for anthology projects televised in 1975 and 1977.

Trilogy of Terror (ABC, March 4, 1975) stars an Emmy-worthy Karen Black as four different women in three stories of psychological horror. "That's a classic," Curtis declared.[1] Black agreed that *Trilogy of Terror* "is a little legend all to itself. It's one of the films I'm most remembered for because there is a lot of me in it."[2]

Curtis developed *Trilogy in Terror* (its pre-production title) for ABC after Matheson offered Curtis some short stories, including "Prey." Matheson remembered, "Nolan adapted two of my stories for *Trilogy of Terror,* and they were not easy stories to adapt. He did a wonderful job with them. And how did I reward him? Being the mean guy that I am, I kept the best story for myself, and that's the one everyone remembers!"[3]

William F. Nolan concurred, "My two stories were totally eclipsed by Matheson's 'Prey,' featuring that evil little doll. That's the one that everybody remembers. It made a terrific impact."[4]

The first story of the trilogy is "Julie," based on Matheson's 1962 short story "The Likeness of Julie" (anthologized in *Alone by Night* and *Shock II*) and adapted by Nolan. Julie Eldridge (Karen Black) is a seemingly shy, mousy English professor who exerts an unexplained, wicked influence over a series of her male students, including Chad Foster (Robert "Skip" Burton). "I didn't really want to do *Trilogy of Terror,*" Black confessed. She continued,

But what happened was the guy who portrayed the student to my teacher was really my husband [Burton]. So I said that I would do it if he would play that part. Otherwise, I really didn't want to do it. What really interested me was that I got to play an older spinster. I knew that it would be many years until I would be asked to do that. You see, I have very small eyes. They're close-set. I thought it would be interesting to play the spinster because I knew I could wear these far-sighted glasses which are like magnifying glasses for the eyes. Also, I wouldn't wear any eye makeup so I could look older and not glamorous. Playing that character is really what interested me, and that's all. The manager I had at that time [Lyle Sudrow] came to my house and sat there in my living-room chair all night saying, "I want you to do this." He really used to talk me into doing stuff, and I still didn't want to do it. Finally, around four o'clock in the morning, I said, "Okay, I'll do it!" So I did it, and they put my husband in the part.[5]

In Matheson's short story, Eddy Foster and Julie Eldridge are both college students. In Nolan's "Julie" teleplay, Chad Foster is a libidinous student, but Julie Eldridge is his prim, overdressed professor of literature. Seeing his teacher meekly carrying her books across the campus, Chad muses, "I just got the weirdest idea: I wonder what she looks like under all those clothes." He admits, "It's kind of like the idea just jumped into my head." According to Matheson's story, "As he watched, the thought came suddenly to him. *Take her.* [...] He had to have her."

> Why? He asked himself the question endlessly, but no logical answer ever came. Still, visions of her were never long out of his mind — the two of them locked in a cabin at the Hiway Motel, the wall heater crowding their lungs with oven air while they rioted in each other's flesh.[6]

In Nolan's teleplay, Chad watches Julie's every move in class and peeks in her windows at night. Finally, he asks his teacher out on a date to a drive-in where "a wonderful old vampire movie" is playing (actually, it is Curtis's own modern classic, *The Night Stalker*). The obsessed young man drugs Julie's soft drink and drives her to the motel. In Matheson's words, "To guarantee his safety afterward, he'd take photographs of her."[7]

Both Matheson's story and Nolan's teleplay are a terrifying study in scopophilia (Sigmund Freud's term for voyeuristic, pleasurable *looking* at people without their knowledge). Matheson's description of the kidnapping, photographing, and raping of Julie demonstrates the power that the student believes that he has over her.

> In falling to the bed, her skirt had pulled up to her thighs. He could see the tops of her stockings and the garter buttons fastened to them. Swallowing, Eddy sat down and drew her up into a sitting position. He took her sweater off. Shakily, he reached around her and unhooked her bra; her breasts slipped free. Quickly, he unzipped her skirt and pulled it down.
>
> In seconds, she was naked. Eddy propped her against the pillows, posing her. *Dear God, the body on her.* Eddy closed his eyes and shuddered. *No,* he thought, this is the important part. First, get the photographs, and you'll be safe. She can't do anything to you then; she'll be too scared. He stood up tensely and got his camera.[8]

Thinking that he has all of the power in this relationship, Chad uses his nude photographs of Julie to force her into sexual submission. However, weeks later over drinks Julie announces to Chad that she is "bored" with their arrangement. The story's twist is that Julie is a kind of succubus who has preyed on *many* male students' minds and bodies over the years and then arranged for them to die in apparent fires or falls when they ceased to amuse her. It was Julie who somehow put lascivious thoughts of herself into Chad's mind so that *she* could dominate *him*. "You drugged me!" Chad gasps. "No, dear," Julie glibly replies, "I've *killed* you." The story ends when Julie begins tutoring a new male student. As Matheson's short story concludes,

> Posing at the window, the drugged Coke, the motel photographs — these were getting dull by now although that place in the woods was wonderful. Especially in the early morning with the mist outside, the car like an oven. That she'd keep for a while — and the violence, of course. The rest would have to go. She'd think of something better next time.[9]

Until the tables turn, this segment of *Trilogy of Terror* is a shocking statement about the objectification and victimization of women. Chad's fantasies of Julie lead to his numerous crimes against her — many of which he photographs just like the murderer (played by Carl Boehm) who makes his own snuff movies in Michael Powell's 1960 film *Peeping Tom*.

Several months after *Trilogy of Terror* aired, film critic Laura Mulvey's groundbreaking article, "Visual Pleasure and Narrative Cinema," was published in the autumn 1975 issue of *Screen*. Written in 1973, the essay introduces Mulvey's concept of the "male gaze" which she claims is predominant in cinema. Because the vast majority of filmmakers are male, Mulvey asserts, visual pleasure in film can come only from the male-centered narrative form. In many movies, men are the active protagonists, and women are looked upon as their passive wives, girlfriends, servants, whores, or victims. As the male-driven camera gazes (often lecherously) at the woman, she becomes an object of either fetishism or sadism. Women have no real viewpoint of their own in film because the male-oriented filmmaking system reduces them to mere objects to be worshiped, denounced, punished, destroyed, or saved.[10]

Mulvey's suggested antidote to this cinematic disempowerment of women is to make self-reflexive films that deliberately expose and denounce male scopophilia to viewers.[11] Her own films — *Penthesiliea: Queen of the Amazons* (1974), *Riddles of the Sphinx* (1977), *Amy!* (1980), *Crystal Gazing* (1982), *The Bad Sister* (TV-1983), *Disgraced Monuments* (1996), and others (some of them co-directed by her husband Peter Wollen) — seek to counteract traditional cinematic methods of filming women. In her 1984 essay "When the Woman Looks," film critic Linda Williams adds that the aforementioned *Peeping Tom* (1960) accomplishes what Mulvey proposes a feminist film should do, i.e. expose and indict the male scopophiliac gaze.[12]

William F. Nolan's "Julie" teleplay serves this same purpose. Dan Curtis's direction and Paul Lohmann's camera explicitly portray Chad's male gaze, first in his sexual fantasies (showing Karen Black ravished on a bed), then in his actual picture-taking, then in his rape of Julie, and finally in his heartless blackmail-and-domination scheme. However, the script and later Julie expose Chad for the creep that he is (and was, even before Julie's psychic prodding). Chad gets his comeuppance, and then the film offers the *female* gaze of Julie's pleased appraisal of her scrapbook of obituary clippings of her accident-prone former students. Finally, her eyes behold her new student, Arthur Moore (played by a young Gregory Harrison), and her power play begins again.

The second segment of *Trilogy of Terror* is "Millicent and Therese," based on Matheson's short story "Needle in the Heart," (published in the October 1969 issue of *Ellery Queen's Mystery Magazine*) and adapted by Nolan. Millicent and Therese Lorimor (both Karen Black) are vastly different sisters who uneasily share their childhood home after the death of their father. Nolan retains the feel of Matheson's epistolary short story by having the prim, proper, brown-haired Millicent write entries in her diary about Therese, her blonde, libertine, immoral sibling. "My sister is evil," Millicent tells Mr. Anmar (Curtis mainstay John Karlen), a character Nolan creates as an example of someone whom Therese has ruined by drawing him into her sadomasochistic sexual practices.

Millicent tells Anmar that when her sister was 16, Therese "seduced" their father, as both father and daughter reveled in their readings in "demonology, pornography, Satanism, voodoo, [and] witchcraft" in their home library. As the scandalized Millicent of Matheson's story writes, "I shall burn the books after I have killed Therese!"

> Thank God our mother died before he started to collect them. Vile man that he was, Therese loved him to the end, of course. She is just like him really — brutish, carnal, and disgusting. I should not be at all surprised to learn that she shared his bed as well as his interests. Oh, God, I will sing a hymn of joy the day she dies![13]

Millicent finds her opportunity to kill her wicked sister when she runs across the book *Voodoo: An Authentic Study.* (Nolan's more sensational title is *Voodoo Rites and Satanism.*) Millicent constructs a voodoo doll sprinkled with Therese's belongings and pierces it with a needle. Later, Dr. Ramsay (George Gaynes), the woman's psychiatrist, finds Therese dead. Removing her blonde *wig*, Ramsay muses, "Hers was a hopeless situation. Millicent Therese Lorimor suffered from the most advanced case of dual personality it has ever been my misfortune to observe."

While Matheson's story suggests that Millicent perhaps only assumes that her sister and their father were having sex, Nolan's teleplay makes the incest a fact. The script's references to incest, sadomasochism, homosexuality, and pornography caused ABC to issue a parental-discretion advisory for *Trilogy of Terror.* What *both* Matheson and Nolan leave the audience to ponder is whether Millicent/Therese seduced Mr. Lorimor or he seduced her. The latter scenario is much more likely and is the probable reason Millicent's psyche split into the pure, pious (although murderous) Millicent and the wild, nymphomaniacal Therese. In order to solidify her existence as the wholly righteous Millicent, she has demonized her version of the totally sinful Therese to the point that Therese *must* have seduced her father and not vice versa. This advanced case of Dissociative Identity Disorder is never remedied before one "sister" dies at the hands of the "other" sister, empowered with voodoo. Is voodoo real? Perhaps it is, but if Millicent/Therese's mind is powerful enough to create two separate personalities, it is probably powerful enough to cause the death of one of them. (Two years later, Karen Black played essentially the same role — a woman with two personalities — in Gordon Hessler's TV-movie *The Strange Possession of Mrs. Oliver* [NBC, February 28 and July 24, 1977], another Richard Matheson story.)

Trilogy of Terror ends with a bang with the classic "Amelia," Matheson's own adaptation of his short story "Prey" (published in the April 1969 issue of *Playboy*). Karen

Black is the only human being seen in this half-hour segment. It can be considered a descendant of "The Invaders," Matheson's similar *Twilight Zone* episode (January 27, 1961), which pits Agnes Moorehead against a tiny invading spaceman.

Amelia is an unhappy, mother-dominated woman who seeks to make a life for herself by moving away from home and dating a gentleman friend. Her friend Arthur, Amelia tells her mother on the phone, is "an anthropology professor at City College." For his birthday Amelia has bought him He Who Kills, a ferocious-looking Zuni warrior fetish doll. Soon the Zuni doll comes to life and stalks Amelia through her highrise apartment. As if the scenes of Amelia's life-and-death struggle with the doll are not memorable enough, the film's final image is the stuff of TV legend. After Amelia succeeds in burning up the doll, the spirit of the Zuni warrior that inhabited the doll enters *her* body. With wild hair, crazed eyes, and jagged teeth, the possessed woman brandishes a knife and lies in wait for her mother. "Then," according to Matheson's story, "she sat down, cross-legged, in the corner. He Who Kills sat, cross-legged, in the corner, in the darkness, waiting for the prey to come."[14]

With one exception, Matheson's "Amelia" teleplay is extremely faithful to his "Prey" short story. In the story, Amelia's mother and boyfriend speak several lines over the telephone; in the film, viewers hear only Amelia's side of the conversations. Karen Black declared,

Trilogy of Terror (1975): Karen Black fights off the Zuni fetish doll in this memorable scene from the climactic "Amelia" ("Prey") segment of the trilogy. *Trancers* and *Dollman* producer Charles Band acknowledged that the Zuni doll was the inspiration for his series of nine *Puppet Master* movies.

I rewrote some of the dialogue with the mother in the beginning with the director, Dan, because I wanted to make it very clear how the mother made Amelia feel. So at the end, it would be justified what she did [i.e. planned to kill her mother]. I wanted the audience to feel her suppression and the way she was made to feel inadequate. I thought that scene on the phone was very important to bring all of that out. Even though Amelia herself couldn't recognize it, the audience could.[15]

Of her director, Black added, "Dan is an excellent

director and excellent at doing suspense. He knows just the right angles. Nobody is better at suspense. Dan should be applauded for his work with it."[16]

Curtis remembered that long before the days of CGI effects, he "did it all with smoke and mirrors. The Zuni doll was a little hand puppet. But it worked. The thing still holds up." Curtis explained,

> The first two stories were pretty straightforward, but when it came time to shoot the Zuni-doll story, I was scared out of my wits because I didn't know what we were going to do. How was I going to make this thing work? All we had was a hand puppet and a little model with hands and legs that could move. So what we did was to build the apartment set on risers. We cut lines into the floor that were covered by the shag carpet, and we had some idiot underneath running [and] moving the Zuni doll by means of a rod stuck up the puppet's ass. Well, forget it. It absolutely didn't work. It was the most awful thing you've ever seen. So I got the idea of chasing Karen Black with a hand-held camera about two inches off the ground. That was very effective, but I still didn't have anything with the doll. When it was over, everybody was going home, and I was sitting there in a total depression. I didn't know what to do. Then, I got one last thought, which saved the picture. I got hold of the puppeteer [Erick Von Buelow, creator of the Pillsbury Doughboy], and we hung a piece of black velvet. And I just shot a ton of close-ups of the doll: opening its mouth, thrashing around, exiting frame. I sent it to the lab and had it skip-framed, and before you know it, it was zipping around. I flipped the film over to make him go from left to right and right to left. The knife would jump from one hand to another, but nobody has ever noticed that! It was against black. I could cut to it any time I wanted. I edited those into the scene, and it was very effective. It absolutely saved me.[17]

So does Walker Edmiston's performance as the terrifying voice of the Zuni doll. Edmiston, who died on February 15, 2007, was an actor (*The Big Valley*) and voice-over artist (*H.R. Pufnstuf*) who later portrayed General Douglas MacArthur in *War and Remembrance*. Also adding to the horrifying effect of *Trilogy of Terror* is Robert Cobert's nerve-wracking music. "I wrote some of the most abstruse music that Dan's ever allowed me to write," Cobert exclaimed. "Really far-out!"[18] Among other instruments, Cobert uses vibraphone for Julie, oboes for Millicent and Therese, and clarinet, bass clarinet, trumpet, strings, and tambourine for Amelia. Cobert's music over the closing credits builds to a shattering climax. Karen Black remarked, "He does an incredible job with the music."[19] She continued,

> It's an interesting study as to *why* [the Zuni-doll story] is *so* scary. It seems to me that maybe it's the little things in life that kill you eventually. But, of course, I'm a woman, and I think it's fine to say this in 2006, but women are afraid of *entry*— you know, vaginal entry — and that's why rats, snakes, and mice are so incredibly frightening. If you watch women draw away from them, they generally close their knees, you see! I don't know if you think that consciously, but certainly you're vulnerable in a way that a man can't be. So I think that small things and women — and being chased by a small thing — might have something to do with why it's *so* scary.[20]

Trilogy of Terror received high ratings and high praise. *Variety* called the film "fodder for a virtuoso performance by Karen Black, who essays a quartet of women, and producer-director Dan Curtis, [who] displays his talents in the horror genre. The beginning and final scene, in which the devil doll prepares her for action, are separated by ghoulish work shrewdly manipulated, realistically managed."[21]

Only a few years after the first two broadcasts, just the "Amelia" story was released on early VHS as *Terror of the Doll*. Later in the 1980s, the entire *Trilogy of Terror* came to VHS, and it was released on DVD in August 2006. Over the years, the Zuni doll and its sentient, murderous antics have influenced the 1984 film *Black Devil Doll from Hell*, three of Joe Dante's movies (*Gremlins* [1984], *Gremlins 2* [1990], *Small Soldiers* [1998]), and the series of *Child's Play* and *Puppet Master* horror films of the late 1980s and the 1990s.[22] All of these films pit pint-sized menaces (dolls, gremlins, or puppets) against hapless humans. In 1996, Dan Curtis himself revisited the Zuni fetish doll in *Trilogy of Terror II*, and in 2006 the doll made a cameo appearance on the first episode (July 12) of TNT's *Nightmares and Dreamscapes*, an anthology series dramatizing the short stories of Stephen King. In "Battleground," another one-character drama, a man (William Hurt) fights vengeful toy soldiers that have come to life in his high-rise apartment. Sitting on his bookshelf is the Zuni fetish doll! Adapting "Battleground" for TV was Richard Christian Matheson, paying homage to his father's horrific creation.

Long before those latter-day productions, Curtis and Matheson reunited for *Dead of Night* (NBC, March 29, 1977), a pilot for a proposed anthology series. The program comes on like an early-television classic. The words DEAD OF NIGHT appear in *Shock Theater*-style wavy letters as a music cue from *Dark Shadows* is heard. The announcer, *Gunsmoke / Twilight Zone* mainstay John Dehner, speaks in the style of *Creature Feature* hosts as he insists that the dead of night is "a state of mind — that dark, unfathomed region of the human consciousness from which all the unknown terrors of our lives emerge." Dehner promises "three tales: one of mystery, one of imagination, and one of terror." What follows is a traditional fantasy/horror anthology — perhaps scarier than *Trilogy of Terror* — but enhanced by Curtis's eye toward modern sensibilities in the final tale of demonology with an all-too-familiar setting.

First comes the tale of imagination, Matheson's adaptation of "Second Chance," a Jack Finney story from the April 1956 issue of *Good Housekeeping*. Frank Cantrell (Ed Begley, Jr.), a present-day senior at Poynt College in Hylesburg, Illinois, restores a ruined 1923 Jordan Playboy automobile, notorious as the death car of a long-ago local couple from nearby Cressville. When he gets the car running, he drives it along an old back road and *back in time* to the Cressville of the year 1926 (1923 in Finney's story). By inadvertently delaying the couple fated to die in a collision with a train, Frank changes history and allows the couple to live, marry, and one day be the grandparents of Helen (Christina Hart), the young woman whom he has met and will marry in the present day.

"Second Chance" has an old-fashioned, Bradburyesque feel, from the vintage cars and clothes to Robert Cobert's use of 'Toot Toot Tootsie Good-Bye" and other period songs to Begley's narration. Unlike the terse, ironic narration which gives the Kolchak and Norliss movies a *film-noir* feel, Begley's warm, sentimental narration imbues "Second Chance" with a quaint, storybook feel — "And just like her grandparents did almost 50 years before, we'd leave on our honeymoon in the very same car." The narration is a carry-over from Matheson's faithful adaptation of Finney's story, in which the narrator speaks directly to the reader about "how driving used to be before people shut themselves behind great sheets of glass and metal and began rushing along super-high-ways, their eyes on the white line."[23] This is a change-of-pace sweet film from Curtis and a warm-up for his two semi-auto-biographical family dramas (1978 and 1980) and, much later (1998), his sensitive filming of Jack Finney's romantic time-travel short story "The Love Letter."

The second *Dead of Night* entry is the tale of mystery: Matheson's adaptation of his short story "No Such Thing as a Vampire" (from *Playboy*, October 1959). This segment was actually filmed in 1973 as a half-hour ABC pilot that never aired. It finally sees the light of day in *Dead of Night* and offers a chilling vampire tale with a twist.

"No Such Thing as a Vampire" has the atmospheric look of the popular films of the Hammer studio in England. Matheson and Curtis were no strangers to that *Brides of Dracula / Curse of the Werewolf* look because Matheson had written

Dead of Night (1977): In "Second Chance," Ed Begley, Jr. (as Frank Cantrell) drives a restored 1923 Jordan Playboy automobile back to the year 1926 (1923 in Jack Finney's short story).

two Hammer films (*Fanatic* [1965] and *The Devil Rides Out* [1968]) and Curtis (consciously or unconsciously) had patterned *House of Dark Shadows* somewhat after Hammer's colorful, sexy vampire movies. "No Such Thing as a Vampire" features an international cast, a European street scene, a castle setting, an especially heavy Cobert score, and more blood than is usually seen on 1970s television (perhaps one reason why this film took four years to reach TV).

The time period is left vague, so a light switch glimpsed in one shot is disconcerting (like the accidental light bulb in *Gone with the Wind* and wristwatch in *Spartacus*). However, this is not a blooper but Curtis's sly message that things are not as they seem in this Hammeresque tale of a vampire's nightly attacks on Dr. Petre Gheria's beautiful young wife Alexis (Anjanette Comer). As it turns out, there is no such thing as a vampire. As in *London After Midnight* (1927), *Mark of the Vampire* (1935), and Curtis and Matheson's own *Scream of the Wolf* (1974), the supernatural attacks are a hoax. The jealous Dr. Gheria (Patrick Macnee) has been surgically draining his sleeping wife's blood. Next he frames their handsome young friend Dr. Michael Vares (Horst Bucholz) by drugging him, bloodying him, and putting him in a coffin for the servant Karel (Elisha Cook, Jr.) to find. As Karel mistakenly drives a stake through Michael's heart, Dr. Gheria whispers to Alexis, "Sleep well, my dear. Your nightmare has ended — or will it just begin when you learn that *your lover* is dead?"

> Dr. Gheria smiled in pleasure for the first time since Alexis and he had returned from Cluj at the end of the summer [when Alexis and Michael had had their affair]. Dear spirits in heaven, would it not be sheer enchantment to watch old Karel drive a stake through Michael Vares's damned, cuckolding heart![24]

Macnee, star of *The Avengers* (1961–1969), gleefully plays against type in this clever and frightening tale. Indeed, *The Hollywood Reporter* acknowledged, "All of the performances are top-rate."[25]

Much scarier still is "Bobby," the tale of terror which attempts to recapture the killer-chases-woman phenomenon of *Trilogy of Terror*. Matheson wrote this story especially for *Dead of Night,* so it is in tune with the times. It incorporates demonology and perpetuates the 1970s-era trend of real horror in an everyday setting (e.g. *The Exorcist* [1973], *The Wicker Man* [1973], *The Texas Chainsaw Massacre* [1974], *Carrie* [1976], *Halloween* [1978]).

After the presumed drowning death of her 12-year-old son Bobby, Alma (Joan Hackett) has retreated from reality (in the opinion of her absent husband) by consulting "phony psychics and spiritualists." Alone in her two-story home on a stormy night, Alma draws demonological symbols on the floor and calls upon arcane, Lovecraftian gods to bring her son back to her. Soon, Bobby (Lee Harcourt Montgomery) does appear — but he is horrifyingly different. A murderous Bobby stalks his mother through the garage and both floors of their house. Finally Alma shoots Bobby, but he still comes

Dead of Night (1977): In "No Such Thing as a Vampire," Horst Bucholtz (as Dr. Michael Vares) comforts Anjanette Comer (as Alexis Gheria).

back. The boy explains that Bobby did not drown by accident: he drowned himself because he wanted to escape his unhappy home life and his cruel mother. "Bobby didn't want to come back," the shadowed figure says, "Bobby hates you, Mommy, so he sent *me* instead." The boy now reveals his true form to be that of a demon (in Frank Westmore's frightening makeup)! Alma has gotten more than she bargained for by calling on the powers of darkness.

In deciding which killer segment — Karen Black's or Joan Hackett's — is better, one encounters the same *Night Stalker / Night Strangler* dilemma. "Amelia" is an undisputed classic — fresh and shocking — but "Bobby," the intentionally similar follow-up, contains more characterization of the woman and especially her adversary. Plus, "Bobby" is terrifying in a much more realistic way. A little doll's attack on a woman is fantastical, but a child's attack on his parent is plausible. "Bobby" continues a trend of evil-child movies (e.g. *The Bad Seed* [1956], *Village of the Damned* [1960], *The Innocents* [1961], *A Little Game* [TV-1971], *The Other* [1972]), but even more importantly, it belongs to the then-current sub-genre of films expressing female anxiety about reproduction, childbirth, and children (e.g. *Rosemary's Baby* [1968], *The Exorcist* [1973], *It's Alive* [1974], Matheson's *The Stranger Within* [TV-1974], *The Brood* [1979]).

Dead of Night (1977): Joan Hackett plays Alma, who is so desperate to bring her drowned son Bobby back to life that she resorts to the dark arts.

In addition to being topical, "Bobby" is an extremely frightening cat-and-mouse game which builds relentlessly to the shocking revelation of the demon at the final fade-out. As always, Curtis's direction is tight and full of low angles (the camera looks *up* at Alma as she hides in the car, runs through the hall, shoots Bobby, etc.), and Cobert makes excellent use of music *and silence.* Whenever either begins, the effect is nerve-jangling. Like *Scream of the Wolf* three years earlier, *Dead of Night* is another underrated gem in Curtis's *oeuvre.* However, one-third of *Dead of Night* lived again, 19 years later, when Dan Curtis and William F. Nolan collaborated on another trilogy of terror.

Because the Zuni fetish doll had become so much a part of popular culture over the years — even being spoofed on an episode of *The Simpsons* and made into a collectible action figure — Curtis decided to film *Trilogy of Terror II* for the USA Network in 1996. It turned out to be his final horror presentation on television. (The 2004 *Dark Shadows* pilot for WB never aired.) *Trilogy of Terror II* proved to be a powerful finale to Curtis's unique brand of horror television. This latter-day sequel is perhaps scarier than either *Trilogy of Terror* or *Dead of Night*, and like each of them, it is in tune with the times.

Stepping into Karen Black's role as the woman around whom each story is built is Lysette Anthony, Angelique from the 1991 *Dark Shadows*. The first story, adapted by Nolan and Curtis, is "The Graveyard Rats," based on the March 1936 *Weird Tales* classic by fantasy author Henry Kuttner (*Dr. Cyclops,* "The Twonky, "Mimsy Were the Borogroves").

Kuttner was a member of the Lovecraft Circle, a group of pulp-fiction writers who corresponded with H.P. Lovecraft, creator of the Cthulhu mythology. Others in the circle were Robert E. Howard, Frank Belknap Long, and Clark Ashton Smith, all of whom were writing for *Weird Tales, Amazing Stories,* and other 1930s pulp magazines. Lovecraft and his circle became mentors to a slightly younger generation of horror/sci-fi literary figures, including Robert Bloch, Fritz Leiber, and Julius Schwartz. Kuttner especially was a mentor to two young men who became two of the leading American fantasy writers of the twentieth century. Kuttner helped Ray Bradbury with his first published horror story, "The Candle," and Richard Matheson dedicated his last-man-on-earth/vampire novel, *I Am Legend,* "to Henry Kuttner, with my grateful thanks for his help and encouragement on this book."

As written for *Weird Tales,* "The Graveyard Rats" is another story of one person versus a horrifying menace. Kuttner's first sentence reveals the circumstances: "Old Masson, the caretaker of one of Salem's oldest and most neglected cemeteries, had a feud with the rats."[26] The enormous rodents, "some as large as good-sized cats,"[27] have dug underground burrows around and through the many wooden coffins buried in the cemetery. According to Kuttner, "The malodorous tunnels were large enough to enable a man to crawl into them on his hands and knees"[28] because "the rats inevitably dragged away the whole cadaver through the hole they gnawed in the coffin."[29]

Often, the creatures beat Old Masson — a grave robber — to a body which he wants for its jewelry, its clothes, or its value to "less reputable doctors who were in need

Dead of Night (1977): Larry Green takes over for Lee Harcourt Montgomery when "Bobby" becomes a demon. "So he sent *me* instead!"

of cadavers and not over-scrupulous as to where these were obtained."[30] On this night, Masson has just dug up a coffin, only to find that "the rats had forestalled him again!"[31] They have chewed through a wooden box and begun to drag off a corpse laden with valuable cuff links and a pearl stick-pin that Masson covets. He jumps into the open coffin and enters the burrow after them.

When Masson crawls through the fetid, claustrophobic tunnel, the relentless horror of Kuttner's story escalates. Nolan and Curtis's expanded adaptation begins long *before* this moment, and it assigns most of Masson's role to Laura Ansford (Lysette Anthony), one of three new major characters. Nolan, a writer of *film-noir* histories and fiction (*Dashiell Hammett: A Casebook* and *Death Is for Losers* et al.), grafts a *noirish* back-story onto the ultimate confrontation under the Salem cemetery.

Laura and her lover Ben Garrick (Geraint Wyn Davies) conspire to kill Roger Ansford (Matt Clark), Laura's rich, older, invalid husband. For inspiration, Garrick watches his "favorite movie," Henry Hathaway and Ben Hecht's 1947 *noir* classic *Kiss of Death*. Featured on the TV screen is the famous scene in which Richard Widmark hurls a wheelchair-bound Mildred Dunnock down a flight of stairs. Laura reluctantly goes along with Ben's plan to break in to her and Ansford's house and let the same apparent accident befall Ansford.

Curtis directs the scenes of the home invasion with great suspense. A truly frightening image is the sight of the helpless terror on Ansford's face and the giddy delight on Ben's face as the latter rapidly pushes Ansford and his wheelchair toward the stairs and the big drop. Ansford dies from this apparent accident, but he foils Ben and Laura by hiding his $700 million fortune in Swiss banks and microfilming the account numbers on a microdot. The microdot is hidden in his antique watch, which has been buried with him in the rat-infested Salem cemetery.

At this point, Kuttner's Masson character, renamed Arleigh Stubbs (Geoffrey Lewis), begins digging up the body in order to steal the dead man's finery. Ben and Laura catch Stubbs in the act, and Ben kills him with a shovel. Ben jumps into the hole with the open coffin and confirms that the watch and the microdot are within. Laura, a bona-fide *film-noir* black widow, promptly shoots Ben to death — but before she can retrieve the watch, Ansford's body begins to slide away!

From this point, what happens to Masson in the short story happens to Laura in the film. Curtis and Nolan's teleplay captures the terrifying atmosphere of Henry Kuttner's story:

> The end of the sarcophagus had been gnawed through, and a gaping hole led into darkness. A black shoe, limp and dragging, was disappearing as Masson watched, and abruptly he realized that the rats had forestalled him by only a few minutes.
>
> He fell on his hands and knees and made a hasty clutch at the shoe, and the flashlight incontinently fell into the coffin and went out. The shoe was tugged from his grasp; he heard a sharp, excited squealing; and then he had the flashlight again and was darting its light into the burrow.[32]

In the 1936 "Rats" story, after Masson begins his crawl through the burrow, Kuttner writes,

Agonizing pain shot through his leg. He felt sharp teeth sink into his flesh, and he kicked frantically. There was a shrill squealing and the scurry of many feet. Flashing the light behind him, Masson caught his breath in a sob of fear as he saw a dozen great rats watching him intently, their slitted eyes glittering in the light. They were great, misshapen things, as large as cats, and behind him he caught a glimpse of a dark shape that stirred and moved swiftly aside into the shadow; and he shuddered at the unbelievable size of the thing.[33]

The "dark shape" in Kuttner's story is his Lovecraftian hint of "ghoulish beings that dwelt far underground,"[34] perhaps the subterranean elder gods which exist in stories written by all of the members of the Lovecraft Circle. "It was almost as though the rats were working under the direction of some impossibly intelligent leader," Kuttner hints.[35] For *Trilogy of Terror II,* Curtis and Nolan discard this supernatural element and tell a straightforward, *noirish* crime drama with the worst possible ending. Trapped by the ferocious graveyard rats deep in the tunnel, Laura sinks "down into the blackness of death with the mad squealing of the rats dinning in [her] ears."[36] With this image, Dan Curtis has succeeded in creating another one of the most horrifying films ever made for television.

The second story is a shot-for-shot remake of "Bobby," Richard Matheson's story from *Dead of Night.* Curtis faithfully follows Matheson's script and almost all of his own camera angles and shots from the 1977 filming of Alma's ordeal at the hands of her demonic son. This time, however, the storm outside is even fiercer, Robert Cobert's dire music adds eerie synthesized effects, Bobby (Blake Heron) is even scarier, and prosthetics specialist Rick Stratton's demon-head appliance is even more grotesque. "Bobby" still packs a punch and explores Matheson's trademark theme of one person, alone, against insurmountable odds (e.g. the last man on earth, the shrinking man, the time traveler, the motorist in *Duel,* Amelia, Bobby's mother Alma, etc.).

William F. Nolan explained that Richard Matheson was not involved with *Trilogy of Terror II.* "Dan simply reshot Matheson's 'Bobby' from his earlier script and put it in as the middle story. Then, he and I wrote the other two as a team. I had always wanted to have a crack at writing about the Zuni doll — since it was all anybody ever talked about from the first *Trilogy* — so it was very satisfying being able to do it at last."[37]

Trilogy of Terror II (1996): In this USA Network publicity still, Lysette Anthony plays Alma in the remake of the "Bobby" story from *Dead of Night.*

Curiously, the third story, "He Who Kills," is both a sequel to and a remake of Matheson's "Amelia" story about the Zuni fetish doll in *Trilogy of Terror.* This story begins soon after Amelia's story has ended. Amelia, possessed by the spirit of the Zuni warrior, has died after killing her mother, and the police take the charred Zuni doll to Dr. Simpson (Lysette Anthony again), a scientist who examines it at her office in a natural-history museum after hours. The Zuni doll comes back to life and stalks her through the museum, and what follows is a close remake of the original segment's frantic, bloody battle of wits between woman and doll.

Co-writers Nolan and Curtis provide some necessary exposition about how "doll and spirit will become one living entity," as well as a new fact. Dr. Simpson announces that the Zuni doll is "not Indian; it's African; I'd say the tribe has been extinct for at least five centuries." After the scientist lays the doll on a table in her office, an eerie touch is Curtis's use of subjective shots: the camera looks at Dr. Simpson sideways through the reclining doll's eyes.

Viewers who saw Amelia's original struggle with the doll can regard "He Who Kills" as a quasi-sequel to "Amelia" except for a drastic change in Amelia's apartment set. Whereas the *Trilogy* apartment was small and claustrophobic, the apartment where the police discover the bodies of *this* Amelia and her mother is a palatial, two-level apartment with a huge wall of windows. Using a much smaller apartment set very similar to the original would have provided more continuity between Amelia's timeless story and this 1996 coda, but *Dark Shadows* devotees familiar with Curtis's use of parallel time are able to account for the differences between the two apartments (and between the Collinwood of the TV *Dark Shadows* and the Collinwood of *House of Dark Shadows* and *Night of Dark Shadows*). According to critic Henry Jenkins, "Fans have found ways to explain away such apparent continuity problems [...] The fans have come to accept that their ideal [...] never aligns perfectly with what producers provide. They have found ways to talk around annoying details."[38]

In addition to the apartment upgrade, *Trilogy of Terror II* (1996) shows a great deal of evidence of the influence of two decades of changes in television and film since the 1975 *Trilogy of Terror.* "He Who Kills" begins as a police procedural not unlike *Law and Order, NYPD Blue,* and *Homicide: Life on the Street,* TV series popular in the mid–1990s. In a symbolic acknowledgement of how culturally pervasive the Zuni fetish doll has become over the decades, the doll is not confined to a small apartment. This time, it runs all over a four-story museum. Reflecting the influence of the slasher movies of the 1980s and 1990s (especially the Chucky movies — themselves an outgrowth of *Trilogy of Terror*), the Zuni doll kills three people instead of one. The tiny menace dispatches Lew (Thomas Mitchell), the younger of the museum's two night watchmen, by manipulating a bow and arrow held by a wax figure on exhibit. The Zuni doll kills Steve (Aron Tager), the older guard, by cutting his throat.

Trilogy of Terror II also anticipates the self-reflexivity of late-1990s horror movies — i.e. how characters know all about horror movies or even know that they are acting like characters *in* horror movies, as in the *Scream, I Know What You Did Last Summer, Urban Legend,* and *Scary Movie* series. In an early scene, Lew reads the fifth issue (summer 1993) of Innovation Comics' *Dark Shadows* comic book. Of course, this film's director created *Dark Shadows,* and this film's leading actress played Angelique on *Dark Shadows!*

The Zuni warrior doll first attacks Dr. Simpson in the museum's elevator. Then the struggle moves through the Dinosaur Gallery. The scientist pushes a suit of armor over onto the doll, but it manages to follow her to her office. From this point, "He Who Kills" stops being a sequel-of-sorts to "Amelia" and becomes a very close remake of "Amelia." Once again, the woman traps the doll in a suitcase, and it cuts its way out. She stabs the doll numerous times, as before, but it continues to make way. Finally, instead of throwing the doll into an oven as Amelia did, Dr. Simpson hurls the doll into a nearby vat of sulfuric acid and closes the lid.

As before, the woman opens the lid to take another look at her adversary, and in the words of Matheson's 1969 short story, "Something dark and stifling rushed across her, and she heard the screaming in her mind once more as hotness flooded over her and *into* her. It was a scream of victory now."[39] Once again, the spirit of the warrior has left the doll and gone into the woman.

All that remains is a remake of the final image of *Trilogy of Terror.* This time, Dr. Simpson's boyfriend Dennis (Pete Keleghan) returns to the museum to pick her up. He presses the elevator button, and when the doors part, a maniacal, jagged-toothed Simpson rushes at him with an axe. In Nolan and Curtis's intentional acknowledgment of how characterization in movies has diminished over the decades, *this* possessed killer murders Pete for no reason other than shock value. The possessed Amelia, like Norman Bates in *Psycho* (1960), committed matricide because of deep-seated resentments. The possessed Dr. Simpson kills Pete when all he has done (as far as the audience knows) is to be a good boyfriend to her — even buying expensive theatre tickets, which she earlier rejected in favor of working late with the charred doll.

In his 1985 essay "Children of the Light," horror-film critic Bruce Kawin laments that many a post–1980 horror movie "deals in spectacle"—"a lot of people get killed, but no one really cares about them; the audience's attention skips from victim to victim until it finds the survivor."[40] If, as in "The Graveyard Rats," "Bobby," and probably this segment, there is *no* survivor, "it doesn't make much difference in the basic formula."[41] The audience is still scared and experiences the catharsis horror affords.

Nevertheless, *Trilogy of Terror II* succeeds in delivering 90 minutes of woman-in-jeopardy chills as Lysette Anthony's characters battle rats, a demon, and a doll. *USA Today* raved that *Trilogy of Terror II* is "not only the best and spookiest new offering of the TV season, but It Is also a wonderful and worthy nod to an old TV classic. Revisiting *Trilogy of Terror* was a clever choice. Equally clever was casting Lysette Anthony."[42] The newspaper dubbed these three stories "more ambitious" than the 1975 stories and added, "From its morbid opening credits to its final shock sequence, *Trilogy of Terror II* is a treat all the way."[43]

The *New York Daily News* declared that the Zuni fetish doll had "lost none of its menace — or teeth — in the intervening years. If you enjoyed the original *Trilogy of Terror,* you'll want to scope out the sequel as well."[44] On December 31, 1996, the *Daily News* named *Trilogy of Terror II* one of the best made-for-TV movies of the year.[45]

Trilogy of Terror II, with its strict remake of "Bobby," its loose remake of "Amelia," and its outstanding new Henry Kuttner adaptation, serves as a synthesis of *Dead of Night* and *Trilogy of Terror,* with new tips of the hat to *Weird Tales* and *film noir* as well. William F. Nolan expressed only one regret: "In my opinion, the best segment of all would have been my adaptation of Philip K. Dick's 'The Father-Thing,' but it got dropped at the last moment and replaced with Matheson's 'Bobby.' My Dick teleplay was very frightening, but no one ever got a chance to see it."[46]

Including a Philip K. Dick story in *Trilogy of Terror II* certainly would have acknowledged yet another contemporary trend in filmmaking: adapting stories and novels by Philip K. Dick. Over and over, Hollywood has turned to Dick's material for movies such as *Blade Runner* (1982), *Total Recall* (1990), *Confessions of a Crap Artist* (1992), *Screamers* (1995), *Imposter* (2002), *Minority Report* (2002), *Paycheck* (2003), *A Scanner Darkly* (2006), and *Next* (2007). "The Father-Thing" is Dick's 1954 short story about a boy who realizes that his father has been replaced by a lookalike alien.

On returning to horror trilogies such as *Dead of Night* and *Trilogy of Terror* after two decades, Dan Curtis admitted,

> It's murder having to compete with yourself. That's the scary part. It gave me a little pause to consider that I was competing against a Dan Curtis who was twenty years younger and maybe smarter. Believe me, I didn't like the competition. Horror stories are the most difficult type of things to do because you need imagination and humor, and you can never make a mistake. The first screw-up, you lose all credibility, and you're dead with the audience. Most people say, "Well, it's a ghost, so we can do whatever we want with it." They're the people who are dead before they start. A logic lapse or the wrong kind of laugh can sink you. Every single word is a deathtrap. That's the worst part of it. Every single line in a horror picture becomes dangerous. A simple "hello" at the wrong place can bring an unwanted laugh. You don't want *any* unwanted laughs. You want chuckles in the right places. You want people smiling with you when you do certain things. So if you can do these kinds of pictures, you can do anything. Most people think just the opposite — that if you can do these kinds of pictures, you can't do anything else. Well, I've proven them wrong.[47]

Trilogy of Terror (ABC, March 4, 1975). Producer: Dan Curtis. Associate producer: Robert Singer. Director: Dan Curtis. "Julie" teleplay: William F. Nolan (based on a story by Richard Matheson). "Millicent and Therese" teleplay: William F. Nolan (based on a story by Richard Matheson). "Amelia" teleplay: Richard Matheson (based on his story). Music: Robert Cobert. Director of photography: Paul Lohmann. Art director: Jan Scott. Makeup: Mike Westmore. Puppet master: Erick M. Von Buelow.

"Julie" Cast: Karen Black (Julie Eldridge), Robert Burton (Chad Foster), James Storm (Eddie Nells), Kathryn Reynolds (Ann Richards), Gregory Harrison (Arthur Moore), Orin Cannon (Motel Desk Clerk).

"Millicent and Therese" Cast: Karen Black (Millicent Lorimor & Therese Lorimor), George Gaynes (Dr. Chester Ramsay), John Karlen (Thomas Anmar), Tracy Curtis (Tracy Stephenson).

"Amelia" Cast: Karen Black (Amelia). 72 minutes.

Dead of Night (NBC, March 29, 1977). Executive producer: Dan Curtis. Producer: Robert Singer. Director: Dan Curtis. "Second Chance" teleplay: Richard Matheson (based on a story by Jack Finney). "No Such Thing as a Vampire" teleplay: Richard Matheson (based on his story). "Bobby" teleplay: Richard Matheson. Music: Robert Cobert. Directors of photography: Ric Waite and Paul Lohmann. Art director: Trevor Williams. Makeup: Frank Westmore.

"Second Chance" Cast: Ed Begley, Jr. (Frank Cantrell), Jean Le Bouvier (Frank's mother), Ann

Doran (Mrs. McCauley), E.J. Andre (Mr. McCauley), Christina Hart (Helen), Orin Cannon (Farmer), Michael Talbott (Young Vince McCauley).

"**No Such Thing as a Vampire**" **Cast:** Patrick Macnee (Dr. Petre Gheria), Anjanette Comer (Alexis Gheria), Horst Bucholz (Michael Vares), Elisha Cook, Jr. (Karel).

"**Bobby**" **Cast:** Joan Hackett (Alma), Lee Harcourt Montgomery (Bobby), Larry Green (Dwarf). 75 minutes.

Trilogy of Terror II (USA, October 30, 1996). Executive producer: Dan Curtis. Producer: Julian Marks. Director: Dan Curtis. "The Graveyard Rats" teleplay: William F. Nolan and Dan Curtis (based on a story by Henry Kuttner). "Bobby" teleplay: Richard Matheson. "He Who Kills" teleplay: William F. Nolan and Dan Curtis (based on the Zuni doll from a story by Richard Matheson). Music: Robert Cobert. Director of photography: Elemer Ragalyi. Art directors: Veronica Hadfield and Elizabeth Calderhead. Makeup: Marie Nardella, Tom Irvin, and Rick Stratton. Creature effects: Eric Allard.

"**The Graveyard Rats**" **Cast:** Lysette Anthony (Laura Ansford), Geraint Wyn Davies (Ben Garrick), Matt Clark (Roger Ansford), Geoffrey Lewis (Arleigh Stubbs), Alan Bridle (Minister).

"**Bobby**" **Cast:** Lysette Anthony (Alma), Blake Heron (Bobby), Joe Gieb (Dwarf).

"**He Who Kills**" **Cast:** Lysette Anthony (Dr. Simpson), Richard Fitzpatrick (Lt. Jerry O'Farrell), Thomas Mitchell (Lew), Aron Tager (Steve). Alex Carter (Breslow), Philip Williams (Pete), Tom Melissis (Sgt. Rothstein), Durwood Allen (Leonard Spaulding), Peter Keleghan (Dennis). 90 minutes.

CHAPTER VIII

Curtis's Pre-*War* Farewell to Horror: *Burnt Offerings* and *Curse of the Black Widow*

In mid–1965, Dan Curtis had literally dreamed up *Dark Shadows* and begun to stake his claim as television's master of horror. A decade later, Curtis was poised to return to the big screen with *Burnt Offerings* (1976), one of the gems of his horror *oeuvre*, and then bid a temporary farewell to the genre after his 1977 TV-movies *Dead of Night* and *Curse of the Black Widow*. (The remake of *Dark Shadows* was more than a dozen years away.) He then made his two family dramas, *When Every Day Was the Fourth of July* (1978) and *The Long Days of Summer* (1980); his only Western, *The Last Ride of the Dalton Gang* (1979); his ill-fated TV series, *Supertrain* (1979); and his two epic miniseries, *The Winds of War* (1983) and *War and Remembrance* (1988, 1989). The summer of 1975 found Curtis filming *Burnt Offerings* in Oakland, California.

Just as the Old Testament tells of believers making sacrifices and burnt offerings to a supernatural higher power of goodness, Robert Marasco's 1973 novel and Dan Curtis's 1976 film *Burnt Offerings* tell the story of human beings who are sacrificed to a supernatural force of evil which resides within — and seems to *be* — an old, dark house. Although it shares a kindred spirit with such works as Henry James's *The Turn of the Screw* (1898), Shirley Jackson's *The Haunting of Hill House* (1959), and Richard Matheson's *Hell House* (1971) — and is a precursor to Stephen King's *The Shining* (1977) — *Burnt Offerings* is a haunted-house novel with a difference. Instead of a house haunted by evil spirits, the house at 17 Shore Road *is* an evil spirit that possesses its inhabitants and ultimately kills or absorbs them in order to use each victim's life-force to revitalize itself. When people move into the house, they do not move out. Their essences merge with the building and continually refurbish the rooms, revive the dying plants, restart the clocks, and brighten the paint job. Even the rotting shingles slough off to reveal a new roof underneath as the house drains its occupants' energy and disposes of them, leaving only their frozen likenesses in an ornate picture collection silently tended by an unseen mother who may or may not really be there.

After schoolteacher Robert Marasco's play *Child's Play* opened on Broadway in

1970 (winning five Tony Awards), he wrote his first novel, *Burnt Offerings*. It is the story of Marian and Ben Rolfe, their son David, Ben's aunt Elizabeth, and the sentient house that engulfs them. In August 1975, Dan Curtis filmed *Burnt Offerings* from a script he co-wrote with William F. Nolan. "I took the back half" of the script, Curtis remembered, "and Nolan wrote the first half."[1]

The movie is an extremely accurate, faithful filming of the novel, up to a point. Virtually everything in the movie is in the book, and vice versa. The only changes of any import come at the conclusion of the film — but they are significant changes. In the novel, Ben and young David meet their demises at the swimming pool on the estate, but in the movie Marian rescues them. Ultimately, no one saves them from the much gorier, more spectacular finishes Curtis and Nolan devise for them. Nolan and Curtis forgo novelist Marasco's nebulous, abstract ending for a more cinematic conclusion, which is a cross between the climaxes of Alfred Hitchcock's *Psycho* (1960) and Curtis's own *Night of Dark Shadows* (1971). Curtis admitted,

> Someone pointed out to me that I stole the ending from what I did in *Night of Dark Shadows* — the concept of the person going back into the house and the car horn beeping outside and the whole *waiting* thing. "What's taking so long?" All I know is I think the last 15 minutes of this film — and I did a lot of scary stuff in my day — is the scariest 15 minutes I have ever seen. Nothing beats the last 15 minutes of this picture.[2]

Burnt Offerings (1976): Oliver Reed (as Ben Rolfe) and Karen Black (as Marian Rolfe) share a tender moment.

Nevertheless, until the final moments *Burnt Offerings* is an extremely faithful filming of the novel. Even a great deal of Marasco's actual dialogue makes it into the screenplay. In both the novel and the film, homeowners Roz Allardyce and her brother Arnold (played in the film by Eileen Heckart and Burgess Meredith) tell Marian and Ben that the house is "practically immortal."[3] The elderly Allardyce siblings offer the house to Ben and Marian — or perhaps it is vice versa — for the entire summer for only $900.00.

In the film, at first, Ben (Oliver Reed), Marian (Karen Black), David (Lee Harcourt Montgomery), and Aunt Elizabeth (Bette Davis) are overjoyed with their summer retreat, but soon disturbing events cast a pall of uneasiness, suspicion, and even terror over 17 Shore Road. Ben tries to drown David in the pool, a rift grows between Ben and Marian, and Aunt Elizabeth loses her energy and begins to wither away. At the same time, Marian neglects her family as she becomes obsessed with caring for the house and possessively looking after the never-seen, 85-year-old Allardyce mother whom Roz and Arnold have left behind in the attic sitting room. According to Marasco's novel, "There was a malevolence in the house, and she [Marian] was being used as its agent."

> Like the Allardyces had suggested, it [the house] was coming alive, bit by bit, and all through her. [...] It was alive, all around her it was alive, and how else had it come alive but through her? And wasn't that the uneasiness she was feeling — the growing awareness of her power in the house, the enormity of the mystery enveloping her life, which, but for the sanctuary of the sitting room, would be unthinkable?[4]

While a graying Marian becomes consumed by her housekeeping, Ben begins to suffer a mental breakdown. These are perhaps the most frightening scenes in the film, as Ben abuses David and later Marian and suffers dreams and hallucinations involving a grim, long-ago funeral and a grinning chauffeur (Anthony James) driving a hearse-like Bentley — which now may be coming back for Ben and his failing aunt. The chauffeur's leering interest in the boy Ben (Todd Turquand) suggests a long-buried abuse which may be at the root of Ben's mistreatment of David and Marian and of the house's exploitation of Ben's fears. Bette Davis's death scene, which anticipates Sylvia Sidney's similar death scene in Don Taylor's *Damien: Omen II* (1978) by two years, is a memorable moment as Aunt Elizabeth and Ben, both terror-stricken, are paralyzed by their fear of what may be approaching the bedroom door. With each new death, the house revitalizes itself. Curtis revealed,

> My whole theory of what is scary and what isn't scary went out the window with this movie because I always believed the premise of "a house that eats people" was so bullshit that it would be like eating Chinese food. In ten minutes, it would be over. But somehow, the inherent terror, the deep-seated, deep-down, psychological *fear* that ran through this picture, came from this "house-restoring-itself" premise. And then, the ending really took care of it completely.[5]

The ending was inconsiderately revealed in United Press International's unsigned, lackluster review of the film. "As horror movies go," UPI opined, "it is very tame except for the climactic scene where Oliver Reed plunges from an attic window, landing upside down with his face smashed through a station-wagon windshield. Don't say you weren't warned."[6] UPI also called *Burnt Offerings* "torturously slow,"[7] but almost all other reviewers understood that the film works *because* it is slow-moving and the frights are spaced out along the two-hour running time. The *Fort Worth Star-Telegram* wrote that "Curtis, the *Dark Shadows* creator, has done a masterful job of bringing to the viewer a tangible sense of dread and then punctuating it with jabs of pure terror."[8]

Films in Review agreed, "This story of a family menaced by psychic forces which plague their summer estate succeeds because producer-director Dan Curtis has enough confidence in his material to pitch the level of suspense at a low key."[9] The *New York Times* added, "Director Curtis times his audience immersions into the ice-bath of terror with skill."[10] Rex Reed, in *Vogue*, also complimented the film's "inwardly churning horror," "visually breathtaking splendor," and "enormous style."[11]

Much of that style comes from Curtis's most frequent use of low angles in any of his horror movies. Curtis claimed,

> I was always known as "Mr. Low Angle." I never want to shoot eye-level, with rare exceptions, because I think it's boring. Either you're going to shoot low, or you're going to shoot high, or you're going to shoot raking angles. I try not to get straight-on stuff because the low angle, to me, is more involving. You somehow feel, as a viewer, that you're in the picture, and you're looking *up* at it, and you are *there*. Visually, it seems to have more depth and be more interesting. You see ceilings, for example.[12]

Another hallmark of the film is Robert Cobert's tantalizing score. Cobert infuses *Burnt Offerings* with *Dark Shadows*-style trembling violins, ominous xylophones, and harsh brass. He adds bells when the grinning chauffeur haunts Ben, and as in *Dark Shadows* and *Dracula*, Cobert uses a music-box theme to great effect. However, Cobert confessed that he and Curtis "fought about" the music for *Burnt Offerings*. "For once, our conceptions had been completely different."[13] After Cobert composed and recorded the various music cues, Curtis moved them to places in the film other than the spots where Cobert had intended them and thereby created a different effect.

"Little things" are what make the movie work, Curtis explained, "like finding the old, rusted bicycle by the graves and the glasses at the bottom of the pool."[14] *Burnt Offerings*, at its core, is the story of a family. Curtis and Nolan's script accentuates the family's happiness in the initial car ride to the house and the group's banter and warmth before the malevolence of the house unhinges Ben, enslaves Marian, and destroys Aunt Elizabeth. After a slowly paced build-up, the characters careen helplessly to their ghastly ends. Elizabeth weakens and dies, Marian merges with the spirit of the house and becomes the new Mrs. Allardyce, Ben dives out the attic window to escape the horror of Marian and the house, and a crumbling chimney falls on David and crushes him.

Burnt Offerings (1976): Bette Davis (as Aunt Elizabeth) and Lee Harcourt Montgomery (as David) ponder the mysteries of the Allardyce home.

In Marasco's novel, Elizabeth weakens and dies, David drowns in the angry waters of the pool, Ben seems to succumb to a vague apoplexy, and Marian nebulously merges with the essence of the house when a strange "hum" compels her to sit in Mrs. Allardyce's chair and surrender her will. What works in prose often cannot be realized on film, and Marasco's abstract conclusion is an example. Curtis was much more blunt: "The book didn't have an ending! It left you thinking, 'What the hell was it all about?!'"[15] Curtis and Nolan dutifully — remarkably — follow Marasco's narrative quite precisely until the end when they dispatch the characters much more visually and viscerally. Nolan remembered, "At the premiere in Lakewood [California], the audience was screaming at them, 'Don't go back into the house! Don't go back in that house!'"[16]

Although the house on Shore Road is supposed to be somewhere on the East Coast, *Burnt Offerings* was filmed at Dunsmuir House, a 37-room mansion in Oakland, California. The Neoclassical Revival home was built in 1899 by Alexander Dunsmuir, the scion of a wealthy Canadian family that had made its fortune in coal. Just as the Lyndhurst estate

Burnt Offerings (1976): "I've been waiting for you, Ben!" Karen Black appears in Al Fleming's old-age makeup as "Mrs. Allardyce."

had had an old swimming pool which had figured prominently (empty of water) in *House of Dark Shadows* and (filled with water) in *Night of Dark Shadows*, Dunsmuir House afforded a similar pool. In the film, Ben and David are seen cleaning out the empty pool and filling it with water before the disturbing "rough-house" scene in which Ben almost drowns his son. The 1953 Bentley that terrifies Ben belonged to San Jose Symphony conductor George Cleve, who appears briefly in Ben's dream of his mother's funeral, attended by the grinning chauffeur. (Three years after *Burnt Offerings*, Dunsmuir House was seen again in Don Coscarelli's horror film *Phantasm* [1979].)

Burnt Offerings ranked number one at the box office for the week of October 13, 1976.[17] Its business was boosted by Lawrence Van Gelder's oft-quoted blurb from the *New York Times*: "an outstanding terror movie [...] that does for summer houses what

Jaws did for a dip in the surf."[18] Rex Reed called *Burnt Offerings* "an amazingly gripping horror film."[19] *Films in Review* noted, "Curtis is one of the few Hollywood producers to employ well-known sci-fi authors regularly to write scripts. This deserves applause at a time when most such movies are being entrusted to people who don't understand or respect the genre."[20] Over the years, *Burnt Offerings* has earned a reputation as being more sophisticated than most contemporary horror films. "The public loved it," William F. Nolan said.[21]

In the genre magazine, *The Old, Dark House*, George LaVoo wrote, "Bette Davis outdoes them all in the role of Aunt Elizabeth. Her death scene, with the chauffeur dragging the coffin up the stairs, is by far the best scene in the movie."[22] In 1977, Davis won the Saturn Award for best supporting actress from the Academy of Science-Fiction, Fantasy, and Horror Films. *Burnt Offerings* also won Saturns for best horror film of 1976 (beating *The Omen*) and best director. Bette Davis and Oliver Reed won acting awards for *Burnt Offerings* at the Antwerp Film Festival.[23]

Essential to the effect and the success of *Burnt Offerings* is Karen Black, whose portrayal of Marian goes from sympathetic to ambivalent to lethal. In a 1976 interview, Dan Curtis revealed that his daughter Tracy, who had acted with Black in *Trilogy of Terror*, "threatened to leave home if I didn't cast Karen Black in *Burnt Offerings*."[24] Curtis had high praise for Black's performances in both films. "She worked her tail off and never, ever let me down."[25] In *Burnt Offerings*, Marian is the lynchpin that first lovingly holds the Rolfe family together and later coldly allows it to disintegrate — all because of, in Marasco's words, "the force in the sitting room that at times made Marian feel like an extension" of the evil of the hungry old house.[26] As the film progresses, Black drastically changes her attitude and even her appearance as Marian's hair grays and she takes on the demeanor of Mrs. Allardyce.

The role is quite physical as well. Marian races through the house in an attempt to open a door or a window, she fends off Ben's unwanted sexual advances, and she jumps into the pool to save David from drowning. "I was four or five months pregnant when I made the movie!" Black declared in the DVD commentary she recorded with Curtis and Nolan. After filming *Burnt Offerings* in August 1975, Black and her second husband, L. Minor "Kit" Carson, welcomed their son Hunter in December. "I'm very long-waisted," Black explained, and that, along with Ann Roth's careful costuming, prevented Marian from looking pregnant in the film.

Black had equally high praise for her director. "Why have I been told by a few hundred people that '*Burnt Offerings* is the scariest movie I've ever seen'? Because of the talent — visual and verbal — and the genius for this genre that the one and only Dan Curtis brings to his great directing career."[27] *Burnt Offerings*, with its downbeat ending, is so frightening because of Curtis's conviction that "the scariest horror movies are the ones that end badly — the ones that end in total disaster."[28] Horror-film critic Bruce Kawin could have been thinking of *Burnt Offerings* (and *Night of Dark Shadows*) when he wrote, "In a good horror story, nobody gets off easy."[29]

The same could be said for *Curse of the Black Widow* (ABC, September 16, 1977), the film that concluded Curtis's horror cycle until his latter-day *Dark Shadows* and *Trilogy of Terror II* projects. If the family in *Burnt Offerings* goes from function to dysfunction, then the family in *Curse of the Black Widow* goes from dysfunction to disaster.

Like *Burnt Offerings, Curse of the Black Widow* is the horrific story of a family, but one cannot overlook the fact that this film is also about a giant spider. As soon as the term "giant spider" comes up in connection with a film, many critics immediately dismiss the movie as grade-Z schlock. Many giant-bug movies *have* been ridiculous, but then there also have been some genre classics along the way.

Huge numbers of people find insects and spiders very disturbing. Bugs make Stephen King's list of the ten key fears that he believes are at the dark heart of most horror writing and horror filmmaking. King names "fear of the dark, fear of 'squishy' things, fear of deformity, fear of snakes, fear of rats, fear of closed-in spaces, fear of insects and spiders, fear of death, fear of other people, and fear for someone else."[30] Giant spiders were considered so unbearably frightening that they were excised from the 1933 prints of *King Kong*, the greatest giant-animal movie of all time.

Giant bugs rampaged through countless sci-fi movies of the 1950s, a time when nature-run-amok was a cinematic metaphor for Americans' uneasiness about rapid scientific advances and the threat of atomic war. Moviegoers screamed at *Tarantula* in 1955, *World Without End* (giant spiders) in 1956, *The Beginning of the End* (giant grasshoppers) and *The Deadly Mantis* in 1957, and *Earth Versus the Spider* in 1958. Bookending these films were two of the best bug movies: *Them!* (1954), a shocking tale of giant ants (effective because the ants are not seen until very late in the film), and *The Fly* (1958), another horrific family drama, this one about a father's scientific experimentation and its terrible effect on his family.

Perhaps cinema's most frightening giant spider is the actually normal-sized arachnid that menaces Richard Matheson's courageous *Incredible Shrinking Man* (1957). Certainly the greatest spoof of 1950s-era giant-bug movies is *Mant*, the self-reflexive movie-within-a-movie in Joe Dante's *Matinee* (1993). A half-century after the bug-eyed monsters of the Eisenhower era, giant spiders finally became respectable when the Academy Award-winning Best Picture of 2003, *The Return of the King*, contained a frightening scene in which a giant spider threatens Frodo Baggins.

Halfway between *Tarantula* and *The Return of the King* was Dan Curtis's *Curse of the Black Widow*, intended as an homage to fifties-era giant-bug thrillers. Curtis once again showed his penchant for casting his favorite character actors, for half the cast of this 1977 TV-movie could have come from a 1950s movie: June Allyson, Sid Caesar, Jeff Corey, June Lockhart, and Vic Morrow. Also starring were Anthony Franciosa, Patty Duke Astin, Donna Mills, Max Gail, and Roz Kelly. Curtis again included his daughter Tracy, as well as his neighborhood handyman Orin Cannon (whom Curtis used in small parts in five of his films).

Writer Robert Blees created the story of *Curse of the Black Widow*, and Blees and Earl Wallace co-wrote the script. Blees had co-written one of the actual giant-bug movies that *Curse of the Black Widow* evokes—*The Black Scorpion* (1957), about giant scorpions in Mexico City. More recently, Blees had co-written *Dr. Phibes Rises Again* and *Frogs* (both 1972). Earl Wallace went on to write *Supertrain* and *The Last Ride of the Dalton Gang* (both 1979) for Curtis. In the 1980s, Wallace was the story editor of

The Winds of War, and he was a full-fledged co-writer (with Dan Curtis and Herman Wouk) of *War and Remembrance*. Between the two *War* miniseries, Wallace won the Academy Award for the Best Original Screenplay of 1985 for co-writing *Witness*, directed by Peter Weir.

In *Curse of the Black Widow*, Mark Higbie (Franciosa) is a private investigator who is drawn into a baffling series of gruesome murders somehow tied to the fraternal twins Leigh and Laura Lockwood and a mysterious brunette named Valerie Steffan. The film pays homage to *film noir* in the scene in which Leigh (Mills) comes to Higbie's office and hires him. Countless *film-noir* thrillers, from *The Maltese Falcon* (1941) to *Chinatown* (1974), have included such a scene in which the beautiful, enigmatic female client hires the gumshoe. *Curse of the Black Widow* also toys with Curtis's Kolchakian formula as Higbie butts heads with Lt. Guillermo "Gilly" Conti (Morrow) and delivers lines such as, "What are you guys trying to hide?" and "I'm going to stay on this thing, and I'm going to find out what you're so scared of!"

Phil "Rags" Ragsdale (Gail), one of Higbie's allies in the police department, surreptitiously aids Higbie in his investigation of these full-moon murders in which men's chests are ripped open and "the bodies drained of blood." Rags tells him of a Chinese legend of "an enchanting woman who appeared to weary travelers and took them to a cave to rest." There she transformed into a giant spider and fed on them. He adds that certain "North American Indians" have a similar legend. Higbie and his outspoken secretary, Florence Ann "Flaps" Parsons (Kelly), research a belief held by "Northern California Indians" of "a spider curse transferred down the female line" and causing transformations, from woman to spider, during the full moon.

The aforementioned characters, with their unusual names and distinctive personalities, lend texture and characterization to *Curse of the Black Widow*. Caesar provides comic relief as Lazlo Cozart, Higbie's ornery neighbor in the office building. H.B. Haggerty plays Marion "Popeye" Sykes, an alcoholic gymnastics coach who witnessed one of the first documented spider-murders. Corey has a memorable scene as Aspa Soldado, a Native American who rescues Higbie after he has a terrifying accident. Dan Curtis's gymnast daughter Tracy even turns a flip in one scene.

While Mark Higbie's storyline is unfolding, the heart of *Curse of the Black Widow* is the story of the Lockwood family. Flaps learns that Leigh and Laura's mother gave birth to the twins in 1947 in the desert after surviving a plane crash that killed their father. Before Aspa Soldado found the woman and her newborns, one of the girls had been bitten numerous times by spiders. Leigh and Laura's mother later died under mysterious circumstances in Rome in 1965. Their family estate is now home to Olga (Allyson), the twins' former nanny, and Jennifer (Rosanna Locke), a young girl of unspecified parentage. Jennifer calls Laura (Duke Astin) "Aunt Laura" and thinks of Olga as her "grandmother." Whenever Laura stays at the house, she goes upstairs to a locked attic room and visits a shadowed figure.

Meanwhile, Leigh Lockwood, Higbie's client, lives in a fashionable beach house. At the beginning of the film, Leigh is engaged to Frank Chatham (James Storm), and Laura is engaged to Jeff Wallace (Robert "Skip" Burton). In the past, each man was linked to the opposite sister. Before the end of the film, both fiancés and a third man,

Carlo Lenzi (Michael DeLano), who encountered Valerie Steffan, have died from the bite of the giant spider.

This family melodrama becomes even more complicated when it is revealed that the spider-bitten twin is cursed, like a werewolf, to transform into a giant spider under the full moon — and that her mother (Lockhart) did not die in Rome but went mad after seeing her daughter change. It is Mrs. Lockwood who lives in the attic room — and it is *Laura* who is the spider-woman. A young man in Rome raped and impregnated Laura — Jennifer is her secret daughter — and Valerie Steffan killed him for Laura. In yet another twist, Valerie is the bewigged alter-ego of Laura, who suffers from both the spider curse and a split personality! Writers Blees and Wallace have hit every note, from *film noir* to monster movies to psychological thrillers. Director Curtis keeps the story moving at a brisk pace, and, as in *Burnt Offerings*, he spaces out the scares and

the deaths. The crazed Mrs. Lockwood's dive out the attic window to escape her spider-daughter is reminiscent of Oliver Reed's plunge in *Burnt Offerings*.

Robert Cobert's music is a Kolchakian blend of detective jazz (a jazz-riff *leit-motif* for Higbie) and his trademark scary music, along with two disco instrumentals as source music. In a change of pace, Cobert scores one scene with solo acoustic guitar (an idea that he considered for *Night of Dark Shadows* but discarded).

In a shot rather daring for 1977 broadcast television, Laura appears in her bra and panties with a black widow spider's red-hourglass mark pulsating far below her navel. Higbie follows the spider-woman to her lair and finds skeletons wrapped in thick webbing. Also covered in webs are Olga, who is dead, and Leigh, who is still alive. Finally the giant spider appears. Curtis wisely mimics *Them!* and keeps his giant bug out of sight until the final reel. This way (as in

Curse of the Black Widow (1977): Anthony Franciosa (as Mark Higbie) and Roz Kelly (as "Flaps" Parsons) face the monstrous-feminine spider.

Them!), the ultimate sight of the monster carries the most shock value, for the audience has had time to accept the real possibility of a giant creature before it actually appears. Higbie sets fire to the spider and her lair, and then escapes with Leigh, who has become his love interest. As in so many 1950s-era monster movies, the surviving couple runs away from a burning, exploding house.

Wallace, Blees, and Curtis have one final shock for the audience: the implication that, as Bruce Kawin writes, "nobody gets off easy."[31] Young Jennifer has come to live with Leigh at her beach house, and Mark Higbie is a frequent visitor. The camera closes in on the bikini-clad youngster — and she, too, carries the red-hourglass shape on her lower abdomen. Jennifer has inherited her mother's curse, so Leigh and Mark's troubles are far from over. The only retro touch that is missing is a big THE END? with a question mark. Curtis's farewell to horror for more than a dozen years is a highly effective, scary/funny, so-bad-it's-good send-up of giant-spider movies — and a sly, winking send-*off* to his own 1966–1977 body of work in the horror genre.

In addition to its classic-horror aspects, *Curse of the Black Widow* has a modern theoretical side. Laura, the murderous spider-woman, is an example of horror-film critic Barbara Creed's concept of the "monstrous-feminine" character in modern horror movies. Creed states that women, by the very fact that they are women, are otherized in the historically male-centered order of society. Women are not men, so they represent a deviant, subversive, or even dangerous element within the male-oriented status quo. When women deviate from their traditional societal roles as wives and mothers, they become truly dangerous and monstrous-feminine. Unmarried heterosexual women, lesbian women, and powerful women represent a considerable deviation from the male-prescribed norm, but women who are killers, witches, vampires, succubi, and spider-creatures constitute a nightmarish, grotesque perversion that jeopardizes the very fabric of the patriarchal society.

Creed adds that the monstrous-feminine character often is linked to myths and legends (e.g. Lilith, Medusa, the Sirens) and to that which is, in critic Julia Kristeva's term, "abject" (i.e. unclean or undesirable), such as bodily fluids, excrement, rotting flesh, and the like. Laura in *Curse of the Black Widow* fits this description. This monstrous-feminine creature subverts male society by seducing and killing men. She is evidence of a multicultural legend, and she leaves gooey webbing in her wake.[32] The climactic scene of the film is a powerful, pre–*Alien* (1979) realization of the monstrous-feminine model, with Laura in her arachnid form in her lair, which is littered with skeletons wrapped in spider webs. Next come the horrific sights of Olga and Leigh enmeshed in webbing and the spider-creature advancing on Higbie, her male prey. After Higbie vanquishes the monstrous-feminine threat, the patriarchy seems to be intact once more, but the ultimate subversion is that the young, seemingly harmless Jennifer is poised to strike at male society at some point in the future.

Curse of the Black Widow can be seen as a feminist film because the women are the ones with all of the power, and the men are powerless, even the so-called star (Franciosa as Higbie). The film spotlights a strong albeit troubled family of only women. The mother survived a plane crash and childbirth in the desert. Of the two daughters, Leigh demonstrates strength by resisting the police's attempts to implicate her in the murders and by hiring Higbie — and Laura, of course, is the dreaded killer of men. The granddaughter is a vessel of future monstrous-feminine power. The family's friend Olga has stepped in and assumed the roles of caregiver (to the insane Mrs. Lockwood and Laura/Valerie) and grandmother (to Jennifer). Although Leigh has been married briefly before and she and Laura have fiancés when the film begins, all three men end up dead. Higbie himself may not fare much better if he continues his involvement with Leigh, the aunt/caregiver of Jennifer the spider-girl.

Another strong character is "Flaps" Parsons, Higbie's wisecracking secretary. Flaps is much more than the stereotype of the sassy, spunky Girl Friday. She is the real brains of Higbie's private-investigating operation. She does the research for him, and it is she, not Higbie, who puts the pieces together. "You ever seen *The Three Faces of Eve?*" she asks Higbie before she explains her correct theory that Valerie and one of the Lockwood sisters are one and the same. In a word, she is smarter than he is.

While the Lockwood women and Flaps are active, the men are passive. Frank, Jeff, and Carlo are murder victims. So were the Italian man who raped Laura and the man who married Leigh. A night watchman (Bryan O'Byrne) is powerless to stop Carlo's death. "Popeye" is still traumatized by his earlier sighting of the giant spider. Lazlo merely complains about how the office building is always too cold. Lt. Conti is clueless and close-minded. Even Mark Higbie coasts along on his charm and depends on his secretary's hard work. He is not quite the driven, determined investigator that Carl Kolchak or David Norliss is. Even though Higbie is the male lead and admittedly defeats one of the two spider-women, he is not as powerful as the women in the film.

Although he never publicly acknowledged feminism in so many words, Dan Curtis always surrounded himself with strong women: his wife Norma, his daughters Tracy and Cathy, his director Lela Swift, his producer Barbara Steele, and his numerous female writers. Two years after *Curse of the Black Widow,* Dan Curtis again showcased a strong woman in his telefilm *Mrs. R's Daughter* (NBC, September 19, 1979), about a mother (Cloris Leachman) who tenaciously battles the male-dominated judicial system when justice is painfully slow to come for her daughter (Season Hubley), who has been raped. As in his horror movies, Curtis's extremely low camera angles in *Mrs. R's Daughter* effect a tone of claustrophobia and despair.

Meanwhile, *Curse of the Black Widow* was another ratings winner for ABC, which used the movie to launch its 1977–1978 TV season. Before receiving a deluxe VHS treatment in 1999, it was released on early home video under the softer title *Love Trap.* Patty Duke laughingly admitted that *Curse of the Black Widow* was one of her sons' favorites of her movies when they were growing up. The role of Laura the spider-woman may not be the most prestigious one in the career of the Academy Award winner and three-time Emmy Award winner, but it is one of the most memorable to the millions of viewers who eagerly anticipated and embraced the many remarkable horror-TV offerings of Dan Curtis, the master of macabre television.

Burnt Offerings (United Artists, 1976). Released October 1976. Producer: Dan Curtis. Associate producer: Robert Singer. Director: Dan Curtis. Screenplay: William F. Nolan and Dan Curtis (based on the novel by Robert Marasco). Music: Robert Cobert. Directors of photography: Jacques Marquette and Stevan Larner. Production designer: Eugene Lourie. Makeup: Al Fleming.

Cast: Karen Black (Marian Rolfe), Oliver Reed (Ben Rolfe), Bette Davis (Aunt Elizabeth), Lee Harcourt Montgomery (David Rolfe), Eileen Heckart (Roz Allardyce), Burgess Meredith (Arnold Allardyce), Dub Taylor (Walker), Anthony James (Grinning Chauffeur), Jim Myers (Dr. Ross), Todd Turquand (Young Ben), Orin Cannon (Minister). 114 minutes.

Curse of the Black Widow (ABC, September 16, 1977). Executive producer: Dan Curtis. Producer: Steven North. Director: Dan Curtis. Teleplay: Robert Blees and Earl Wallace. Music: Robert Cobert. Directors of photography: Paul Lohmann and Stevan Larner. Art director: Phil Barber. Makeup: Mike Westmore and Richard Cobos.

Cast: Anthony Franciosa (Mark Higbie), Donna Mills (Leigh Lockwood), Patty Duke Astin (Laura Lockwood/"Valerie Steffan"), June Allyson (Olga), June Lockhart (Mrs. Lockwood), Roz Kelly (Florence Ann "Flaps" Parsons), Vic Morrow (Lt. Guillermo "Gilly" Conti), Max Gail (Phil "Rags" Ragsdale), Sid Caesar (Lazlo Cozart), Jeff Corey (Aspa Soldado), Robert Burton (Jeff Wallace), James Storm (Frank Chatham), Michael DeLano (Carlo Lenzi), H.B. Haggerty (Marion "Popeye" Sykes), Robert Nadder (Morgue Attendant), Bryan O'Byrne (Watchman), Rosanna Locke (Jennifer), Orin Cannon (Minister). 97 minutes.

Conclusion: Dan Curtis and the Emergence of Participatory Fan Culture

It was inevitable that some of the young people who grew up watching *Dark Shadows, The Night Stalker,* and *Trilogy of Terror* (or later *The Winds of War, War and Remembrance,* and the 1991 *Dark Shadows*) would remember the work of Dan Curtis when they too became writers, producers, and directors. Throughout the 1990s, Chris Carter, creator of *The X-Files,* acknowledged in interviews that *The Night Stalker* had inspired him to create his landmark paranormal drama series.[1] Critic Mark Dawidziak heard Carter say so as early as July 1993, two months before *The X-Files* premiered.[2] Later, in 1997, Carter told *Emmy* magazine that when he was young, he "loved" *The Night Stalker,* so when he grew up, he "knew what I wanted to do. That was it. I wanted to scare people!"[3] Carter even brought Darren McGavin on to *The X-Files* as Arthur Dales, a Carl Kolchak-type character who had founded the X-Files, and Carter cast Raymond J. Barry as Senator Richard Matheson, who was a supporter of the X-Files.

In the mid–1990s, two motion pictures set in the year 1970 acknowledged *Dark Shadows.* In Lesli Linka Glatter's *Now and Then* (1995), a young girl has a poster of Barnabas Collins on her wall. In Robert Tinnell's *Frankenstein and Me,* a.k.a. *Mojave Frankenstein* (1996), two young brothers build Aurora monster models and watch *Dark Shadows.* On 1990s/2000s television, characters on both *Northern Exposure* and *Gilmore Girls* discussed the 1967 Barnabas-kidnaps-Maggie storyline on *Dark Shadows.* The Zuni fetish doll found its way back to TV in Dan Curtis's own *Trilogy of Terror II* (1996) and in a 2006 episode of *Stephen King's Nightmares and Dreamscapes.* Also, Lukas Haas's character in Rian Johnson's 2005 film *Brick* dresses like Barnabas Collins, and Jill Clayburgh's character in Ryan Murphy's 2006 film *Running with Scissors* watches *Dark Shadows* reruns. Vampire P.I. Mick St. John of *Moonlight* (2007–2008) is appealing to TV viewers because he is a reluctant vampire just like Barnabas Collins. The productions of Dan Curtis have made a lasting impression upon popular culture.

One of Curtis's most impressive feats is that *Dark Shadows* (1966–1971) and his five adaptations of the classics (1968, 1973–1974) served as a bridge from classic film horror to modern film horror in the United States, just as the films of the Hammer Studio were doing in England. Dan Curtis was producing *Dark Shadows, House of Dark Shadows,* and *Night of Dark Shadows* — as well as the five adaptations of the classics, the two *Night Stalker* movies, *The Norliss Tapes, Scream of the Wolf,* and *Trilogy of Terror* — at a time (1966–1975) when cinematic horror was becoming more brutally terrifying and realistic. As movie horror was evolving from *The Reptile, The Witches,* and *Island of Terror* (all 1966) to *The Stepford Wives, Shivers,* and *Jaws* (all 1975), Curtis was mixing elements from two different horror styles — haunted-house settings, classic monsters, and less-is-more suggestion of horror, blended with urban settings, increased bloodletting, and an innovative mixture of horror, humor, and *film noir.* Curtis characterized *The Night Stalker* (1972) as "a great story — so traditional yet so modern — and it had a sense of humor!"[4]

Curtis's work reflected the worlds of both classic horror (e.g. *Dark Shadows, The Strange Case of Dr. Jekyll and Mr. Hyde, Dracula, The Turn of the Screw*) and modern horror (e.g. *House of Dark Shadows, The Night Strangler, The Norliss Tapes, Trilogy of Terror*). *Curse of the Black Widow* (1977), the finale to Curtis's 1966–1977 horror cycle, was an extremely effective amalgam of classic and modern horror. The 1991 *Dark Shadows* and the 1996 *Trilogy of Terror II* were even more skillful modernizations of classic themes. They, along with the 2005 sex-abuse drama *Our Fathers* (a different kind of horror story), are Curtis's latter-day modern classics which were noted in many of the director's March-April 2006 obituaries.

On Sunday August 27, 2006, Curtis's work and memory were honored once again. At the 58th Prime-Time Emmy Awards ceremony in Los Angeles, Dan Curtis was included in the "In Memoriam" segment along with Darren McGavin (seen as Kolchak in a clip), Gloria Monty, Anthony Franciosa, Maureen Stapleton, Don Knotts, and other television luminaries who had died in 2005–2006. Curtis was seen directing Ali McGraw as the logos of *Dark Shadows* and *The Winds of War* flashed across the screen.

No few seconds or few hours can sum up the impact on television and popular culture that Dan Curtis had in the 1960s with *Dark Shadows* and *The Strange Case of Dr. Jekyll and Mr. Hyde,* in the 1970s with his numerous horror classics, in the 1980s with his unsurpassed World War II epics, or in the 1990s with *Dark Shadows* and *The Love Letter.* In the 2000s, as his output slowed down, he was finally gaining a richly deserved reputation as an elder statesman of television horror and drama. At the end of his career, *Our Fathers* (2005), one of his finest dramas, became his swan song before his rapid decline and death, just 20 days after the passing of his beloved Norma.

Dan Curtis's effect upon the popular-culture landscape will continue to be felt as new generations of fans keep *Dark Shadows* alive; Majestic Studios, Inc., manufactures action figures of Barnabas, Quentin, and the Zuni doll; interest in Kolchak remains high because of new *Night Stalker* comic books and short stories from Moonstone Books; MPI Home Video continues to release DVDs of Curtis's rarest productions, including additional footage from "No Such Thing as a Vampire"; David Selby and other *Dark Shadows* actors lend their voices to new *Dark Shadows* audio dramas on compact discs from Big Finish Productions; and Hollywood writers and producers keep pitching new concepts as *Dark Shadows*-meets-this (e.g. *Dante's Cove, Blood Ties*) or *The Night Stalker*-meets-that (e.g. *Supernatural, The Dresden Files*).

William F. Nolan, who wrote almost one dozen scripts for Curtis, observed, "Horror does not work until you have the mood and the atmosphere to go with it. The material is one thing, but it's how you treat the material, and Dan has always done that very well. *The Norliss Tapes* was great — he kept it raining all through the movie."[5]

Dean Jones, who played Curtis's father on television and who was his dear friend in real life, agreed, "It is evident from Dan's work that he's one of the finest film directors/producers in the world. He's also a man with one of the most tender hearts toward family, friends, and country that it has ever been my joy to meet. God bless him."[6]

Hart Bochner, who co-starred in *War and Remembrance* and who served as a pallbearer at Curtis's funeral, mused that "working with the guy scared the crap out of everyone. But after a year stuck in a submarine with him, I realized not only that it was his passion manifesting, but it was the easiest way for him to hog all the attention. I love the man and hope he wills me his testosterone."[7]

One day after the death of Dan Curtis, *Orlando Sentinel* film critic Hal Boedeker called Curtis "a showman" and wrote,

> Producer-director Dan Curtis should be remembered for thinking big, a quality that's in short supply these days on television. His willingness to think big continues in a few pockets of television — think HBO. By thinking big, television grows. In that respect, Curtis was a vital pioneer in television history.[8]

At the same time, fan websites such as Jim Pierson's *Dark Shadows Festival,* Stuart Manning's *Dark Shadows Journal,* Craig Hamrick's *Dark Shadows Online,* Dan Silvio's *Shadows of the Night,* and Tim Lucas's *Video Watchblog* posted comprehensive tributes to Curtis. Countless other websites and blogs carried heartfelt comments from fans and admirers. Bill Gibron of *Pop Matters* wrote, "Curtis was happy to carry the torch for terror, arguing for character over carnage. He remained true to his passions to the end."[9] A *House of Irony* blogger known only as Steve added, "For people of a particular age, Dan Curtis is the man most responsible for many a sleepless night. Thanks for the nightmares, Mr. Curtis."[10]

Indeed, one legacy Curtis leaves is the participatory culture — fans and fandom — that his productions inspired and perpetuated. Henry Jenkins, author of *Textual Poachers: Television Fans and Participatory Culture* (1992), maintains that fandom allows for "the translation of program material into new texts that more perfectly serve fan interests, the sense of possession that the fan feels toward favored media products, [and] the celebration of intense emotional commitments"[11] not only to the beloved television series but also to fellow fans who share the same devotion to the TV series. For *Dark Shadows* fandom, these pursuits are manifested in fan writing and other creative arts, in memorabilia collecting, and in the annual Dark Shadows Festival fan gatherings.

Any cult television series — be it *Star Trek, Space: 1999, Beauty and the Beast, Moonlight,* or *Dark Shadows* — generates a huge amount of fan-produced writing — fiction and non-fiction that reveal creative insights into the TV characters and accurate news about their real-life portrayers. Fandom is a community of like-minded, usually amicable people who enjoy sharing their ideas, enthusiasm, creations, and opinions with other fans across the country or across the world. Fan writing takes the forms of letters, e-mails, newsletters, fanzines (short for "fan magazines"), newszines (all-news fanzines), APA-zines (collaborative, round-robin fanzines, now obsolete), one-shot publications, websites, blogs, list-serves, chat rooms, and posting boards (i.e. cyberspace forums for written messages received by small or large groups of fans).

Published continuously since 1975 (the year that *Dark Shadows* resurfaced in syndicated reruns), *The World of Dark Shadows* is the definitive *Dark Shadows* fanzine. Kathleen Resch's publication features long and short *Dark Shadows* fiction, *Dark Shadows* poetry and song lyrics, artwork, rare photographs, Dark Shadows Festival reports, star biographies and interviews, classified ads, letters of comment, book reviews, the discussion series "The Collinsport Debating Society," and long-running fiction serials such as *Journey through the Shadows* and *The Stranger in the Mirror*. Resch, who also has published fanzines devoted to *Star Trek*, *Blake's 7*, and *Beauty and the Beast*, has written several *Dark Shadows* novels, including *Beginnings: The Island of Ghosts*, and, since 1977, has spent years at a time researching and writing extremely detailed *Dark Shadows Concordances* chronicling the TV storylines set in 1795 (two editions), 1968 (two volumes), 1897 (two editions), 1970 Parallel Time, and 1840. In 1992, Resch published *Shadows in the 90s: The Dark Shadows Concordance 1991*.

In *Textual Poachers*, Henry Jenkins takes notice of Resch's *Concordances*[12] and observes that such copious attention to plot and character intricacies is a hallmark of dedicated fans and their fandoms. Jenkins writes,

> Fans often display a close attention to the particularity of television narratives that puts academic critics to shame. Within the realm of popular culture, fans are the true experts; they constitute a competing educational elite. [...] The fan, while recognizing the story's constructedness, treats it as if its narrative world were a real place that can be inhabited and explored and as if the characters maintained a life beyond what was represented on the screen; fans draw close to that world in order to enjoy more fully the pleasures that it offers them. This degree of closeness, however, can be sustained only as long as the imagined world maintains both credibility and coherence, and hence the importance that the fans place on even the most seemingly trivial detail.[13]

One year before the publication of *Textual Poachers*, Kathleen Resch and Marcy Robin wrote in their book *Dark Shadows in the Afternoon* (1991), "Back in the 1960s, for 30 minutes a day, we [fans] had the chance to share the lives of the Collins family and their friends and enemies. Those small, daily segments of time infiltrated our minds. Characters and situations seeped into our consciousness, giving us insights"[14] which developed into fan-written stories and novels that filled in blanks, answered questions, rationalized plot discrepancies, and created back-stories concerning major and often minor characters in the *Dark Shadows* universe.

Following Resch's lead, Dale Clark began publishing his long-running fanzine *Inside the Old House* in 1978. *Inside the Old House* features fiction, poetry, artwork, photographs, the character-biography series "Who's Who in Collinsport," and long-running fiction serials such as *The Collins Story* and *The 1840 Cycle*. Like Resch, Dale Clark has written quite a few acclaimed fan novels, including *Resolutions in Time*, *Reunion*, and *Destiny*. His eight volumes of *The Dark Shadows Book of Questions and Answers* address almost every conceivable query about the complicated TV story-lines.

While *The World of Dark Shadows* and *Inside the Old House* effectively cover the literary and artistic aspects of *Dark Shadows* fandom, Marcy Robin's *Shadowgram* newszine is the only official source of confirmed hard news and current events. Delivering late-breaking news to its readers every few weeks since 1979, *Shadowgram* features detailed, accurate, and official reports on the Dark Shadows Festival fan conventions, the MPI Home Video DVD releases and collectibles, the status of possible *Dark Shadows* reunion projects (including Johnny Depp's intention to portray Barnabas Collins in a 2011 film for Warner Brothers), the latest CD audio dramas from Big Finish Productions, and all of the *Dark Shadows* personnel's current professional and personal activities (e.g. film roles, TV appearances, stage work, book deals, awards, travels, marriages, births, deaths, etc.). *Shadowgram* also includes a column called "Fan News," in which the fans can inform each other (and the *Dark Shadows* personnel reading *Shadowgram*) of their own milestones and accomplishments.

In addition to this triumvirate of fan publications, numerous other *Dark Shadows* fanzines sprang up and flourished in the period from 1983 to 1997, the heyday of printed *Dark Shadows* fanzines before most of them either joined or were eclipsed by the Internet revolution of the mid–1990s. Late-1980s/early-1990s *Dark Shadows* fans had their choice of such regional and national fanzines as *Chasing Shadows, The Collinsport Call, Collinwood Chronicle, Collinwood Revisited, Dark Shadows Announcement, Dark Shadows Collectibles Classified, Dark Shadows Digest, The Eagle Hill Sentinel, Lone Star Shadows, The Music Box, The Parallel Times, Shades of Shadows, Shadows of the Night, Wolf Tracks,* and *Wyndcliffe Watch.* Some fanzines, such as the *David Selby Official Fan Club Newsletter, Karlenzine,* the one-shot *Starring Jonathan Frid* (1985), and the one-shot *Lara Zine* (1993), focused on a favorite *Dark Shadows* actor. Another one-shot fanzine, *Victoria Winters* (1993), presented fans' stories about the life of the young governess. Soon after the 1985 death of Grayson Hall, the one-shot publication *A Gift of Memory* (1987) collected fans' appreciations and reminiscences of the Academy Award-nominated actress while the one-shot fanzine *Tales of Hoffman* (1988) anthologized fans' stories about almost every aspect of Dr. Julia Hoffman's life and experiences before, during, and after her time in Collinsport, Maine. Still other one-shot fanzines documented fandom itself—*Dark Shadows Memories Are Made of This: 25 Years of Letters, Memoirs, Interviews, and Highlights, 1966–1991; Dark Shadows Festival Memory Book, 1983–1993;* and *Fangs for the Memories: Memoirs of Dark Shadows Fans and Cast Members* (1996).

In the 2000s, *Shadowgram, Shadows of the Night,* the Dark Shadows Festival, and other *Dark Shadows* publications and organizations have a presence on the Internet, and new e-zines (electronic fanzines) such as *Dark Shadows Online, The Barbarian Chronicles, Dark Shadows Reborn, Barnabas Undead, Dark Shadows DVD, Phil's Stairway through Time, HODS Is 30,* and the superb British website *Dark Shadows Journal* have advanced *Dark Shadows* fan publishing into international cyberspace. Whether mimeographed, desktop-published, or strictly electronic, fanzines and fan writings allow *Dark Shadows* devotees to participate in the perpetuation, personalization, and recontextualization of their favorite television series. Diehard fans want to know the name of David Selby's latest book of poetry, and they want to imagine what the immortal Quentin Collins was doing in the 1920s or the 1950s. They want to keep up with the professional endeavors of the late Grayson Hall's husband Sam and son Matthew, and they want to fill in the details of Dr. Julia Hoffman's life in medical school. Writing fact and fiction about the world of *Dark Shadows* allows fans to celebrate *Dark Shadows* in active, creative ways — to make the show their own, in a way — and to capitalize on their personal interests through their own creativity.

Fans' creativity does not stop with writing fanzines. *Dark Shadows* fans have made costumes, drawn pictures, painted portraits, produced plays, created music videos, constructed websites, written songs, and made short films about the TV show and its characters. While not personally interested in such things himself, Dan Curtis was well aware of the sunburst of creativity which *Dark Shadows, The Night Stalker,* and some of his other productions had inspired among countless fans. He never objected to or interfered with fans' honest, well-meaning pursuits of writing, painting, costuming, filmmaking, and the like. The only practice of which he disapproved was a few fans' attempts to sell *Dark Shadows* episodes they had taped off of local TV stations or the Sci-Fi Channel. In the 1980s and early 1990s, lawyers for Dan Curtis Productions issued several warning letters to such video pirates.

Beginning in the late 1960s, D.C.P. attorneys were busy with the licensing of official *Dark Shadows* merchandise — memorabilia that fans avidly collect to this day. Because a large percentage of the *Dark Shadows* audience was children and teenagers, merchandisers released dozens of youth-oriented products based on the TV show. Ironically, kids spent millions of dollars on these products, but they were *not* the demographic group that was buying the household products advertised on *Dark Shadows* (and all other soap operas) — an economic failing that led to the cancellation of the TV series faster than its falling but still respectable ratings.

The wave of memorabilia began in late 1966 when Paperback Library started publishing Gothic novels based on *Dark Shadows* and written by Canadian author Dan Ross (*China Shadow, Moscow Mists, The Vampire Contessa*). Between late 1966 and early 1972, Ross, one of the leading Gothic novelists of the 1960s and 1970s, wrote 32 novels featuring Barnabas, Julia, Quentin, Maggie, and his own original characters. Most fans agree that the best book in the series is novel number six, the poignant *Barnabas Collins* (November 1968), but Ross's own personal favorites in the series were *Barnabas, Quentin, and the Frightened Bride* (#22, October 1970), partially set during World War I; *Barnabas, Quentin, and Dr. Jekyll's Son* (#27, April 1971), echoing Robert Louis Stevenson's classic; and *Barnabas, Quentin, and the Vampire Beauty* (#32, March 1972), partially set in Switzerland. Ross's novelization of *House of Dark Shadows* (October 1970) closely followed Sam Hall and Gordon Russell's original script and dramatized several scenes that were either cut from the movie or never filmed. (There was no novelization of *Night of Dark Shadows*.) Before his death at 82 in November 1995, Dan Ross had written 358 Gothic, mystery, Western, spy, nurse, romance, and historical novels under 21 different pseudonyms, including Marilyn Ross (his wife's name), Clarissa Ross, Dana Ross, W.E.D. Ross, Dan Roberts, and Tex Steele. (In 1969–1970, fans also collected a few non–Ross paperbacks: a *Dark Shadows* cook book, a joke book, and Jonathan Frid's *Personal Picture Album*.)

Between late 1968 and late 1975, Gold Key Comics published 35 issues of the *Dark Shadows* comic book. One of the writers was Arnold Drake, who created Deadman and the Doom Patrol for DC Comics. When diehard fans balked that some of the comic books' stories and characterizations veered too far from what had been established on the television series, Drake (who died on March 12, 2007) explained,

> My goal was to write a good story. The fans are interested beyond the normal interest in a story. Their interest becomes almost like a religion or something bordering on it. So they are interested ritualistically: they want everything to be observed in a particular kind of way. The writer is not interested in the ritual of *Dark Shadows*. He is interested in the people, yes; in the characters, of course; and in the best darn stories that he can get out of them, but not in whether he observes precisely what Jonathan [Frid as Barnabas Collins] should do under these precise conditions so that it will be in agreement with 20 other [comic-book] stories that came before [or be in agreement with the television series]. If the writer involves himself that much in the ritual of *Dark Shadows*, he isn't going to get a decent story. He's going to be restricted — bound — too much by what has been done.[15]

Fans' strong desires to experience stories that *do* precisely align with the mythos of the television series prompt them to participate in fan culture by writing their own scenarios in which Barnabas, Julia, Roger, Elizabeth and the rest do exactly what they would do or are supposed to do according to the facts that have been established on the TV show. Because the plots of the *Dark Shadows* comic books and paperback novels take liberties with the TV show's parameters, some fans do not enjoy them as much as the primary incarnation of Barnabas and company. Many other fans, however, trust their parallel-time sensibilities and realize that these adventures take place in alternate realities (just as *House of Dark Shadows* and *Night of Dark Shadows* occupy *their* own universe apart from the televised text).

Because of their obvious fidelity to the TV series in the pre–VCR years of the sixties and seventies, the favorite *Dark Shadows* collectibles of many fans were Philadelphia Chewing-Gum Company's *Dark Shadows* trading cards and GAF's *Dark Shadows* View-Master packet, all of which visually recreated *Dark Shadows*. The first series of trading cards, released in 1968, featured red-bordered photographs from the TV show's 1967, 1795, and 1968 storylines. One year later, the second series (the green-bordered set, as fans call it) pictured the show's extremely popular 1897 storyline. Also released in 1969, the three-dimensional View-Master reels presented actual scenes from the 1968 Adam/Eve/Nicholas storyline.

In 1968, Whitman released a *Dark Shadows* board game. Players moved along an obstacle-laden track on an atmospheric game board that pictured a cemetery, several nocturnal animals, a bloody hand, a ghostly woman who resembled Angelique, and a fairly authentic drawing of Seaview Terrace, the TV Collinwood. In 1969, Milton Bradley followed with the Barnabas Collins *Dark Shadows* Game, which was simply a glorified Cootie game in which players raced to assemble a skeleton. Added frills were an ornate spinner, a Barnabas Collins coffin, miniature wooden stakes, and plastic glow-in-the-dark fangs. Also in 1969, Whitman released two *Dark Shadows* jigsaw puzzles and two Magic Slates.

Both the ratings and the merchandising of *Dark Shadows* peaked in 1969 when children and teenagers flocked to stores to find the novels, the comic books, the trading cards, the View-Master reels, the games, the puzzles, the rare Magic Slates, Philadelphia Chewing-Gum Company's sets of 12 *Quentin Post Cards* and 16 *1897 Pin-Ups,* Ben Cooper's Barnabas Collins Halloween costume, Edward Roberts's rare Barnabas Collins wristwatch, Western Publishing's Barnabas Glow-in-the-Dark Poster, Timco's rare Barnabas Collins Ring, and Model Products Corporation's plastic model kits of Barnabas, the Werewolf, and the Barnabas Vampire Van — not to mention Benlar's rare, curious *Groovy Horror Head Pillows* of Barnabas, the Werewolf, and the Witch.

Also in 1969, Robert Cobert's all-important music from *Dark Shadows* appeared in record stores and on *Billboard* music charts. In July, Philips Records released *The Original Music from Dark Shadows,* a best-selling LP featuring Cobert's eerie music along with moody narrations by Jonathan Frid and David Selby. The soundtrack album remained on the *Billboard* music charts for 19 weeks, "Quentin's Theme" was issued on sheet music and piano roll and was nominated for a Grammy Award, and the LP is still (as of 2008) among the top five best-selling TV soundtrack albums of all time. In 1969–1970, both Cobert and his sometimes collaborator Charles Randolph Grean released several LP records and 45 RPM singles of Cobert's music. At the same time, "Shadows of the Night (Quentin's Theme)" became a modern standard when vocal and instrumental versions were recorded by more than two dozen easy-listening artists including Ray Conniff, Claudine Longet, Henry Mancini, Mantovani, Lawrence Welk, and Andy Williams. Completist fans still scramble to acquire *all* of these recordings of "Quentin's Theme," including the almost impossible-to-find versions by The Magic Organ, banjoist Paul Buskirk, The Electronic Harmonica with The New Group, and Pierre Andre and The Golden Leaves.

By 1970, when Paul Randolf Associates released the rare Josette's Music Box, Curnor Music had published the sheet music for "Ode to Angelique," and Gold Key Comics had printed the one-shot *Dark Shadows Story Digest Magazine, Dark Shadows* had saturated the market — and popular culture. It remains the non–Saturday-morning daytime-TV series that has inspired the most merchandise, and it rivals many nighttime shows (e.g. *Batman, Star Trek, The Brady Bunch, Charlie's Angels*) in its sheer number of collectibles. Even *House of Dark Shadows* and *Night of Dark Shadows* generated some memorabilia (e.g. posters, lobby cards, stickers, VAMPIRE POWER badges, a tiny Angelique ghost doll), and Register Tribune's daily *Dark Shadows* newspaper comic strip ran in newspapers from March 14, 1971, to March 5, 1972. Seeking out and acquiring as many *Dark Shadows* collectibles as possible cements "the sense of possession that the fan feels toward favored media products," according to Henry Jenkins.[16] When fans buy all of the memorabilia and then enhance their collection with stories, artwork, costumes, and music that they create themselves, they feel that they truly own *Dark Shadows* and have helped to perpetuate and even shape the phenomenon.

Fans find true community when they bring their "intense emotional commitments" (Jenkins's words again),[17] their ideas, and their handiwork to a Dark Shadows Festival and share them with like-minded lovers of Dan Curtis's dream. *Dark Shadows* conventions, attended by fans and stars alike, began in the late 1970s and early 1980s with the *Dark Shadows* programming components at several Shadowcon and Timecon science-fiction conventions. Then, in 1983, the prominent *Dark Shadows* fans Jeffrey Arsenault, Maria Barbosa, Dale Clark, Melody Clark, Robert Finocchio, Jean Graham, Beth Klapper, Janet Meehan, Jim Pierson, Kathleen Resch, Marcy Robin, and Ann Wilson co-founded the Dark Shadows Festival, an annual three-day *Dark Shadows*-only convention which has been held once or twice each year in New Jersey, New York, California, Texas, or Nevada for the past quarter century—five times longer than the run of *Dark Shadows* itself.

Unlike Creation Con and *Fangoria* Weekend of Horrors, which are profit-making, corporate affairs, the Dark Shadows Festival is a homespun gathering run *by* fans *for* fans,

At Dark Shadows Festivals in the 1980s and early 1990s, Jeff Thompson often played Barnabas Collins in the Collinsport Players' productions, such as *The More Things Change 1990,* written and directed by Thompson (from the author's collection).

The Collinsport Players—(from left) Walter Down, Harriet Stich, Jeff Thompson, Darryl Schaffer, and Charles Ellis—perform *The Times, They Change,* written and directed by Muninn Venetis, at the 1990 Dark Shadows Festival in New York (from the author's collection).

with proceeds going to charity (often AIDS, cancer, juvenile diabetes, or Alzheimer's research). Although Festivals in the 1990s and 2000s have attracted up to 20 celebrity guests, the emphasis at the Dark Shadows Festival is on the fans and the fan experience. It is an extremely interactive gathering featuring trivia contests, poster-caption contests, living-caption contests, and filksinging (i.e. putting *Dark Shadows*-related lyrics to well-known popular songs and Christmas carols). Fan-made music videos run on big screens, and fans' *Dark Shadows*-inspired drawings and paintings hang in the Art Room. The Dealers' Room sells fanzines, *Concordances,* costumes, artwork, dolls, jewelry, and other fan-made crafts, as well as old *TV Guides* and the avidly sought aforementioned *Dark Shadows* memorabilia from the late 1960s and early 1970s. The Storyfest is a round-robin story-writing exercise among fans, and the Fan Panel updates the audience on fan clubs, fanzines, writing tips, and more. Other panels have focused on vampirism, time travel, and the many time periods featured on *Dark Shadows.* (In addition to the main time periods of 1795, 1897, et al., several episodes were set in 1949, 1692, and even 1680 Parallel Time.)

Dozens of fans participate in the Festival's Costume Gala, which began as a costume contest with prizes but later evolved into a non-competitive show-and-tell extravaganza of costumes, tableaux, and scenarios. Each year an equal number of women and men dress in elaborate, often home-made costumes depicting Naomi, Angelique, Laura, Abigail, Kitty, Barnabas, Quentin, Nicholas, Count Petofi, the werewolf, and many other *Dark Shadows* characters. Often, the participants perform brief songs or recitations as their characters. Also, female impersonation is a frequent part of the Costume Gala as men dress and sing as Julia, Carolyn, Magda, Josette, Carlotta, and other drag characters. All types of expression — occasionally even depictions of non–*Dark Shadows* Gothic characters — are encouraged and embraced at the Costume Gala, directed since the very first Festival by *Shadowgram* publisher Marcy Robin.

Another highly fan-participatory staple of the Dark Shadows Festival is the Collinsport Players, the fan acting troupe that Dr. Laura Brodian Freas and I co-founded in 1984. Each year the Collinsport Players present fans' humorous one-act plays based on *Dark Shadows.* The elaborate skits feature costumes, props, set pieces, sound effects, and music (either Robert Cobert's recordings or live music

The Collinsport Players — (from left) Ira Lipper, Eileen Farrar, and Jeff Thompson — perform *A Julia Carol,* written and directed by Thompson, at the 1991 Dark Shadows Festival in New York (from the author's collection).

performed by ensembles of fan musicians). The productions have spoofed every major storyline seen on *Dark Shadows* (1966–1971 and 1991), as well as the plots of *House of Dark Shadows* and *Night of Dark Shadows.* Other plays have blended *Dark Shadows* with the universes of *Austin Powers, Home Alone, Saturday Night Live, Scooby-Doo, The Newlywed Game,* Broadway musicals, *The Golden Girls,* and *A Christmas Carol* (partially fulfilling Dan Curtis's own dream of merging *Dark Shadows* and Charles

The Collinsport Players — Jonathan Harrison (left), Jeff Thompson, Joan Stewart, and Eileen Berger — perform *Curtains,* written and directed by Thompson, at Dracula 97: A Centennial Celebration in Los Angeles on August 15, 1997. Harrison directed a revival of *Curtains* at the 2008 Dark Shadows Festival in Burbank (from the author's collection).

Dickens's novel). A few of my more self-reflexive skits (including *Quiet on the Set!* and *Double Play*) have included Curtis himself as a gruff character named D.C. the Director.

The real Dan Curtis never attended a Dark Shadows Festival, but he occasionally autographed pictures, scripts, sheet music, and trading cards that were auctioned off to fans at the annual Charity Auction. The auction, which often features garments, props, fangs, scripts, and paintings from the two *Dark Shadows* series, allows fans a rare opportunity to possess an actual piece of *Dark Shadows.* At the Charity Auction at the 1985 Festival in Newark, New Jersey, the actual *Dorian Gray*-style portrait of Quentin Collins seen during the 1897 storyline sold for $800, and the portrait of Angelique first seen in 1968 went for $2,900. At the 2006 Dark Shadows Festival in Brooklyn, New York, the 22½" × 32" portrait of Barnabas seen in *House of Dark*

Although Dan Curtis never attended a Dark Shadows Festival, he signed various pictures, scripts, and trading cards that were auctioned for charity at the conventions.

Shadows sold for $13,000, with the proceeds going to Alzheimer's research in memory of Norma and Dan Curtis.

Every year since 1983, numerous personnel from the original *Dark Shadows* and later the 1991 series have appeared at the Festival to meet fans, answer questions, sign autographs, reminisce about *Dark Shadows,* and even have dinner with fans at various tables at the Sunday-night banquet. Not only the actors (e.g. Frid, Karlen, Millay, Parker, Selby, Scott, Wallace, and many others) but also the writers, costumers, hairstylists, and cameramen of *Dark Shadows* have attended various Festivals, and Robert Cobert has appeared at several conventions to discuss his music for *Dark Shadows* and many other Dan Curtis productions. Taking their cue from the Costume Gala participants and the Collinsport Players, the stars themselves now act in skits with each other, give dramatic readings, perform their cabaret acts, re-enact TV episodes, and stage new radio dramas. Additionally, some of the *Dark Shadows* stars and even their children have acted in the Collinsport Players' skits. As the Festivals have progressed, there has been a blurring of the line between fan and star as increased interaction and familiarity have lent the conventions the atmosphere of a family reunion. Attendance has risen from 100 in 1983 to 775 in 1985 to 2000 in 1993. When the European Sci-Fi Channel began showing *Dark Shadows* in England, attendees from overseas further increased the crowds. Three thousand fans attended the 1997 Dark Shadows Festival at the Marriott Marquis Hotel in Times Square. In more recent years, attendance has ranged from 2000 in Brooklyn in 2003 to 800 in Tarrytown in 2004 to 1000 in Hollywood in 2005 to 1400 back in Tarrytown in 2007 to 1500 in Burbank in 2008.

On August 25–27, 2006, when 1200 fans and one dozen stars gathered in Brooklyn for the 24th annual Dark Shadows Festival, they held several Dan Curtis tribute programs of videos and testimonials. Kathryn Leigh Scott, David Selby, John Karlen, and other *Dark Shadows* alumni shared their memories of Curtis, and Marie Wallace revealed that the last time she saw Curtis, in New York, her director told her how much he "loved" her as an actress and a human being. Festival chairman Jim Pierson, who is also an executive of both Dan Curtis Productions and MPI Home Video,

Roger Davis and Lara Parker perform an impromptu skit at the 1989 Dark Shadows Festival in New York. (from the author's collection).

showed the retrospective videos that had been presented at Curtis's March 30 funeral and May 13 memorial service.

Dan Curtis's mid–1965 dream of the girl on the train has begotten an entire fandom — indeed, an entire way of life for thousands of people who have been moved and inspired by *Dark Shadows* and who eagerly await the planned remake starring Johnny Depp. A slogan among fans is F.I.A.W.O.L. (Fandom Is A Way Of Life), and *Dark Shadows* devotees best demonstrate this philosophy at the Dark Shadows Festival. The convention is a euphoric weekend of sharing, remembering, collaborating, and celebrating.

Louis Edmonds poses for a picture at the 1990 Dark Shadows Festival in New York. (from the author's collection).

Perhaps most importantly, the fans adoringly watch and rewatch the many productions of Dan Curtis — *Dark Shadows* episodes, *A Darkness at Blaisedon,* the two Kolchak films, *The Norliss Tapes, The Great Ice Rip-Off, Intruders,* and many others. As they communally experience the shows, they discuss the effect that Curtis's television horror has had on their interests, the high quality and ratings of Curtis's groundbreaking productions, and the enormous influence that Curtis's work has had on subsequent media and on their own lives.

In terms of impact, ratings, innovation, quality, and influence, the television horror of Dan Curtis commands a very special place in popular culture. Its legacy will be felt for years to come. The words A DAN CURTIS PRODUCTION will not soon be forgotten. Neither will Dan Curtis the man. On Thursday October 26, 2006, *Dark Shadows* stars and

David Selby poses for a picture with Jeff Thompson at the 2008 Dark Shadows Resurrected Weekend in Burbank. (from the author's collection).

fans reconvened at the Vista Theatre in Los Angeles, California, for the Dark Shadows 40th Anniversary Haunted Halloween Party. Paying tribute to Curtis in speeches to the crowd were Barbara Steele, Lara Parker, and Karen Black. The star of *Trilogy of Terror* and *Burnt Offerings* said,

> I had never worked with anyone quite like Dan. He was ferocious and forthcoming. He had a very big heart and large intentions — and he was going to get that shot *right* no matter *what* — and it was usually a low shot. [...] He was really *with* the actor; he was very supportive of me. He was very open and very loving with me. Dan Curtis had a huge impact on my career. [...] When he was on his way [i.e. near death], he had a brain tumor, and he couldn't speak. Jim Pierson was very kind. He let me go and see Dan. Dan was lying on a couch, but he was still *Dan*. I knelt by him, and he held my hand and stroked my hair. He was just as feisty and as beautiful as ever. We had a lovely good-bye. I don't know if you believe in energy or whether you believe people become air or you believe people become another lifetime, but if you are ever in your backyard and this huge gust of air — *wind* — comes around you, or if you feel a sudden, really strong, electric, outrageous burst of energy, or if you see a little baby who's kicking up a horrible fuss, then you can say hello — to Dan.[18]

Chapter Notes

Introduction

1. J. Gordon Melton, *The Vampire Book,* 1st edition (Detroit: Visible Ink Press, 1994), 150.

2. Mark Dawidziak, *The Night Stalker Companion* (Los Angeles: Pomegranate Press, 1977), 63; Jim Pierson, *Produced and Directed by Dan Curtis* (Los Angeles: Pomegranate Press, 2004), 18.

3. Radu Florescu, *In Search of Frankenstein* (Boston: New York Graphic Society, 1975), 236.

4. Quoted in Marcy Robin, "Dan Curtis News," *Shadowgram,* no. 108 (June 2006): 8.

5. Quoted in Pierson, *Produced and Directed by Dan Curtis,* 14.

6. Bruce Kawin, "Children of the Light," in *Film Genre Reader II,* ed. Barry Keith Grant (Austin: University of Texas Press, 1995), 325.

7. *Ibid.*

8. Isabel Pinedo, "Recreational Terror: Postmodern Elements of the Contemporary Horror Film," *Journal of Film and Video,* vol. 48, no. 1/2 (Spring-Summer 1996): 20.

9. Gregory Waller, "Introduction to *American Horrors,*" in *The Horror Reader,* ed. Ken Gelder (London: Routledge, 2000), 257.

10. *Ibid.,* 257–258.

11. Paul Wells, *The Horror Genre: From Beelzebub to Blair Witch* (London: Wallflower, 2000), 74.

12. Wells, 75.

13. Quoted in Dawidziak, 40.

14. Quoted in *Richard Matheson: Terror Scribe,* dir. David Gregory, in *Trilogy of Terror* DVD (Dark Sky Films, 2006).

Chapter I

1. Dan Curtis, *The Night Stalker: Dan Curtis Interview,* dir. Greg Carson, in *The Night Stalker & The Night Strangler* DVD (MGM Home Entertainment, 2004).

2. *Ibid.*

3. Dan Curtis, *A Novel for Television,* dir. Don-ald Beck, in *The Winds of War, Part V* (Paramount DVD: 2004).

4. Quoted in Pierson, *Produced and Directed by Dan Curtis,* 205.

5. *Ibid.,* 14.

6. *Ibid.,* 205

7. Quoted in Zan Stewart, "Bob Cobert Scores His Own Victory in *War and Remembrance,*" *Shadowgram,* no. 45 (January 1989): 13.

8. Quoted in *Dark Shadows Behind the Scenes,* prod. Jim Pierson, in *Dark Shadows Special Edition* (MPI Home Video, 1999).

9. Dan Curtis, DVD Interview, *Dark Shadows DVD Collection 2* (MPI Home Video, 2002).

10. Quoted in "Director/Co-Producer Dan Curtis," *Drama-Logue,* October 14, 1993, 11.

11. Quoted in Pierson, *Produced and Directed by Dan Curtis,* 21.

12. Dan Curtis, DVD Interview, *Dark Shadows DVD Collection 16* (MPI Home Video, 2005).

13. Kathryn Leigh Scott and Jim Pierson, *Dark Shadows Almanac,* Millennium edition (Los Angeles: Pomegranate Press, 2000), 104.

14. Dan Curtis, DVD Interview, *Dark Shadows DVD Collection 16.*

15. Dawidziak, 63; Pierson, *Produced and Directed by Dan Curtis,* 18; Marcy Robin, "Dan Curtis News," *Shadowgram,* no. 107 (April 2006): 13.

16. Quoted in Pierson, *Produced and Directed by Dan Curtis,* 93.

17. *Ibid.*

18. *Ibid.,* 94.

19. *Ibid.,* 107.

20. *Ibid.,* 205.

21. *Ibid.,* 114.

22. Quoted in *Three Colors Black,* dir. David Gregory, in *Trilogy of Terror* DVD (Dark Sky Films, 2006).

23. Quoted in Pierson, *Produced and Directed by Dan Curtis,* 24.

24. *Ibid.,* 132.

25. *Ibid.*

26. *Ibid.,* 24.

27. *Ibid.*, 131.

28. *Ibid.*, 136–137.

29. *Ibid.*, 25.

30. Quoted in Robin, "Dan Curtis News," *Shadowgram,* no. 107: 22.

31. Dan Curtis, DVD interview, *Dan Curtis and the Daltons,* prod. Jim Pierson, in *The Last Ride of the Dalton Gang* (MPI Home Video, 2005).

32. Quoted in Pierson, *Produced and Directed by Dan Curtis,* 142.

33. Pierson, *Produced and Directed by Dan Curtis,* 145–146.

34. Quoted in Pierson, *Produced and Directed by Dan Curtis,* 146.

35. Quoted in *A Novel for Television.*

36. *Ibid.*

37. Quoted in "Director/Co-Producer Dan Curtis," 11.

38. Quoted in *Making The Winds of War,* dir. Donald Beck, in *The Winds of War, Part V* (Paramount DVD, 2004).

39. Pierson, *Produced and Directed by Dan Curtis,* 156.

40. Quoted in Pierson, *Produced and Directed by Dan Curtis,* 208.

41. Quoted in *A Novel for Television.*

42. Quoted in Pierson, *Produced and Directed by Dan Curtis,* 205.

43. Quoted in *Making the Winds of War.*

44. Marcy Robin, "Dan Curtis News," *Shadowgram,* no. 41 (February 1988):5.

45. Quoted in *Making The Winds of War.*

46. Quoted in Pierson, *Produced and Directed by Dan Curtis,* 156.

47. *Ibid.*

48. *Ibid.*

49. *Ibid.*

50. Thomas O'Neil, *The Emmys,* 3rd edition (New York: Berkley, 1998), 299–300, 303–307.

51. Quoted in *Making of War and Remembrance,* dir. Donald Beck, in *War and Remembrance: The Final Chapter, Parts V-VII* (MPI Home Video, 2003).

52. Marcy Robin, "Dan Curtis News," *Shadowgram,* no. 41:5.

53. *Making of War and Remembrance.*

54. Morgan Gendel, "ABC at War Again with Miniseries, Maxi-Sequel," *Los Angeles Times,* September 6, 1986), 10-F.

55 Marcy Robin, "Dan Curtis News," *Shadowgram,* no. 47 (August, 1989): 7.

56. Gendel, 10-F.

57. Quoted in *Making of War and Remembrance.*

58. Pierson, *Produced and Directed by Dan Curtis,* 168.

59. *Ibid.*

60. Quoted in Rick DuBrow, "*Winds of War II:* The Saga Continues," *Los Angeles Herald-Examiner,* May 17, 1984, 4-F.

61. Pierson, *Produced and Directed by Dan Curtis,* 168.

62. Quoted in Pierson, *Produced and Directed by Dan Curtis,* 208.

63. *Ibid.*, 205.

64. *Ibid.*, 206.

65. Quoted in Stewart, 13.

66. Quoted in, *Making of War and Remembrance*; Stewart, 13.

67. Quoted in Stewart, 13.

68. Quoted in Pierson, *Produced and Directed by Dan Curtis,* 169.

69. *Ibid.*

70. *Ibid.*

71. *Ibid.*

72. *Ibid.*

73. *Ibid.*

74. *Ibid.*, 168.

75. Quoted in Marcy Robin, "Dan Curtis News," *Shadowgram,* no. 46 (April 1989): 9.

76. *Ibid.*

77. O'Neil, 396, 400–406; Pierson, *Produced and Directed by Dan Curtis,* 168.

78. O'Neil, 396.

79. *Ibid.*, 400–406.

80. Marcy Robin, "Dan Curtis News," *Shadowgram,* no. 82 (February 1998):10.

81. Marcy Robin, "Dan Curtis News, *Shadowgram,* no. 47: 7.

82. *Ibid.*

83. Quoted in *Making of War and Remembrance.*

84. Dan Curtis, "Remember *Remembrance*," in *Shadowgram,* no. 79 (May 1997): 9.

85. Quoted in Marcy Robin, "*Dark Shadows News*," *Shadowgram,* no. 54/55 (January 1991): 15.

86. Quoted in Pierson, *Produced and Directed by Dan Curtis,* 180.

87. Jim Pierson, *Dark Shadows Resurrected* (Los Angeles: Pomegranate Press, 1992), 20.

88. O'Neil, 446.

89. Quoted in Marcy Robin, "Dan Curtis News," *Shadowgram,* no. 61 (August 1992): 15.

90. Quoted in Pierson, *Produced and Directed by Dan Curtis,* 188.

91. Quoted in Robin, "Dan Curtis News," *Shadowgram,* no. 61: 15.

92. Quoted in Pierson, *Produced and Directed by Dan Curtis,* 188.

93. Quoted in "Director/Co-Producer Dan Curtis," 10–11.

94. Quoted in Marcy Robin, "Dan Curtis News," *Shadowgram,* no. 67 (January 1994): 15.

95. *Ibid.*

96. *Ibid.*

97. *Ibid.*

98. *Ibid.*

99. Quoted in Marcy Robin, "Dan Curtis News," *Shadowgram,* no. 78 (February 1997): 10.

100. Quoted in Marcy Robin, "Dan Curtis News," *Shadowgram,* no. 79 (May 1997): 9.

101. Dawidziak, 194.

102. Robin, "Dan Curtis News," *Shadowgram,* no. 82: 10.

103. Quoted in Pierson, *Produced and Directed by Dan Curtis,* 202.

104. Quoted in Robin, "Dan Curtis News," *Shadowgram,* no. 82: 10.

105. *Ibid.*

106. *Ibid.*

107. Quoted in Pierson, *Produced and Directed by Dan Curtis,* 202.

108. *Ibid.*

109. *Ibid.,* 206.

110. Quoted in *Dark Shadows Reunion: 35th Anniversary Celebration,* prod. Jim Pierson (MPI Home Video, 2003).

111. Darren Gross, "*Dark Shadows* Staked!" *Fangoria,* no. 239 (January 2005): 62.

112. Pierson, *Produced and Directed by Dan Curtis,* 213.

113. Quoted in Marcy Robin, "Dan Curtis News," *Shadowgram,* no. 104 (April 2005): 11.

114. *Ibid.*

115. Quoted in Pierson, *Produced and Directed by Dan Curtis,* 213.

116. *Ibid.*

117. *Ibid.* 215–216.

118. Quoted in Marcy Robin, "Dan Curtis News," *Shadowgram,* no. 106 (October 2005): 9.

119. *Ibid.*

120. Quoted in Pierson, *Produced and Directed by Dan Curtis,* 216.

121. Quoted in Robin, "Dan Curtis News," *Shadowgram,* no. 106: 9.

122. *Ibid.*

123. *Ibid.*

124. *Ibid.*

125. *Ibid.*

126. Quoted in Robin, "Dan Curtis News," *Shadowgram,* no. 107: 13.

127. Scott, letter to the author, June 15, 2006.

128. Robin, "Dan Curtis News," *Shadowgram,* no. 107:12–13.

129. *Ibid.*

130. All quoted in Robin, "Dan Curtis News," *Shadowgram,* no. 108: 8.

131. Quoted in Pierson, *Produced and Directed by Dan Curtis,* 206.

132. Quoted in Robin, "Dan Curtis News," *Shadowgram,* no. 108: 8.

133. Scott, letter to the author, June 15, 2006.

134. Quoted in Robin, "Dan Curtis News," *Shadowgram,* no. 108: 8.

135. Quoted in David Del Valle, "Memories of Dan Curtis, *Films in Review,* March 28, 2006, http://www.filmsinreview.com/Features/dancurtis.html.

136. *Ibid.*

137. Quoted in Dawidziak, 95; Pierson, *Produced and Directed by Dan Curtis,* 29.

Chapter II

1. Quoted in *Dark Shadows Behind the Scenes.*

2. Quoted in Kathleen Resch and Marcy Robin, *Dark Shadows in the Afternoon* (New York: Image Publishing, 1991), 7, 71.

3. Quoted in Curtis, *Dark Shadows DVD Collection 2.*

4. Quoted in Robin, "Dan Curtis News," *Shadowgram,* no. 97 (October 2002): 10.

5. Quoted in *Dark Shadows Behind the Scenes.*

6. *Ibid.*

7. *Ibid.*

8. Quoted in *Dark Shadows Reunion: 35th Anniversary Celebration.*

9. Dan Curtis, DVD Interview, prod. Jim Pierson, in *Dark Shadows DVD Collection 11* (MPI Home Video, 2004).

10. Scott and Pierson, *Dark Shadows Almanac,* Millennium edition, 104.

11. Quoted in Curtis, DVD Interview, *Dark Shadows DVD Collection 11.*

12. Scott and Pierson, *Dark Shadows Almanac,* Millennium edition, 104.

13. Quoted in Dan Curtis, DVD interview, *Inside the Shadows,* prod. Jim Pierson, in *Dark Shadows Special Edition* (MPI Home Video: 1999).

14. *Ibid.*

15. Quoted in Quoted in *Dark Shadows Behind the Scenes.*

16. Henry Jenkins, *Textual Poachers: Television Fans and Participatory Culture* (New York: Routledge, 1992), 137.

17. Scott and Pierson, *Dark Shadows Almanac,* Millennium edition, 102, 135.

18. *Ibid.*

19. *Ibid.,* 102.

20. Quoted in "Director/Co-Producer Dan Curtis," 11.

21. Scott, letter to the author, June 15, 2006.

22. Quoted in Robin, "Dan Curtis News," *Shadowgram,* no. 97: 10.

23. Quoted in Curtis, DVD Interview, *Inside the Shadows.*

24. Quoted in Curtis, DVD Interview, *Dark Shadows DVD Collection 16.*

25. Quoted in *Dark Shadows Behind the Scenes* .

26. Quoted in Curtis, DVD Interview, *Inside the Shadows.*

27. Stephen King, *Stephen King's Danse Macabre* (New York: Berkley Books, 1981), 188.

28. Resch and Robin, 24.

29. Scott and Pierson, *Dark Shadows Almanac,* Millennium edition, 104.

30. Marilyn Ross, *The Vampire Contessa: From the Journal of Jeremy Quentain* (New York: Pinnacle Books, 1974), 34.

31. Katherine Ramsland, *Prism of the Night: A Biography of Anne Rice,* 2nd edition (New York: Plume, 1994), 105.

32. *Ibid.,* 149.

33. Pierson, *Dark Shadows Resurrected,* 9.

34. *Ibid.,* 24.

35. *Ibid.*

36. *Ibid.,* 23.

37. *Ibid.,* 19.

38. Quoted in Pierson, *Produced and Directed by Dan Curtis,* 180.

39. *Ibid.*
40. *Ibid.*
41. *Ibid.*
42. Gross, "*Dark Shadows* Staked!" 64.
43. Resch and Robin, 7, 71.
44. Quoted in Gross, "*Dark Shadows* Staked!" 64.
45. *Ibid.*
46. *Ibid.*, 65.
47. *Ibid.*
48. *Ibid.*, 82.
49. Quoted in Dan Curtis, DVD Interview, *Dark Shadows DVD Collection 24* (MPI Home Video: 2006).

Chapter III

1. Quoted in *Dark Shadows Reunion: 35th Anniversary Celebration.*
2. Jim Pierson, Liner notes, *House of Dark Shadows and Night of Dark Shadows*, composed and conducted by Robert Cobert (Turner Classic Movies Music: 1996), 8.
3. Kathryn Leigh Scott and Jim Pierson, *The Dark Shadows Movie Book* (Los Angeles: Pomegranate Press, 2000), 9.
4. Quoted in Scott and Pierson, *The Dark Shadows Movie Book*, 18.
5. *Ibid.*, 19.
6. Kathryn Leigh Scott, letter to the author, June 15, 2006.
7. Scott and Pierson, *The Dark Shadows Movie Book*, 19.
8. Quoted in Pierson, *Produced and Directed by Dan Curtis*, 52.
9. Quoted in Scott and Pierson, *The Dark Shadows Movie Book*, 20.
10. Quoted in Curtis, DVD Interview, *Inside the Shadows.*
11. Quoted in Scott and Pierson, *The Dark Shadows Movie Book*, 22.
12. Lyndon Joslin, *Count Dracula Goes to the Movies: Stoker's Novel Adapted, 1922–1995* (Jefferson, NC: McFarland, 1999), 142.
13. "*House of Dark Shadows* Stresses the Sinister," *New York Times Online*, October 29, 1970, http://movies2.nytimes.com/mem/movies/review.html.
14. *Ibid.*
15. Quoted in "Featured Filmmaker — Dan Curtis — The Career of the Man Behind *Dark Shadows* and Kolchak," *Film Force*, July 8, 2003, http://filmforce.ign.com/articles/427/427516pl.html.
16. Roger Ebert, "*House of Dark Shadows*," *Chicago Sun–Times Online*, October 6, 1970, http://rogerebert.suntimes.com/apps/pbcs.dll/article?AID=/19701006/REVW.
17. Quoted in Pierson, *Produced and Directed by Dan Curtis*, 52.
18. Donald Glut, *The Dracula Book* (Metuchen: Scarecrow, 1975), 305.

19. Quoted in Pierson, *Produced and Directed by Dan Curtis*, 16.
20. Scott and Pierson, *The Dark Shadows Movie Book*, 23.
21. Tim Lucas, "*House of Dark Shadows* and *Night of Dark Shadows*," *Video Watchdog*, no. 22 (March-April 1994): 67.
22. Quoted in Pierson, *Produced and Directed by Dan Curtis*, 57.
23. Lucas, "*House of Dark Shadows* and *Night of Dark Shadows*," 67.
24. Quoted in Scott and Pierson, *The Dark Shadows Movie Book*, 26.
25. A. H. Weiler, "*Night of Dark Shadows* Arrives," *New York Times Online*, October 14, 1971, http://movies2.nytimes.com/mem/movies/review.html.
26. Quoted in Pierson, *Produced and Directed by Dan Curtis*, 57.
27. *Ibid.*
28. Roger Ebert, "*Night of Dark Shadows*," *Chicago Sun–Times Online*, September 21, 1971, http://rogerebert.suntimes.com/apps/pbcs/dll/article?AID=/19710921/REVW.
29. Scott and Pierson, *Dark Shadows Almanac*, Millennium edition, 162.
30. Anthony Ambrogio, "Tell Me When It's Over: The Rise and Fall of the Downbeat Ending," *Midnight Marquee*, no. 67/68 (2003): 37.
31. Scott and Pierson, *The Dark Shadows Movie Book*, 26.
32. Quoted in Pierson, *Produced and Directed by Dan Curtis*, 16.
33. Quoted in Scott and Pierson, *The Dark Shadows Movie Book*, 16.

Chapter IV

1. Quoted in Dan Curtis, DVD Interview, *Dark Shadows DVD Collection 8* (MPI Home Video, 2003).
2. *Ibid.*
3. Elaine Showalter, "Dr. Jekyll's Closet," in *The Horror Reader*, ed. Ken Gelder (London: Routledge, 2000), 197.
4. Robert Louis Stevenson, *The Strange Case of Dr. Jekyll and Mr. Hyde* (New York: Books, Inc., n.d.), 79.
5. *Ibid.*, 77.
6. *Ibid.*, 55.
7. Quoted in Pierson, *Produced and Directed by Dan Curtis*, 16.
8. *Ibid.*, 43.
9. *Ibid.*, 44.
10. *Ibid.*
11. Quoted in John Burlingame, Liner notes, *The Night Stalker and Other Classic Thrillers*, composed and conducted by Robert Cobert (Varese Sarabande, 2000).
12. Quoted in Pierson, *Produced and Directed by Dan Curtis*, 11.

13. O'Neil, 124–128.

14. Quoted in Pierson, *Produced and Directed by Dan Curtis,* 44.

15. Florescu, 198.

16. Mary Shelley, *Frankenstein, or The Modern Prometheus* (London: Penguin, 1992), 58.

17. Paul O'Flinn, "Production and Reproduction: The Case of *Frankenstein,*" in *The Horror Reader,* ed. Ken Gelder (London: Routledge, 2000), 114.

18. *Ibid.,* 115, 120.

19. Quoted in Pierson, *Produced and Directed by Dan Curtis,* 19.

20. Shelly, 19.

21. Quoted in Burlingame, Liner notes, *The Night Stalker and Other Classic Thrillers.*

22. Quoted in Pierson, *Produced and Directed by Dan Curtis,* 69.

23. *Ibid.*

24. Florescu, 236.

25. Dan Curtis, "A Frank Explanation of Producer's Version," reported in *Shadowgram,* no. 63 (January 1993): 10.

26. Quoted in Pierson, *Produced and Directed by Dan Curtis,* 75.

27. Quoted in Kevin Shinnick, "Come Back, Shane Briant," *Scarlet Street,* no. 42 (2001): 49.

28. *Ibid.,* 51.

29. *Ibid.,* 50.

30. Quoted in Pierson, *Produced and Directed by Dan Curtis,* 75.

31. Oscar Wilde, *The Picture of Dorian Gray* (New York: Modern Library, 2004), 254.

32. Quoted in Pierson, *Produced and Directed by Dan Curtis,* 21.

33. Bram Stoker, *Dracula* (New York: Signet Classic, 1992), 320.

34. Quoted in Dan Curtis, DVD Interview, prod. Jim Pierson, in *The Dan Curtis Macabre Collection* (MPI Home Video: 2002).

35. *Ibid.*

36. Quoted in Pierson, *Produced and Directed by Dan Curtis,* 85.

37. *Ibid.*

38. Quoted in Jack Palance, DVD Interview, prod. Jim Pierson, in *The Dan Curtis Macabre Collection* (MPI Home Video: 2002).

39. Glut, *The Dracula Book,* 293.

40. J. Gordon Melton, *The Vampire Book: The Encyclopedia of the Undead,* 2nd ed. (Detroit: Visible Ink Press, 1999), 758–764.

41. Stoker, 29.

42. *Ibid.,* 30.

43. *Ibid.,* 30–31.

44. *Ibid.,* 241–242.

45. Melton, *The Vampire Book,* 2nd ed., 702–703.

46. *Ibid.,* 603–604.

47. J. Gordon Melton, *The Vampire Book,* 1st ed., 669.

48. Stoker, 303–304.

49. Quoted in Burlingame, Liner notes, *The Night Stalker and Other Classic Thrillers.*

50. Raymond McNally and Radu Florescu, *In Search of Dracula,* New ed. (Boston: Houghton Mifflin, 1994), 273.

51. Melton, *The Vampire Book,* 1st ed., 670.

52. Quoted in Dan Curtis, DVD Interview, *The Dan Curtis Macabre Collection.*

53. Quoted in Pierson, *Produced and Directed by Dan Curtis,* 86.

54. Quoted in Dan Curtis, DVD Interview, *The Dan Curtis Macabre Collection.*

55. Quoted in Michael McCarty, "William F. Nolan Looks Back at the Legacy of *Logan's Run* and Looks Forward to Bryan Singer's Remake," *Sci-Fi* (2005), http://www.scifi.com/sfw/issue403/interview.html.

56. Quoted in Dan Curtis, DVD Interview, *The Dan Curtis Macabre Collection.*

57. *Ibid.*

58. *Ibid.*

59. Quoted in McCarty, "Nolan Looks Back."

60. Henry James, *The Turn of the Screw* (New York: Dover, 1991), 12.

61. *Ibid.*

62. *Ibid.,* 58.

63. *Ibid.,* 75.

64. *Ibid.,* 76.

65. Edmund Wilson, "The Ambiguity of Henry James," *Hound and Horn* VII (April–June 1934): 385–406.

66. James, 8.

67. *Ibid.,* 15.

68. *Ibid.,* 86.

69. Quoted in Dan Curtis, DVD Interview, *The Dan Curtis Macabre Collection.*

70. *Ibid.*

71. Quoted in Pierson, *Produced and Directed by Dan Curtis,* 99.

72. *Ibid.*

73. Quoted in "Director/Co-Producer Dan Curtis," 10-11.

Chapter V

1. Dawidziak, 63; Michael Karol, *The ABC Movie of the Week: A Loving Tribute to the Classic Series* (New York: iUniverse, 2005), 4; Pierson, *Produced and Directed by Dan Curtis,* 18.

2. Robin, "Dan Curtis News," *Shadowgram,* no. 78: 10.

3. Robin, "Dan Curtis News," *Shadowgram,* no. 107:13.

4. Quoted in Mark Scott Zicree, *The Twilight Zone Companion* (New York: Bantam Books, 1982), 57.

5. Quoted in Dawidziak, 31.

6. *Ibid.,* 31–32.

7. *Ibid.,* 32.

8. *Ibid.,* 46.

9. Quoted in Pierson, *Produced and Directed by Dan Curtis,* 17.

10. *Ibid.*

11. *Ibid.*
12. Quoted in Pierson, *Produced and Directed by Dan Curtis,* 17–18.
13. Quoted in Dawidziak, 55.
14. All quoted in Marcy Robin, "Dan Curtis News," *Shadowgram,* no. 81 (November 1997): 11.
15. Quoted in Dawidziak, 21.
16. Quoted in Burlingame, Liner notes, *The Night Stalker and Other Classic Thrillers.*
17. Quoted in Dawidziak, 63.
18. Quoted in Pierson, *Produced and Directed by Dan Curtis,* 20.
19. Quoted in Dawidziak, 79.
20. Quoted in Pierson, *Produced and Directed by Dan Curtis,* 19.
21. Quoted in Dan Curtis, DVD Interview, *Directing the Night Stranger,* dir. Greg Carson, in *The Night Stalker & The Night Strangler* (MPI Home Entertainment: 2004).
22. Quoted in "Thayer David Quotes," *Brainy Quotes,* 2006, http://www.brainyquote.com/quotes/authors/t/thayer_david.html.
23. Jonathan Lampley, letter to the author, May 25, 2007.
24. Quoted in Pierson, *Produced and Directed by Dan Curtis,* 66.
25. *Ibid.*
26. *Ibid.*
27. Quoted in Dawidziak, 83.
28. *Ibid.*
29. Quoted in Burlingame, Liner notes, *The Night Stalker and Other Classic Thrillers.*
30. Quoted in Dawidziak, 81.
31. Quoted in Dan Curtis, DVD Interview, *The Night Stalker: Dan Curtis Interview,* dir. Greg Carson, in *The Night Stalker & The Night Strangler* (MGM Home Entertainment, 2004).
32. *Ibid.*

Chapter VI

1. Quoted in Dawidziak, 90.
2. *Ibid.,* 99.
3. Quoted in McCarty, "Nolan Looks Back."
4. *Ibid.*
5. *Ibid.*
6. Quoted in Pierson, *Produced and Directed by Dan Curtis,* 73.
7. *Ibid.*
8. *Ibid.*
9. Quoted in Pierson, *Produced and Directed by Dan Curtis,* 208.
10. Quoted in Michael McCarty, "Dan Curtis Continues to Thrive in the *Dark Shadows,*" *Sci-Fi* (2002), http://www.scifi.com/sfw/issue272/interview.html.
11. Quoted in Dawidziak, 89; John Javna, *Cult TV* (New York: St. Martin's Press, 1985), 174; Pierson, *Produced and Directed by Dan Curtis,* 14.
12. Javna, 174.

13. Quoted in Pierson, *Produced and Directed by Dan Curtis,* 206.

Chapter VII

1. Quoted in Curtis, DVD Interview, *The Night Stalker: Dan Curtis Interview.*
2. Quoted in Pierson, *Produced and Directed by Dan Curtis,* 205; Robin, 96:9
3. Quoted in Pierson, *Produced and Directed by Dan Curtis,* 22.
4. Quoted in McCarty, "Nolan Looks Back."
5. Quoted in Scott Bosco, Liner notes, *Trilogy of Terror,* videocassette (Anchor Bay Entertainment, 1999).
6. Richard Matheson, "The Likeness of Julie," in *Shock II* (New York: Dell, 1964), 80–81.
7. *Ibid.,* 82.
8. *Ibid.,* 86–87.
9. *Ibid.,* 90.
10. Laura Mulvey, "Visual Pleasure and Narrative Cinema," in *The Norton Anthology of Theory and Criticism,* ed. Vincent Leitch (New York: W. W. Norton, 2001), 2184–2191.
11. *Ibid.,* 2192.
12. Linda, Williams, "When the Woman Looks," in *Re-Vision: Essays in Feminist Film Criticism,* ed. Mary Ann Doane, Patricia Mellencamp, and Linda Williams (Frederick, MD: American Film Institute Monograph Series, University Publications of America, 1984), 96–97.
13. Richard Matheson, "Needle in the Heart," a.k.a. "Therese," in *Shock Waves* (New York: Dell, 1970), 109.
14. Richard Matheson, "Prey," in *Shock Waves* (New York: Dell, 1970), 195.
15. Quoted in Bosco.
16. *Ibid.*
17. Quoted in Pierson, *Produced and Directed by Dan Curtis,* 22–23.
18. Quoted in Burlingame, Liner notes, *The Night Stalker and Other Classic Thrillers.*
19. Quoted in Karen Black and William F. Nolan, DVD Commentary, in *Trilogy of Terror* (Dark Sky Films, 2006).
20. Quoted in *Three Colors Black.*
21. Quoted in Pierson, *Produced and Directed by Dan Curtis,* 109.
22. Karol, 96.
23. Jack Finney, "Second Chance," in *The Third Level* (New York: Dell, 1959), 158.
24. Richard Matheson, "No Such Thing as a Vampire," in *Shock II* (New York: Dell, 1964), 38.
25. Quoted in Pierson, *Produced and Directed by Dan Curtis,* 126.
26. Henry Kuttner, "The Graveyard Rats," in *Dying of Fright,* ed. Les Daniels (New York: Scribner's, 1976), 190.
27. *Ibid.*
28. *Ibid.*
29. *Ibid.,* 191.

30. *Ibid.*
31. *Ibid.*
32. *Ibid.*
33. *Ibid.*, 192.
34. *Ibid.*, 190.
35. *Ibid.*, 191.
36. *Ibid.*, 195.
37. Quoted in McCarty, "Nolan Looks Back."
38. Jenkins, 104.
39. Matheson, "Prey," 194.
40. Kawin, 309.
41. *Ibid.*
42. Quoted in Pierson, *Produced and Directed by Dan Curtis,* 198; Robin, "Dan Curtis News," *Shadowgram,* no. 78: 10.
43. Quoted in Robin, "Dan Curtis News," *Shadowgram,* no. 78: 10.
44. Quoted in Robin, "Dan Curtis News," *Shadowgram,* no. 79: 9.
45. *Ibid.*
46. Quoted in McCarty, "Nolan Looks Back."
47. Quoted in Pierson, *Produced and Directed by Dan Curtis,* 29.

Chapter VIII

1. Quoted in Dan Curtis, William F. Nolan, and Karen Black, DVD Commentary, *Burnt Offerings* (MGM Home Entertainment, 2003).
2. *Ibid.*
3. Robert Marasco, *Burnt Offerings* (New York, Delacorte Press, 1973), 55.
4. *Ibid.*, 226, 190, 214.
5. Quoted in Curtis, Nolan, and Black, DVD Commentary, *Burnt Offerings.*
6. "*Burnt Offerings* Not So Very Well Done," *The Tennessean,* November 19, 1976, 6-D.
7. *Ibid.*
8. Quoted in Pierson, *Produced and Directed by Dan Curtis,* 120.
9. *Ibid.*
10. "*Burnt Offerings* Is an Outstanding Terror Movie," *New York Times Online,* September 30, 1976, http://movies2.nytimes.com/mem/movies/review.html?title1=&title2.
11. Quoted in Pierson, *Produced and Directed by Dan Curtis,* 120.
12. Quoted in Curtis, Nolan, and Black, DVD Commentary, *Burnt Offerings.*
13. Quoted in Burlingame, Liner notes, *The Night Stalker and Other Classic Thrillers.*
14. Quoted in Curtis, Nolan, and Black, DVD Commentary, *Burnt Offerings.*
15. *Ibid.*
16. *Ibid.*
17. Quoted in Pierson, *Produced and Directed by Dan Curtis,* 119.
18. "*Burnt Offerings* Is an Outstanding Terror Movie."
19. Quoted in Pierson, *Produced and Directed by Dan Curtis,* 120.

20. *Ibid.*
21. Quoted in McCarty, "Nolan Looks Back."
22. George LaVoo, "*Burnt Offerings* Filmbook," *The Old, Dark House,* no. 1 (Winter 1976–1977): 7.
23. Quoted in Pierson, *Produced and Directed by Dan Curtis,* 119.
24. Quoted in LaVoo, 10.
25. Quoted in Curtis, Nolan, and Black, DVD Commentary, *Burnt Offerings.*
26. Marasco, 222.
27. Quoted in Pierson, *Produced and Directed by Dan Curtis,* 205.
28. Quoted in Curtis, Nolan, and Black, DVD Commentary, *Burnt Offerings.*
29. Kawin, 309.
30. Stephen King, "Why We Crave Horror Movies," in *The Prose Reader: Essays for Thinking, Reading, and Writing,* 6th edition, ed. Kim Flachmann and Michael Flachmann (Upper Saddle River, NJ: Prentice Hall, 2002), 452–453.
31. Kawin, 309.
32. Barbara Creed, *The Monstrous Feminine: Film, Feminism, Psychoanalysis* (London: Routledge, 1993), 49–54; Laura Mulvey, *Fetishism and Curiosity* (Bloomington: Indiana University Press, 1996), 14.

Conclusion

1. Karol, 5; Robin, "Dan Curtis News," *Shadowgram,* no. 108: 8.
2. Quoted in Dawidziak, 13–18.
3. Quoted in Robin, "Dan Curtis News," *Shadowgram,* no. 82: 10.
4. Quoted in Pierson, *Produced and Directed by Dan Curtis,* 17.
5. Quoted in Curtis, Nolan, and Black, DVD Commentary, *Burnt Offerings.*
6. Quoted in Pierson, *Produced and Directed by Dan Curtis,* 206.
7. *Ibid.*, 205.
8. Hal Boedeker, "Dan Curtis Thought Big," *Orlando Sentinel Blog,* March 28, 2006, http://blogs.orlandosentinel.com/entertainment_tv_tvblog.html.
9. Bill Gibron, "Character over Carnage: Dan Curtis," *Pop Matters,* April 3, 2006, http://www.popmatters.com/tv/features/060403-dancurtis.shtml.
10. Steve, "Dan Curtis Has Passed Away," *House of Irony,* June 18, 2006, http://houseofirony.com/2006/03/27/dan-curtis-1928-2006/.
11. Jenkins, 251.
12. *Ibid.*, 69–70.
13. *Ibid.*, 86, 115.
14. Resch and Robin, 106.
15. Quoted in Jeff Thompson, ""Four-Colour Shadows: The Gold Key Comics," *Dark Shadows Journal,* March 19, 2006, http://www.collinwood.net/features/cards/goldkey.htm.
16. Jenkins, 251.
17. *Ibid.*
18. Quoted in *DS Halloween Party,* dir. Joe Integlia, in *Vista Theatre DS Events* (JT Video, 2006).

Bibliography

Ambrogio, Anthony. "Dracula, Schmacula! Misinformation Never Dies." *Video Watchdog,* no. 19 (Sept.–Oct. 1993): 32–47.

_____. "Tell Me When It's Over: The Rise and Fall of the Downbeat Ending." *Midnight Marquee,* no. 67/68 (2003): 34–43.

Black, Karen. DVD interview. *Three Colors Black.* Dir. David Gregory. *Trilogy of Terror.* Dark Sky Films, 2006.

_____, and William F. Nolan. DVD commentary. *Trilogy of Terror.* Dark Sky Films, 2006.

Bloch, Robert. *Psycho.* New York: Crest Books, 1959.

Boedeker, Hal. "Dan Curtis Thought Big." *Orlando Sentinel Blog.* March 28, 2006. http://blogs.orlandosentinel.com/entertainment_tv_tvblog.html.

Bosco, Scott. Liner notes. *Trilogy of Terror.* Videocassette. Anchor Bay Entertainment, 1999.

Brooks, Tim, and Earle Marsh. *The Complete Directory to Prime-Time Network and Cable-TV Shows 1946–Present.* 8th ed. New York: Ballantine Books, 2003.

Brosnan, John. *The Horror People.* New York: Plume Books, 1976.

Burlingame, John. Liner notes. *The Night Stalker and Other Classic Thrillers.* Composed and conducted by Robert Cobert. Varese Sarabande, 2000.

Burnt Offerings. Dir. Dan Curtis. United Artists, 1976.

"*Burnt Offerings* Is an Outstanding Terror Movie." *New York Times Online,* September 30, 1976.. http://movies2.nytimes.com/mem/movies/review.html?title1=&title2.

"*Burnt Offerings* Not So Very Well Done." *The Tennessean,* November 19, 1976, 6-D.

Carroll, David, and Kyla Ward. "The Horror Timeline." *Tabula Rasa.* http://www.tabularasa.info/DarkAges/Timeline1.html.

Cast and Characters. Dir. Donald Beck. *The Winds of War, Part V.* Paramount DVD, 2004.

Clover, Carol. "Her Body, Himself." In *The Horror Reader,* edited by Ken Gelder, 294–307. London: Routledge, 2000.

_____. *Men, Women, and Chainsaws: Gender in the Modern Horror Film.* Princeton, NJ: Princeton University Press, 1992.

Cobert, Robert. DVD interview. *The Music of War and Remembrance.* Dir. Donald Beck. *War and Remembrance: The Final Chapter, Parts XI–XII.* MPI Home Video, 2003.

_____. Liner notes. *War and Remembrance.* Composed and conducted by Robert Cobert. MPI Music, 2003.

Creed, Barbara. "Kristeva, Femininity, Abjection." In *The Horror Reader,* edited by Ken Gelder, 64–70. London: Routledge, 2000.

_____. *The Monstrous Feminine: Film, Feminism, Psychoanalysis.* London: Routledge, 1993.

Curse of the Black Widow. Dir. Dan Curtis. ABC Circle Films, 1977.

Curtis, Dan. DVD Commentary. *War and Remembrance: The Final Chapter, Parts XI–XII.* MPI Home Video, 2003.

_____. DVD Interview. *Dan Curtis and the Daltons.* Prod. Jim Pierson. *The Last Ride of the Dalton Gang.* MPI Home Video, 2005.

_____. DVD Interview. *Directing The Night Strangler.* Prod. & dir. Greg Carson. *The Night Stalker & The Night Strangler.* MGM Home Entertainment, 2004.

_____. DVD Interview. *Inside the Shadows.* Prod. Jim Pierson. *Dark Shadows Special Edition.* MPI Home Video, 1999.

_____. DVD Interview. *The Night Stalker: Dan Curtis Interview.* Prod. & dir. Greg Carson.

The Night Stalker & The Night Strangler. MGM Home Entertainment, 2004.

_____. DVD Interview. Prod. Jim Pierson. *The Dan Curtis Macabre Collection.* MPI Home Video, 2002.

_____. DVD Interview. Prod. Jim Pierson. *Dark Shadows DVD Collection 2.* MPI Home Video, 2002.

_____. DVD Interview. Prod. Jim Pierson. *Dark Shadows DVD Collection 8.* MPI Home Video, 2003.

_____. DVD Interview. Prod. Jim Pierson. *Dark Shadows DVD Collection 11.* MPI Home Video, 2004.

_____. DVD Interview. Prod. Jim Pierson. *Dark Shadows DVD Collection 16.* MPI Home Video, 2005.

_____. DVD Interview. Prod. Jim Pierson. *Dark Shadows DVD Collection 24.* MPI Home Video, 2006.

_____. Foreword to *Dark Shadows Resurrected,* by Jim Pierson. Los Angeles: Pomegranate Press, 1992.

_____. "A Frank Explanation of Producer's Version." Reported in *Shadowgram,* no. 63 (January 1993): 10.

_____. "Remember *Remembrance.*" Reported in *Shadowgram,* no. 79 (May 1997): 9.

_____, William F. Nolan, and Karen Black. DVD commentary. *Burnt Offerings.* MGM Home Entertainment, 2003.

_____, and Lynn Redgrave. DVD interview. Prod. Jim Pierson. *The Dan Curtis Macabre Collection.* MPI Home Video, 2002.

Dark Shadows. Dir. Dan Curtis, Lela Swift, et al. ABC-TV, 1966–1971.

Dark Shadows. Dir. Dan Curtis, Rob Bowman, et al. NBC-TV, 1991.

Dark Shadows. Dir. P.J. Hogan. Filmed for the WB television network in April 2004 but never aired.

Dark Shadows Behind the Scenes. Prod. Jim Pierson. *Dark Shadows Special Edition.* MPI Home Video, 1999.

Dark Shadows Reunion: 35th Anniversary Celebration. Prod. Jim Pierson. MPI Home Video, 2003.

Dawidziak, Mark. *The Night Stalker Companion: A 25th Anniversary Tribute.* Los Angeles: Pomegranate Press, 1997.

Dead of Night. Dir. Dan Curtis. Perf. Ed Begly, Jr., Patrick Macnee, Joan Hackett, Lee Montgomery. Dan Curtis Productions, 1977.

Del Valle, David. "Memories of Dan Curtis." *Films in Review,* March 28, 2006. http:// www.filmsinreview.com/Features/dancurtis. html.

"Director/Co-Producer Dan Curtis." *Drama-Logue,* October 14, 1993: 10–11.

Dracula. Dir. Dan Curtis. Dan Curtis Productions, 1974.

DS Halloween Party. Directed by Joe Integlia. *Vista Theatre DS Events.* JT Video, 2006.

DuBrow, Rick. "*Winds of War II:* The Saga Continues." *Los Angeles Herald-Examiner,* May 17, 1984, 4-F.

Ebert, Roger. "*House of Dark Shadows.*" *Chicago Sun–Times Online,* October 6, 1970. http://rogerebert.suntimes.com/apps/pbcs.dll/article?AID=/19701006/REVW.

_____. "*Night of Dark Shadows.*" *Chicago Sun–Times Online,* September 21, 1971. http://rogerebert.suntimes.com/apps/pbcs/dll/article?AID=/19710921/REVW.

Everson, William. *Classics of the Horror Film.* Secaucus: Citadel Press, 1974.

"Featured Filmmaker — Dan Curtis — The Career of the Man Behind *Dark Shadows* and Kolchak." *Film Force,* July 8, 2003. http://filmforce.ign.com/articles/427/427516p1.html.

Finney, Jack. "Second Chance." In *The Third Level,* 153–172. New York: Dell, 1959.

Florescu, Radu. *In Search of Frankenstein.* Boston: New York Graphic Society, 1975.

_____, and Raymond McNally. *Dracula: Prince of Many Faces.* Boston: Little, Brown, and Co., 1989.

Frankenstein. Dir. Glenn Jordan. Dan Curtis Productions, 1973.

Gendel, Morgan. "ABC at *War* Again with Miniseries, Maxi-Sequel." *Los Angeles Times,* September 6, 1986, 10-F.

Gibron, Bill. "Character over Carnage: Dan Curtis." *Pop Matters,* April 3, 2006. http://www.popmatters.com/tv/features/060403-dancurtis.shtml.

Gifford, Denis. *A Pictorial History of Horror Movies.* London: Hamlyn, 1973.

Glut, Donald. *Classic Movie Monsters.* Metuchen: Scarecrow, 1978.

_____. *The Dracula Book.* Metuchen: Scarecrow, 1975.

Gross, Darren. "Closed Rooms in the *House of Dark Shadows.*" *Video Watchdog,* no. 40 (1997): 26–31.

_____. "*Dark Shadows* Staked!" *Fangoria,* no. 239 (January 2005): 62 ff.

_____. "Illuminating *Night of Dark Shadows.*" *Video Watchdog,* no. 40 (1997): 32–45.

Gross, Edward. "Dan Curtis." *Dark Shadows Tribute.* Las Vegas: Pioneer Books, 1990.

_____. "Dan Curtis: His 'Dream' Started It All." *The Dark Shadows Interviews.* Las Vegas: Schuster & Schuster, 1988.

Hogan, Ron. *The Stewardess Is Flying the Plane! American Films of the 1970s.* New York: Bullfinch Press, 2005.

House of Dark Shadows. Dir. Dan Curtis. MGM, 1970.

"*House of Dark Shadows* Stresses the Sinister." *New York Times Online,* October 29, 1970. http://movies2.nytimes.com/mem/movies/review.html.

Howard, Malia. *Jonathan Frid: An Actor's Curious Journey.* Fort Worth: Howard Books, 2001.

James, Henry. *The Turn of the Screw.* New York: Dover, 1991.

Jamison, R.J. *Grayson Hall: A Hard Act to Follow.* New York: iUniverse, 2006.

Javna, John. *Cult TV.* New York: St. Martin's Press, 1985.

Jenkins, Henry. *Textual Poachers: Television Fans and Participatory Culture.* New York: Routledge, 1992.

Joslin, Lyndon. *Count Dracula Goes to the Movies: Stoker's Novel Adapted, 1922–1995.* Jefferson, NC: McFarland, 1999.

Karol, Michael. *The ABC Movie of the Week: A Loving Tribute to the Classic Series.* New York: iUniverse, 2005.

Katz, Ephraim. *The Film Encyclopedia.* 5th ed. New York: Harper Collins, 2005.

Kawin, Bruce. "Children of the Light." In *Film Genre Reader II,* edited by Barry Keith Grant, 308–329. Austin: University of Texas Press, 1995.

King, Stephen. *Stephen King's Danse Macabre.* New York: Berkley Books, 1981.

_____. "Why We Crave Horror Movies." In *The Prose Reader: Essays for Thinking, Reading, and Writing,* 6th edition, edited by Kim Flachmann and Michael Flachmann, 452–455. Upper Saddle River, NJ: Prentice Hall, 2002.

Kristeva, Julia. *Powers of Horror: An Essay on Abjection.* New York: Columbia University Press, 1982.

Kuttner, Henry. "The Graveyard Rats." In *Dying of Fright,* edited by Les Daniels, 189–195. New York: Scribner's, 1976.

Lampley, Jonathan. Letter to the author (May 25, 2007).

LaVoo, George. "*Burnt Offerings* Filmbook." *The Old, Dark House,* no. 1 (Winter 1976–1977): 4–13.

Loban, Leila, and Richard Valley. "The Pictures of Dorian Gray." *Scarlet Street,* no. 41 (2001): 36 ff.

_____. "The Pictures of Dorian Gray, Part II." *Scarlet Street,* no. 42 (2001): 52 ff.

_____. "The Pictures of Dorian Gray, Part III." *Scarlet Street,* no. 43 (2001): 48 ff.

Lucas, Tim. "*Dracula.*" *Video Watchdog,* no. 15 (January–February 1993): 11–12.

_____. "*House of Dark Shadows* and *Night of Dark Shadows.*" *Video Watchdog,* no. 22 (March–April 1994): 65–67.

The Making of War and Remembrance. Dir. Donald Beck. *War and Remembrance: The Final Chapter, Parts V–VII.* MPI Home Video, 2003.

Making the Winds of War. Dir. Donald Beck. *The Winds of War, Part V.* Paramount DVD, 2004.

Manning, Stuart. "Remembering Dan Curtis." *Dark Shadows Journal,* March 28, 2006. http://www.collinwood.net.

Marasco, Robert. *Burnt Offerings.* New York: Delacorte Press, 1973.

Marill, Alvin. *Movies Made for Television 1964–1979.* Westport, CT: Arlington House, 1980.

_____. *Movies Made for Television 1964–1984.* New York: New York Zoetrope, 1984.

_____. *Movies Made for Television 1964–2004.* 5 vols. Lanham, MD: Scarecrow Press, 2005.

Matheson, Richard. DVD interview. *Richard Matheson: Terror Scribe.* Dir. David Gregory. *Trilogy of Terror.* Dark Sky Films, 2006.

_____. *I Am Legend.* Garden City, NY: Nelson Doubleday, 1954.

_____. "The Likeness of Julie." In *Shock II,* 79–90. New York: Dell, 1964.

_____. "Needle in the Heart," a.k.a. "Therese." In *Shock Waves,* 109–111. New York: Dell, 1970.

_____. "No Such Thing as a Vampire." In *Shock II,* 27–38. New York: Dell, 1964.

_____. "Prey." In *Shock Waves.* New York: Dell, 1970.

_____. *Shock!* New York: Dell, 1961.

_____. *Shock III.* New York: Dell, 1966.

McCarty, Michael. "Dan Curtis Continues to Thrive in the *Dark Shadows.*" *Sci-Fi,* 2002. http://www.scifi.com/sfw/issue272/interview.html.

_____. "William F. Nolan Looks Back at the Legacy of *Logan's Run* and Looks Forward to Bryan Singer's Remake." *Sci-Fi,* 2005. http://www.scifi.com/sfw/issue403/interview.html.

McNally, Raymond, and Radu Florescu. *In Search of Dracula.* New ed. Boston: Houghton Mifflin, 1994.

McNeil, Alex. *Total Television.* 4th ed. New York: Penguin Books, 1996.

Meikle, Denis. *A History of Horrors: The Rise and Fall of the House of Hammer.* Lanham, MD: Scarecrow Press, 1996.

Melton, J. Gordon. *The Vampire Book: The Encyclopedia of the Undead.* Detroit: Visible Ink Press, 1994.

_____. *The Vampire Book: The Encyclopedia of the Undead.* 2nd ed. Detroit: Visible Ink Press, 1999.

_____. *Vampires on Video.* Detroit: Visible Ink Press, 1997.

Mulvey, Laura. *Fetishism and Curiosity.* Bloomington: Indiana University Press, 1996.

_____. *Visual and Other Pleasures.* Bloomington: Indiana University Press, 1989.

_____. "Visual Pleasure and Narrative Cinema." In *The Norton Anthology of Theory and Criticism,* edited by Vincent Leitch, 2181–2192. New York: W.W. Norton, 2001.

Nance, Scott. *Bloodsuckers: Vampires at the Movies.* Las Vegas: Pioneer Books, 1992.

Night of Dark Shadows. Dir. Dan Curtis. MGM, 1971.

The Night Stalker. Dir. John Llewellyn Moxey. ABC Circle Films, 1972.

The Night Strangler. Dir. Dan Curtis. ABC Circle Films, 1973.

The Norliss Tapes. Dir. Dan Curtis. Dan Curtis Productions & Metromedia, 1973.

A Novel for Television. Dir. Donald Beck. *The Winds of War, Part V.* Paramount DVD, 2004.

O'Flinn, Paul. "Production and Reproduction: The Case of *Frankenstein.*" In *The Horror Reader,* edited by Ken Gelder, 114–127. London: Routledge, 2000.

O'Neil, Thomas. *The Emmys.* 3rd ed. New York: Berkley, 1998.

On Location. Dir. Donald Beck. *The Winds of War, Part V.* Paramount DVD, 2004.

Palance, Jack. DVD interview. Prod. Jim Pierson. *The Dan Curtis Macabre Collection.* MPI Home Video, 2002.

Pattison, Barrie. *The Seal of Dracula.* New York: Bounty Books, 1975.

The Picture of Dorian Gray. Dir. Glenn Jordan. Dan Curtis Productions, 1973.

Pierson, Jim, ed. *Dark Shadows Festival Memory Book 1983–1993.* Maplewood, NJ: Dark Shadows Festival, 1994.

_____. *Dark Shadows Resurrected.* Los Angeles: Pomegranate Press, 1992.

_____. Liner notes. *Dark Shadows: The 30th Anniversary Collection.* Composed by Robert Cobert. Varese Sarabande, 1996.

_____. Liner notes. *House of Dark Shadows and Night of Dark Shadows.* Composed and conducted by Robert Cobert. Turner Classic Movies Music, 1996.

_____. *Produced and Directed by Dan Curtis.* Los Angeles: Pomegranate Press, 2004.

Pinedo, Isabel. "Recreational Terror: Postmodern Elements of the Contemporary Horror Film." *Journal of Film and Video,* vol. 48, no. 1/2 (Spring-Summer 1996): 17–31.

_____. *Recreational Terror: Women and the Pleasure of Horror-Film Viewing.* Albany: State University of New York Press, 1997.

Ramsland, Katherine. *Prism of the Night: A Biography of Anne Rice.* 2nd ed. New York: Plume, 1994.

Rathbun, Mark, and Graeme Flanagan. *Richard Matheson: He Is Legend.* Chico, CA: Rio Lindo, 1984.

Redgrave, Lynn. DVD interview. Prod. Jim Pierson. *The Dan Curtis Macabre Collection.* MPI Home Video, 2002.

Resch, Kathleen, and Marcy Robin. *Dark Shadows in the Afternoon.* New York: Image Publishing, 1991.

Rice, Jeff. *The Night Stalker.* New York: Pocket Books, 1973.

_____. *The Night Strangler.* New York: Pocket Books, 1974.

Robin, Marcy, ed. "Dan Curtis News." *Shadowgram,* no. 41 (February 1988): 5.

_____. "Dan Curtis News." *Shadowgram,* no. 46 (April 1989): 9.

_____. "Dan Curtis News." *Shadowgram,* no. 47 (August 1989): 7.

_____. "Dan Curtis News." *Shadowgram,* no. 54/55 (January 1991): 2.

_____. "Dan Curtis News." *Shadowgram,* no. 61 (August 1992): 15.

_____. "Dan Curtis News." *Shadowgram,* no. 67 (January 1994): 15.

_____. "Dan Curtis News." *Shadowgram,* no. 78 (February 1997): 10–11.

_____. "Dan Curtis News." *Shadowgram,* no. 79 (May 1997): 9.

_____. "Dan Curtis News." *Shadowgram,* no. 81 (November 1997): 11.

_____. "Dan Curtis News." *Shadowgram,* no. 82 (February 1998): 10.

_____. "Dan Curtis News." *Shadowgram,* no. 87 (November 1999): 10.

_____. "Dan Curtis News." *Shadowgram,* no. 94 (November 2001): 10.

_____. "Dan Curtis News." *Shadowgram,* no. 96 (June 2002): 9.

_____. "Dan Curtis News." *Shadowgram,* no. 97 (October 2002): 10.

_____. "Dan Curtis News." *Shadowgram,,* no. 104 (April 2005): 11.

_____. "Dan Curtis News." *Shadowgram,* no. 106 (October 2005): 8–9.

_____. "Dan Curtis News." *Shadowgram,* no. 107 (April 2006): 12–13, 22–23.

_____. "Dan Curtis News." *Shadowgram,* no. 108 (June 2006): 8–10.

_____. "*Dark Shadows* News." *Shadowgram,* no. 54/55 (January 1991): 15–16.

_____. "Robert Cobert News." *Shadowgram,* no. 49 (January 1990): 9.

Ross, Marilyn. *The Vampire Contessa: From the Journal of Jeremy Quentain.* New York: Pinnacle Books, 1974.

Samaras, Helen, ed. *Fangs for the Memories: Memoirs of Dark Shadows Fans and Cast Members.* West Hempstead, NY: Evil Twin Publishing, 1996.

Schow, David, and Jeffrey Frentzen. *The Outer Limits: The Official Companion.* New York: Ace Science-Fiction Books, 1986.

Scott, Kathryn Leigh. *The Dark Shadows Companion.* Los Angeles: Pomegranate Press, 1990.

_____. *Dark Shadows Memories.* Los Angeles: Pomegranate Press, 2001.

_____. Letter to the author (June 15, 2006).

_____. *My Scrapbook Memories of Dark Shadows.* Los Angeles: Pomegranate Press, 1986.

_____. *Dark Shadows Almanac.* Millennium edition. Los Angeles: Pomegranate Press, 2000.

_____. *The Dark Shadows Movie Book.* Los Angeles: Pomegranate Press, 1998.

_____, and Jim Pierson, eds. *Dark Shadows Almanac.* Los Angeles: Pomegranate Press, 1995.

Scott, Lesley. "The Vamp in the Mirror: How Popular Culture's Obsession with the Undead Reveals What We're Really Afraid Of." *Stitch,* vol. 1, no. 4 (December 2003): 104–109.

Scream of the Wolf. Dir. Dan Curtis. Dan Curtis Productions & Metromedia, 1974.

Selby, David. *In and Out of the Shadows.* New York: Locust Grove Press, 1999.

Shelley, Mary. *Frankenstein, or The Modern Prometheus.* London: Penguin, 1992.

Shinnick, Kevin. "Come Back, Shane Briant." *Scarlet Street,* no. 42 (2001): 46 ff.

Showalter, Elaine. "Dr. Jekyll's Closet." In *The Horror Reader,* edited by Ken Gelder, 190–197. London: Routledge, 2000.

Silver, Alain, and James Ursini. *The Vampire Film.* 2nd ed. New York: Limelight Editions, 1993.

Skal, David. *The Monster Show: A Cultural History of Horror.* 2nd ed. New York: Faber and Faber, 2001.

Steve. "Dan Curtis Has Passed Away." *House of Irony,* June 18, 2006. http://houseofirony.com/ 2006/03/27/dan-curtis-1928-2006/.

Stevenson, Robert Louis. *The Strange Case of Dr. Jekyll and Mr. Hyde.* New York: Books, Inc., n.d.

Stewart, Zan. "Bob Cobert Scores His Own Victory in *War and Remembrance.*" Reported in *Shadowgram,* no. 45 (January 1989): 13.

Stoker, Bram. *Dracula.* New York: Signet Classic, 1992.

The Strange Case of Dr. Jekyll and Mr. Hyde. Dir. Charles Jarrott. Dan Curtis Productions & CBC-TV, 1968.

"Terror on TV: 1969–1983." *The Terror Trap,* 1998. http://www.terrortrap.com/television/ televisionterror.htm.

"Thayer David Quotes." *Brainy Quotes,* 2006. http://www.brainyquote.com/quotes/authors /t/thayer_david.html.

Thompson, Jeff. "Breathing Down Our Necks: The 1970 Leviathan Storyline." *The Music Box,* no. 9 (Summer 1993): 21–23.

_____. "*Burnt Offerings.*" *Movie Club,* no. 12 (Autumn 1997): 14–15.

_____. "*Burnt Offerings.*" In *You're Next! Loss of Identity in the Horror Film,* edited by Anthony Ambrogio. Baltimore: Midnight Marquee Press, 2008.

_____. *The Dark Shadows Comic Books.* Los Angeles: Joseph Collins Publications, 1988.

_____. "*Dark Shadows* in the 1970s: Best Episodes." *Shadows of the Night,* January 20, 2006. http://www.sotnight.com.

_____. *The Dark Shadows Memorabilia Slide Show.* Slide program. 1985–1992.

_____. "*Death at Love House.*" In *You're Next! Loss of Identity in the Horror Film,* edited by Anthony Ambrogio. Baltimore: Midnight Marquee Press, 2008.

_____. "*Die! Die! My Darling!*" *Midnight Marquee,* no. 57 (Summer 1998): 13.

_____. *The Effective Use of Actual Persons and Events in the Historical Novels of Dan Ross.* Thesis. Tennessee State University, 1991.

_____. "The Films of Barbara Steele." *Movie Club,* no. 7 (summer 1996): 40–41.

_____. "Four-Colour Shadows: The Gold Key Comics." *Dark Shadows Journal,* March 19, 2006. http://www.collinwood.net/features/ cards/goldkey.htm.

_____. "A History of the East Coast Dark Shadows Festivals, 1983–1993." In *Dark Shadows Festival Memory Book, 1983–1993,* edited by Jim Pierson, 93–99. Maplewood, NJ: Dark Shadows Festival, 1994.

_____. "*House of Dark Shadows.*" In *You're Next! Loss of Identity in the Horror Film,* edited by Anthony Ambrogio. Baltimore: Midnight Marquee Press, 2008.

_____. "In Memoriam: Dan Curtis." *Scoop,* 2006. http://scoop.diamondgalleries.com/ scoop_article.asp?ai=11718&si-122.

_____. "Life from a Coffin: How *Dark Shadows* Has Affected My Life." In *Fangs for the Memories: Memoirs of Dark Shadows Fans and Cast*

Members, edited by Helen Samaras, 61–64. West Hempstead, NY: Evil Twin Publishing, 1996.

_____. "*Matinee.*" In *Science-Fiction Invasions,* edited by Don Dohler, 29–30. Baltimore: Movie Club, 1998.

_____. "*Night of Dark Shadows.*" In *You're Next! Loss of Identity in the Horror Film,* edited by Anthony Ambrogio. Baltimore: Midnight Marquee Press, 2008.

_____. "An Overview of *Dark Shadows* Fandom." *The Southern Fandom Confederation Bulletin,* no. 8 (January 1991): 18–21.

_____. "Soap and Sorcery: Lara Parker." *Femme Fatales,* vol. 4, no. 1 (Summer 1995): 28–31 ff.

_____. "*The Strange Possession of Mrs. Oliver.*" In *You're Next! Loss of Identity in the Horror Film,* edited by Anthony Ambrogio. Baltimore: Midnight Marquee Press, 2008.

_____. "Timeless Loves: *Titanic* and *Somewhere in Time.*" *Scarlet Street,* no. 28 (Mid-1998): 29–31.

_____. "*Trilogy of Terror.*" In *You're Next! Loss of Identity in the Horror Film,* edited by Anthony Ambrogio. Baltimore: Midnight Marquee Press, 2008.

_____. "*Trilogy of Terror II.*" In *You're Next! Loss of Identity in the Horror Film,* edited by Anthony Ambrogio. Baltimore: Midnight Marquee Press, 2008.

_____. "A Visit with Marilyn and Dan Ross." In *Dark Shadows Lives!,* edited by James Van Hise, 57–67. Las Vegas: Schuster & Schuster, 1988.

_____. "*The Winds of War.*" *The World of Dark Shadows,* no. 36 (December 1983): 52–53.

Thompson, Jeff, and Connie Jonas, eds. *The Collinsport Players Companion, Volume I.* Portland, OR: Harmony Road Press, 1993.

Trilogy of Terror. Dir. Dan Curtis. ABC Circle Films, 1975.

Trilogy of Terror II. Dir. Dan Curtis. Dan Curtis & Power Pictures & Wilshire Court Productions, 1996.

The Turn of the Screw. Dir. Dan Curtis. Dan Curtis Productions, 1974.

"TV Terror: Dan Curtis." *The Terror Trap,* 1998. http://www.terrortrap.com/television/televisioncurtis.htm.

Wallace, Marie. *On Stage and in Shadows.* New York: iUniverse, 2005.

Waller, Gregory. "Introduction to *American Horrors.*" In *The Horror Reader,* edited by Ken Gelder, 256–264. London: Routledge, 2000.

War and Remembrance: Behind the Scenes. Exec. Prod. Jim Pierson. *War and Remembrance: The Final Chapter, Parts XI–XII.* MPI Home Video, 2003.

Weiler, A.H. "*Night of Dark Shadows* Arrives." *New York Times Online,* October 14, 1971. http://movies2.nytimes.com/mem/movies/review.html.

Wells, Paul. *The Horror Genre: From Beelzebub to Blair Witch.* London: Wallflower, 2000.

"What a Doll!" *TV Guide* (March 1, 1975): 12–13.

Wilde, Oscar. *The Picture of Dorian Gray.* New York: Modern Library, 2004.

Williams, Linda. "When the Woman Looks." In *Re-Vision: Essays in Feminist Film Criticism,* edited by Mary Ann Doane, Patricia Mellencamp, and Linda Williams, 83–99. Frederick, MD: American Film Institute Monograph Series, University Publications of America, 1984.

Wilson, Edmund. "The Ambiguity of Henry James." *Hound and Horn* VII (April–June 1934): 385–406.

Winkle, Michael. "The Measure of Success." *Geocities,* 1999. http://www.geocities.com/laxaria/success.html?200621.

Wood, Robin. "The American Nightmare: Horror in the 1970s." In *Horror, the Film Reader,* edited by Mark Jancovich, 25–32. London: Routledge, 2002.

Zahl, Paul. "A Sad but Important Week." *Trinity Episcopal School for Ministry,* April 3, 2006. http://www.tesm.edu/deans-corner/dcblog/curtis.

Zicree, Mark Scott. *The Twilight Zone Companion.* New York: Bantam Books, 1982.

Index

Page numbers in **bold italics** refer to illustrations.